THE EMPIRE'S NEW CLOTHES

PHILIP MURPHY

The Empire's New Clothes

The Myth of the Commonwealth

OXFORD
UNIVERSITY PRESS

OXFORD
UNIVERSITY PRESS

Oxford University Press is a department of the
University of Oxford. It furthers the University's objective
of excellence in research, scholarship, and education
by publishing worldwide.

Oxford   New York

Auckland   Cape Town   Dar es Salaam   Hong Kong   Karachi
Kuala Lumpur   Madrid   Melbourne   Mexico City   Nairobi
New Delhi   Shanghai   Taipei   Toronto

With offices in

Argentina   Austria   Brazil   Chile   Czech Republic   France   Greece
Guatemala   Hungary   Italy   Japan   Poland   Portugal   Singapore
South Korea   Switzerland   Thailand   Turkey   Ukraine   Vietnam

Oxford is a registered trade mark of Oxford University Press
in the UK and certain other countries.

Published in the United States of America by
Oxford University Press
198 Madison Avenue, New York, NY 10016

Library of Congress Cataloging-in-Publication Data is available
Philip Murphy.
The Empire's New Clothes: The Myth of the Commonwealth.
ISBN: 9780190911157

Printed in the United Kingdom by
Bell & Bain Ltd, Glasgow

To my family

CONTENTS

PREFACE

We are all familiar with the kind of news item that begins, 'A major academic study has just found...' It's the sort of thing that always produces a warm glow among senior university administrators, regularly called upon to show their institution making an 'impact' in wider society. And, occasionally, it provides harmless amusement for everyone else. This generally occurs when the research findings appear to be things that one could easily intuit without the benefit of hundreds of thousands of pounds of Research Council funding: 'eating yoghurt and fruit for breakfast produces better health results than waffles and cigarettes'; 'owners of cats tend to have lower blood pressure than owners of Rottweilers'; 'photocopiers really are more likely to break down when you're in a hurry'.

The main argument of this book, which itself draws heavily on a fairly hefty piece of externally-funded academic research, risks provoking a similarly wry smile. It is, essentially, that the Commonwealth has lost almost all of the limited significance it once possessed, and has become something of a mirage in the field of British foreign policy. To which the informed reader might respond, "And?", while the slightly less well-informed might confess, "I didn't know the Commonwealth still existed".

Yet there are a number of reasons why this book still seemed worth writing. I began work on it shortly after the June 2016 referendum on British membership of the European Union. As we shall see, in this vote the issue of the Commonwealth was a significant although not pivotal one. Typical of the magical thinking surrounding the Leave campaign, it was sometimes suggested that the Commonwealth had the potential to represent, for a free-trading UK, an alternative market to the EU. And once the result was announced—a victory for Leave—even some Commonwealth enthusiasts who had remained relatively quiet in the run-up to the vote now announced that this was a wonderful opportunity for the UK to revive the organization.

Many of those who presented the contemporary Commonwealth as an alternative destination for British trade ahead of the referendum seemed to have only the vaguest sense of its reality. The lack of a really penetrating, critical analysis of the organization became painfully apparent, and at the risk of closing the stable door after the horse had bolted, I set out to write one. In any case, as the British prime minister prepares to become the Commonwealth's chair-in-office following the April 2018 Commonwealth summit in London, the project remains timely.

The gap in the literature about the Commonwealth is easy to explain. In the way of marginal organizations that attract devoted followers, it tends to be supporters who feel that it is actually worthy of study. A case in point is one of the most recent books, published in 2008 by Tim Shaw, a predecessor of mine as director of the Institute of Commonwealth Studies.[1] Its political science approach is a veritable alphabet soup of serious-sounding acronyms relating to serious-sounding bodies and committees, giving an overall impression of extreme seriousness. Yet anyone who is actually familiar with the contemporary Commonwealth might suspect that there is a certain mismatch here between the analytical tools and the object of study. It is reminiscent of the calculation made by the seventeenth-century Biblical scholar, James Ussher, that the act of Creation began at around 6pm on

22 October 4,004 BCE. In a similarly incongruous application of precision, Shaw's book sees an attempt to chart, in the clear-cut language of international relations, a phenomenon probably better described in terms of collective imagination, not to say fantasy. It gives a misleading sense of solidity to something strikingly impalpable.

A glance through social media—an area where the Commonwealth has upped its game considerably since 2016—might prove equally misleading. The Twitter feeds of the Secretariat and its associated bodies give the impression that they are performing good works across an astonishingly wide spectrum of public policy. Indeed, if the measure of an institution's worth were its ability to generate a blizzard of laudable hashtags, the Commonwealth would be an unparalleled success. Let's hear it for #peace, #technicalassistance, #youth, #humanrights, #education, #trade, #genderequality, #smallstates. What's not to like? Yet one does not have to spend very long observing the organization at close quarters before a nagging question begins to form in the back of one's mind. Eventually, out of bemusement, frustration or simple curiosity, one finds oneself enquiring, 'So, what has the Commonwealth actually achieved?' Like the little boy who asks in all innocence why the emperor has no clothes, one is likely to encounter an embarrassed, even shocked silence.

This brings me to the main reason for wanting to write the book. Since becoming director of the Institute of Commonwealth Studies at the University of London's School of Advanced Study in 2009, I have had an ideally close but detached vantage point from which to observe the Commonwealth in action. The tale of 'The Emperor's New Clothes', to which the title of this book alludes, is essentially an outrageous comic parable. It asks why a group of people should collude in the fantasy that something completely insubstantial is in fact real and magnificent. The answer the fable offers is that people are drawn into such collective illusions by a range of human frailties—prominent among them greed, gullibility and insecurity. The gap between fantasy and reality that the tale exposes is the very stuff of comedy.

In the same way, I hope this book—which examines the gulf between the Commonwealth's lofty rhetoric and its actual achievements—will provide readers with some amusement. But it should also be acknowledged that many of the principles that the Commonwealth espouses are, indeed, laudable ones. Over the years it has secured the loyal support of many good people, whose backing for it is based on the very best of motives. Nothing in what follows is intended to belittle them or their ideals. Rather, this book suggests that the current state of the organization has left it vulnerable to exploitation by those whose motives are far less enlightened.

The Empire's New Clothes draws heavily on material generated by a project run out of the Institute of Commonwealth Studies, on which I served as principal investigator. Entitled 'An Oral History of the Modern Commonwealth', this was generously funded by two separate grants from the UK Arts and Humanities Research Council (AHRC), the first (AH/J006548/1) supporting the main phase of the research from 2012 to 2015 and the second (AH/N003934/1) supporting the broader dissemination of the findings.

In the course of the project, we interviewed over seventy leading figures in the development of the organization since 1965, including prime ministers, foreign ministers, heads of Commonwealth-related organizations, and senior officials in the Secretariat, including all of the surviving former Secretaries-General. The vast majority of the interviews were conducted with consummate skill by my colleague, Sue Onslow, who acted as lead researcher on the project. They have been transcribed and made freely available via a unique online archive, at https://commonwealthoralhistories.org/. Unlike this book, which represents my own very personal view of the Commonwealth, the project sought to present a wide variety of perspectives on and experiences of the organization. Nevertheless, the study that follows would have been impossible without it. So my warmest thanks to all our distinguished interviewees, and the academic co-investigators and other researchers who worked on the project: Sue herself and Leo Zeilig, Ruth Craggs, Eva Namusoke, Chris Moffat and Vanessa Rockel. This book draws not only on the interview materials themselves, but also on Eva and Sue's blog articles for the Commonwealth Oral History Project. The site also offers a useful chronology of the modern Commonwealth and some key documents charting its development. Paul Sullivan and Chloe Pieters provided invaluable administrative support during the inception and execution of the project, and Chloe deserves particular thanks for giving this book its title.

It has been my immense privilege during my time at the Institute to work closely with and have access to the insights of people whose knowledge of the Commonwealth far surpassed my own. I would mention in this context Daisy Cooper, Richard Bourne, David McIntyre, Derek Ingram, James Manor and James Mayall. They bear absolutely no responsibility for the views that follow, many of which they may well disagree with. But they all played a significant part in inducting me into the legend and lore of the Commonwealth. It has also been my great pleasure to supervise the excellent doctoral theses of Matthew Battey and Charles Rukwengye, which have deepened my knowledge, respectively, of the Commonwealth's role in the field of development and of its relations with the Idi Amin regime in Uganda. David Laven kindly commented on an early draft of Chapter One. My partner, Christina Britzolakis, has always been a wise and insightful sounding board for my thoughts on the Commonwealth and has supported me emotionally and intellectually throughout the writing of this book. My warm thanks to Michael Dwyer of

PREFACE

Hurst for the confidence he has shown in this project, and to the two anonymous readers of the book for providing such useful suggestions on how it might be strengthened. I have been blessed by having as my copy editor, Lara Weisweiller-Wu, whose work has been invaluable. All remaining imperfections are, of course, entirely down to me.

PVM, Institute of Commonwealth Studies, 1 January 2018

"WHAT DOES THE COMMONWEALTH MEAN TO YOU?"

"So, Professor Murphy," came the voice at the end of the line, "what does the Commonwealth mean to you?" This was in 2014, and I had agreed to do a live interview about the organization for a radio talk show, from my London office in Senate House. Media interest had been sparked by the staging of the Commonwealth Games in Glasgow, and while I waited, phone in hand, for my turn to speak, the presenter was busily soliciting Commonwealth-related thoughts and anecdotes from anyone he could find on the Glaswegian streets that morning.

Finally, just as the clock was ticking towards the very end of the show and the presenter had scared away every sentient being within range, he turned his attentions to me. But I was stumped by the question—and slightly affronted. I was all ready to dig into my little rattle bag of 'expert's' facts, figures and cute analogies. But what they wanted was some sort of heartfelt personal anecdote: "My passionate attachment to the Commonwealth really began as a small child, hearing the wonderful stories of my grandfather, who had been a judge in Madras in the 1930s"; "Well, my eyes were really opened to the value of the Commonwealth during a sponsored cycle-ride across Malawi in my gap year."

What does the Commonwealth mean to me? It was only since I had become director of the Institute of Commonwealth Studies (ICwS) that it had 'meant' anything much at all. And what was that meaning? Lots of drinks receptions in the hollowed-out citadels of Britain's former imperial power? Endless well-meaning conferences exploring how the Commonwealth could achieve its 'true potential'? The reassuring prospect of never again having to teach the compulsory first-year undergraduate module on the Era of the Two World Wars at the University of Reading? No—none of those would do. In the three-and-a-half seconds while all this was racing through my head, the presenter correctly anticipated that a cheery anecdote would not be forthcoming, and moved on to the more concrete question: "What does the Commonwealth actually do?" I blurted out something spectacularly feeble along the lines of "Well it doesn't *do* very much, but then it doesn't *cost* very much". I could almost see the patronising grin on the presenter's face as he thought to himself, "We got more sense out of the manager of the Buchanan Street Pound Shop." And that was it—straight into the ten o'clock news and traffic roundup. Not my finest hour.

I wasn't prepared for the question. But it was a variant of something I'd been asked regularly over the five years since I'd become director of the ICwS: "How did you become interested in the Commonwealth?" Behind this was always the implication that my interest must have been sparked by some element of my upbringing or family history. But there was nothing I could really point to. I grew up in Hull. Very occasionally we did go 'overseas' on family holidays, but only to the Isle of Man.

There is a lazy assumption implicitly shared by many within the academic community: that the British are afflicted by a form of 'imperial nostalgia' of which the survival of the Commonwealth is a prominent symptom. As we shall see later on, this has informed much of the recent controversy about whether particular statues or other reminders of Britain's imperial past should be banished from the public domain. But the concept is at best a blunt instrument in understanding how Empire continues to live in the public imagination and the relationship between this and the contemporary Commonwealth.

There has been a debate raging for some decades now among historians of imperialism about the depth and durability of the imprint made by Empire on British society. Its context was set in 1978, when Edward Said, a professor of literature at Columbia University, published one of the most influential academic studies of the post-war era: *Orientalism*. In it he traced a process whereby, from the eighteenth century onwards, a variety of explorers, missionaries, traders and administrators sought to make the East explicable to the West by immersing themselves in 'Eastern' cultures, languages and religions. While this might have seemed a relatively benign objective, Said argued that these activities represented an essential element of the extension of Western imperial power. In order to control a society in any meaningful way, you need to 'understand' it. And the Orientalists provided the imperial conquerors with enough information to give them the impression that they did.

At the same time, however, the 'knowledge' generated by the Orientalists was essentially flawed. They were not faithfully and impartially recording some sort of external reality; they were 'constructing' identities. And these constructions were filtered through the distorting mirrors of Western self-interest and self-perception. 'Oriental' societies were defined in opposition to that self-image, so that if Western society was rational, scientific and orderly, and imbued with 'manly values', the Orient was irrational, superstitious, despotic and effeminate. The Orient was 'the other'. But if Orientalist 'discourse' was irredeemably tainted, it did serve an important purpose: to justify the West imposing its will on the East, the better to cure it of its manifold ills. It seeped comprehensively into the West's scholarly and popular representations of the East: in anthropology, in travel writing, in political speeches and even in fiction. All of this served to imbue in Western European populations the sense that the imperial ambitions of their rulers were part of the natural order of things.

Orientalism and Said's subsequent magnum opus *Culture and Imperialism* were signposts that pointed in strictly one direction: the reality that Western culture, from top to bottom, was run through with traces of the imperial project. And if that sometimes wasn't immediately apparent, it just meant you hadn't looked hard enough. This treasure hunt reached the academic field of British imperial history in a less theoretically encumbered guise. It did so initially through the works of John M. MacKenzie in the 1980s: his monograph, *Propaganda and Empire*, and his edited volume, *Imperialism and Popular Culture*. MacKenzie wasn't in any sense an orthodox 'Saidian', and he managed to avoid some of the intellectual contortions that result from following the various strands of Said's thought to their logical conclusions. His essential point was a simpler one: that the Empire, despite being based thousands of miles from home, was from the late nineteenth century a daily presence to ordinary Britons. Indeed, it was wherever they looked: in advertising, in the music hall and then the cinema, in youth movements, in popular fiction and in the popular press. So the Empire did 'mean' something to them, to such an extent that imperial jingoism became a popular political rallying cry when the time came to harvest the votes of those eligible to cast one. Again, the search was on for examples, and another academic cottage industry was duly inaugurated.

Then, in 2004, Bernard Porter published *The Absent-Minded Imperialists: Empire, Society, and Culture in Britain*, a deeply heretical cry of dissent. Porter was a highly respected historian of imperialism. But his new work was certainly not met with universal acclaim. He argued that what was really interesting about the Empire was its relatively small impact on British culture and society. The reason for this wasn't difficult to explain. The British, like most other imperial powers throughout history, liked to do Empire on the cheap. This meant co-opting a variety of local elites in the occupied countries to do the basic heavy lifting for them: collecting taxes, raising troops and enforcing basic law and order. This low-maintenance form of imperialism allowed inter-war British India—a subcontinent of 350 million souls—to be ruled by a British administrative cadre of only around 1,000 officers.

Of course, there were other elements to the flotsam and jetsam that made up the British presence overseas: missionaries, businessmen, soldiers and the like. But only a small fraction of the British population had any real relationship with the imperial project, and it tended to be drawn heavily from what we might call the 'ruling class'. Even then, elite culture in Britain seemed relatively untouched by Empire. Where were the great late Victorian canonical novels with explicitly imperial themes? Where were the great classical buildings of the metropolis recalling the earlier empires of Greece and Rome? At the very point when the map was turning red, the British were embracing a Neo-Gothic architectural style that harked back to a pre-imperial Merrie Olde England.

Porter was not without his supporters. But, generally speaking, his book was received with the sort of opprobrium usually reserved for someone who turns up in an umbrella-manufacturing town with the patent for a sunshine-generating machine. This wasn't just wrong-headed: for hundreds of scholars who had built their careers in the field of Saidian post-colonial studies, it was positively bad for business. My own view was that, however imperfectly, Porter had touched on an important truth. 'Empire' might indeed have proved a rallying cry on the British political right, but even in its heyday and even within the Conservative Party only a small minority of the leading figures took an active interest in its reality, or thought it should be at the heart of Britain's external diplomatic or economic policy. And it is certainly difficult to think of a single general election over the century since 1918 in which British imperial or Commonwealth issues has played a significant role in determining the outcome.

For the purposes of this discussion, however, the key point is that notions like popular enthusiasm for Empire—whether contemporary or historical—are notoriously difficult to measure or evaluate. The period under scrutiny in the great MacKenzie-Porter debate was the turn of the twentieth century, generally regarded as the zenith of British imperial self-confidence. Yet the degree to which Empire captured the imagination of the British people in that period has still been a matter of profound and closely argued disagreement between two distinguished historians. A definitive verdict on British attitudes to Empire is even more elusive when it comes to the following period, when Empire was formally dissolved and its remnants, legacy and memory played, at best, a marginal role in British political discourse. It is more challenging still to incorporate British attitudes into an argument about the future survival of today's Commonwealth, an organization which, in its more radical incarnation, tried to define itself in terms of virtually everything the British Empire was not.

Perhaps the key reason for this complexity was that, for the vast majority of the British population, Empire was not a 'lived' experience; at least, not as it was for their compatriots who crossed the seas to live and work in it. As such, for those growing up in the 'decolonizing' Britain of the post-war decades, the surviving meaning, if any, of the Empire/Commonwealth continued to be heavily determined by factors such as region, class and even religion. As such, I don't pretend that my own experiences were in any way typical, though they might have been representative in some respects. But they are perhaps worth sketching out, if only to question some contemporary assumptions about the *mentalité* of the white, middle-aged, male, Oxbridge-educated British historian of Empire.

I can't remember my schools in Hull in the 1970s and '80s ever marking or even mentioning Commonwealth Day. Had they been fee-paying public schools, where a good smattering of the families would probably have had records of imperial 'service', the situation might have been different. But they most decidedly were not. Nor do I recall any attempt to inculcate in us pride in the great imperial endeavours of Clive, Stanley or Rhodes. We were Catholics. Our folk heroes were essentially oppositional figures, many of whom had actually been executed by the British. My middle school in Hull—St John Fisher—was actually named after one of them. Although I'd certainly read a fair amount of history as a teenager, the story of the British Empire/Commonwealth didn't really register. Why should it have done, when there were all those folks like Catherine the Great, Napoleon, Disraeli and Hitler to become acquainted with? I only really became interested in things imperial as an undergraduate, and by chance had the opportunity to continue my studies at doctoral level. Even then, they didn't take me very far afield. My chosen topic was the way in which the British Conservative Party reacted to the decolonization of Africa. The party's papers were all in the Bodleian Library in Oxford where I was based, and my longer-haul research trips didn't tend to take me much further than the Public Record Office in Kew.

I became familiar with the idea of the Commonwealth as a great, soothing comfort blanket for the party's dwindling band of post-war imperial enthusiasts. They could reassure themselves that the sad business of granting independence to British colonies wasn't really the end of the line. Like the souls of the faithful departed, these countries would simply join the heavenly throng of the Commonwealth and live in eternal peace and harmony. But mine were essentially the findings of an archive rat poring over files from the 1950s and '60s. My personal experience of the Commonwealth—as something actually 'out there' in the wider world—didn't really expand by one iota. For the next twenty years or so, my research into the Commonwealth and its history remained a largely paper exercise. So, although I came to the ICwS with a more detailed knowledge of the history of the Commonwealth than most of my fellow British citizens, I couldn't claim to have much greater direct experience of it, either as an organization or as a collection of countries. I had no gut feeling of belonging or identification. Insofar as I thought about the Commonwealth, it was largely as a relatively minor aspect of British foreign policy in the post-war period, which had briefly been enlivened in the 1980s by some truly epic struggles between Mrs Thatcher and the then Commonwealth secretary-general, Sonny Ramphal, over South Africa.

Porter's point about so few British people having had direct, personal experience of Empire might seem obtuse if one thinks about imperialism as an ideological construct. Seen in those terms, it would be perfectly possible for the British public to have been inculcated with pride in 'Empire' as an abstract signifier of national power and prestige without the majority of them ever having strayed far beyond the place of their birth. But at a deeper level of understanding and personal identification, there is no substitute for direct contact. I was powerfully reminded of this a few years ago when my colleague at the ICwS, the distinguished Indian politics expert Professor James Manor, learned to his horror that I had never visited the subcontinent, and thereafter made it his business to 'educate' me. And educate me he certainly did. He invited me to a conference he was organizing at the Indian Institute of Advanced Studies in Shimla, the old summer capital of the Raj.

On the way, I got my first taste of Delhi. Of course, I knew the basic story. In 1911, the British announced that they were going to relocate the main administrative capital of the Indian Empire there, and commissioned the architects Edward Lutyens and Herbert Baker to draw up suitably grandiose plans. But nothing I'd read had prepared me for the sheer, dizzying folly of the enterprise. My taxi excursion took me past the India Gate and down the Rajpath, Lutyens' steroid-fuelled answer to the Mall, and between the two vast Secretariat buildings. We stopped by a set of gigantic gates. Directly ahead, shimmering in the distance, was the 340-room Rashtrapati Bhavan, now the official residence of the Indian president, but originally the Viceroy's Palace. At every stage of this unfolding spectacle, my only thought was, "Holy shit! What is *this*?"

In the grey, battle-scarred era between the world wars, the age of Lowry's hunched, shadow-like Lancashire factory workers, the British had constructed a capital city 4,000 miles from home, on a scale Albert Speer would probably have found intolerably extravagant and bombastic. And only sixteen years after 'New Delhi' was formally inaugurated in 1931, the British were gone, sent packing back to Lowry-land. "And what should they know of England, who only England know?" asked Rudyard Kipling rhetorically. Well, quite; but the differences between England and its Empire were thanks in no small part to the crazy, megalomaniac schemes of some of Kipling's closest friends and allies. Empire, in its wide variety of manifestations, was too remote from the daily experience of most people in the UK to be easily imaginable, let alone an object of nostalgia once it was gone.

So the blanket term 'imperial nostalgia' risks missing an important distinction between those people in Britain who had close personal or family associations with the now Commonwealth countries, and those who did not. The former group has always tended to be drawn disproportionately from the upper levels of British society. It is among those individuals that one senses a genuine, personal nostalgia for Empire, and in many cases that feeling of identification translated itself into an enthusiasm for the Commonwealth. That is not to say that all Commonwealth enthusiasts share this sense. Many of those most closely engaged in the activities of London's tight network of Commonwealth groups identify instead with the more radical trajectory on which the organization seemed set in the 1960s and '70s. Then, the Commonwealth worked closely with Britain's former colonies to deliver their ambitions for a bright, post-independence future.

Yet what such individuals did share with the 'imperial nostalgics' was direct experience of the member states. As a rule, if someone effortlessly drops references to the Commonwealth into their everyday conversation, the chances are they're either the head of a Commonwealth 'civil society' organization or a member of the British royal family. The correlation between social class and Commonwealth awareness only seems to break down when we come to the UK's various diaspora communities, many of which retain close links to particular Commonwealth countries.

For the rest of the British population, 'Empire' and 'Commonwealth' were what academics sometimes call 'floating signifiers', untethered to personal experience and so changing over time in line with broader ideological undercurrents. By the time I was growing up in the '70s and '80s, the collective memory of Empire was heavily infused with a sense of irony, not to say absurdity. I was reminded of this when I told my friends that I'd been appointed director of the Institute of Commonwealth Studies. The comic references came thick and fast: 'Carry on up the Khyber'; 'It Ain't Half Hot, Mum'; 'Roger of the Raj'; and, of course, the mandatory "Will you be having tea with the Queen?"

"WHAT DOES THE COMMONWEALTH MEAN TO YOU?"

As Karl Marx definitely never said, history on the telly always repeats itself: first as drama and second as parody. 'Carry on up the Khyber' seemed to be on constant repeat during the BBC2 early evening slot in the 1970s, to the extent that by the time we reached puberty we could recite the script almost word-for-word. As a kid, you tended to get the parody version of something first, making it a bit difficult to keep a straight face when the 'serious' version came along—and, in the '60s and '70s, the parody version of Empire was generally all there was to be had.

In the aftermath of the rapid liquidation of colonial rule, the British people were waking up from what seemed like a bizarre, psychedelic dream. And what stuck in the collective memory was the kitschy, camp surrealism of those imperial dreamscapes. The fantastic uniforms of the viceroy and his staff were recycled by the trendy boutiques of Carnaby Street and sold on to London's beautiful people with an added sheen of playful irony. The Kinks devoted a whole concept album to the theme of 'Arthur (or the Decline and Fall of the British Empire)'. And when Sergeant Pepper first taught the band to play, it was probably in the foot-hills of the Himalayas, to a restless audience of imperial functionaries retreating from the summer heat of Delhi.

The popular perception of the Commonwealth was also changing, in a far darker and less playfully ironical sense. From the mid-1960s onwards, Commonwealth gatherings became the scenes of pitched battles between Britain and many of its newly independent former colonies over the latter's determination to end white minority rule in Southern Rhodesia and South Africa. Meanwhile, as Bill Schwarz has noted in *The White Man's World*, Rhodesian Prime Minister Ian Smith was able to deck himself out in the borrowed robes of the classic imperial hero.[1] Here was the plucky Second World War fighter pilot battling to preserve 'white civilization' on a far-flung subtropical frontier.

For much of the Conservative Party and its mouthpieces in Fleet Street, the old assumption that the Commonwealth would be some sort of ersatz Empire was neatly and swiftly inverted. Its public enemy number one embodied the true spirit of Empire, and the Commonwealth itself had become the real threat to British interests—both in Southern Africa, where it seemed hell-bent on replacing stable, pro-Western regimes with Marxist dictatorships, and at home, where it became synonymous with non-white immigration. As East African Asians were expelled first from Kenya in 1968 and from Uganda in 1972, the right-wing press in the UK vilified both victims and perpetrators, and governments from both major British parties vied with each other successively to remove the last remaining rights of Commonwealth citizens to enter the UK. Those who had already settled in the country found themselves viciously mocked by popular comedians on primetime national television, a phenom-enon as redolent of British culture in the 1970s as David Bowie or the chopper bike.

All this time, the Commonwealth itself was really getting going as a sensible and serious operation. A Commonwealth Secretariat, fully independent of the British government, was established in 1965. Six years later, the first Commonwealth Heads of Government Meeting in Singapore issued a ringing condemnation of racial discrimination—something as inextrica-bly linked to British imperialism as ice cream and jelly. 1971 also witnessed the establishment of the Commonwealth Fund for Technical Cooperation (CFTC), a body consciously engineered to challenge the old North-to-South model of social and eco-nomic development and to encourage a South-to-South transfer of expertise. But, set beside the vivid, brightly coloured flash-backs of the great imperial reverie, very few of these good works truly resonated in the British collective consciousness. As far as we know, Jimmy Perry and David Croft never pitched to the BBC the idea of a sitcom set in the CFTC offices.

There was one notable attempt to capture the public imagina-tion. This came in the form of the Commonwealth Institute, an unlovely modernist edifice still visible today from Kensington High Street, which was opened in 1962. The Commonwealth Institute housed a permanent exhibition intended to serve as a shop-front for the new, progressive, modernizing Common-wealth—albeit under a roof of copper donated by the then Northern Rhodesian Chamber of Mines. Until 2000, the Institute was funded by the UK Foreign Office. It was then transferred to a trust managed by the Commonwealth's UK-based high commissioners (always a recipe for disaster), and only two years later had closed its doors permanently to the public. Between then and its reopening in 2016 as a design museum, the building was unused and uncared for—a great big copper-topped white elephant. Many people still remember visits to the Commonwealth Institute as a nice childhood excursion on a wet Sunday afternoon. But, in general, it's difficult to arouse passions about something as painfully well-meaning as the modern Commonwealth. Against the far-from-well-meaning British Empire, the contrast is as stark as the architectural one between inter-war Delhi and post-war Coventry.

The projection of a stable image of the Commonwealth to the British public has partly been hindered by the fact that Britain's rulers have so frequently been unsure precisely what to do with it. As we shall see in the following chapter, during the post-war period, the organization moved from being seen as an essential prop of Britain's 'great power' status to representing a puzzle, then an irritant, and finally a constant source of disappointment. It has maintained a loyal band of supporters, mostly concentrated in a series of London-based affiliated organizations. Yet even they often seem at a loss to explain the reasons for their enthusiasm.

In recent years, such organizations have found an unlikely guru in the form of David Howell, or Lord Howell of Guildford, to give him his full title. Howell had served as a minister in the early Thatcher administrations and had enjoyed a brief renaissance under David Cameron as minister of state at the Foreign and Commonwealth Office in 2010–12. He had long been identifiable as one of the more thoughtful contributors to the House of Lords' periodic debates on the Commonwealth—in that he occasionally strayed from recalling gap years in Kenya or thanking the Queen for her distinguished service, to make an abstract point of more general relevance.

In 2013 Howell published *Old Links and New Ties: Power and Persuasion in an Age of Networks*. It certainly managed to bottle some thoughts then very much in the air. Howell drew heavily on the Harvard professor Joseph Nye's concept of 'soft power', which, in a post-Cold War world, had furnished the theme for countless conferences on international diplomacy—and not surprisingly. The cheery assumption of Tony Blair's New Labour government—that the armed forces were simply the international wing of the British social services—had come somewhat unstuck in Afghanistan and Iraq. When Howell descended from his SW1 Mount Sinai with his very own tablets of stone, they said roughly this: *the era of states, super-states and superpowers is over. Hard power is out and soft power is in. We live in a globalized world in which people are increasingly connected by global networks. And, by a unique act of providence, the UK is the inheritor of the greatest global network of them all: the Commonwealth. Now go forth and use it!* Church bells rang out across London. The capital's Commonwealth true-believers finally had the sacred text they had always lacked.

I remained unconvinced. When, during the Cold War, the CIA generously poured money into the abstract expressionist movement, this was undoubtedly 'soft power'. It served to demonstrate that, in stark contrast to the Soviet Union, where artists were dragooned, on pain of imprisonment, into churning out endless socialist realist depictions of sunsets over the collective farm, in the US—the land of the free—artists were able to go really, splattery-crazy on canvas. It's far less obvious how the Commonwealth, composed of countries which display widely varying attitudes towards things like religious and press freedom, LGBT rights and the death penalty, can serve as an effective instrument of British soft power. And when the organization, in its wisdom, allows a leader with a seriously tarnished international reputation to become its chair-in-office, as it did in 2013, it's unlikely that the British government will be able to bask in much reflected glory. In any case, it doesn't help that the Commonwealth is seen by many as merely a relic of British imperialism. As such, it could hinder just as well as help the UK's self-projection on the world stage as a modern, liberal, humane society.

As for networks, one might have thought that an important sign of belonging to a significant one would be awareness of the fact. As a child growing up in Hull, I don't remember anyone attempting to make us proud of the Commonwealth. But that's probably because they were too busy trying to make us intensely proud of a truly great global network: the Roman Catholic Church—and intensely proud of it we were. It spanned all parts of the globe and had a history going back considerably further than 1949. There was no creative ambiguity about what membership entailed or who was in control. Unlike the authority of the head or secretary-general of the Commonwealth, whose respective remits have always been something of a sacred mystery, the Catholic Church's order of battle was crystal clear. Chief of staff was the Pope—the direct descendent of St Peter, Christ's representative on earth. And the Pope has the sort of global influence—soft power—that the Commonwealth secretary-general could only dream of. If I or any of the other Murphys, O'Neills, O'Connors, O'Rourkes, McNamaras or Mcquillans at my school had actually stumbled across the Commonwealth, this pale Protestant replica would hardly have made much of an impression.

One can sense this slight inferiority complex in the way the modern Commonwealth chooses to present itself on public occasions. It even has a sort of profane version of the Nicene Creed, rather awkwardly recited by the congregation at the annual Commonwealth Day Observance service in Westminster Abbey. It begins:

We affirm that every person possesses unique worth and dignity.

We affirm our respect for nature, and that we will be stewards of the earth by caring for every part of it, and for it as a whole.

We affirm our belief in justice for everyone, and peace between peoples and nations.

There may only be 1.2 billion Catholics in the world, compared with 2.4 billion members of the Commonwealth. The difference is that the vast majority of the former actually know they're Catholics. They also know roughly what that entails, and it's a significant part of their personal identity. The same cannot be said for most of the inhabitants of the Commonwealth. When, in 2010, the Royal Commonwealth Society published a survey of attitudes across its member states, the level of knowledge and engagement it uncovered was not encouraging. For example, only half of those questioned knew that the Queen was head of the Commonwealth. A quarter of Jamaicans thought it was the US president, Barack Obama, and 10 per cent of South Africans and Indians thought it was the former UN secretary-general, Kofi Annan. It's difficult to get a network to function effectively if most of its supposed members have only the haziest notion of its existence.

The irony is that, before being quietly shuffled out of government, Lord Howell himself spent two years from 2010 grappling bravely—but unsuccessfully—with these very conundrums. A large part of the problem he faced, as countless British policy-makers had faced before him, was making sense of the byzantine and slightly dysfunctional nature of the 'Commonwealth network'. For Britain's administrative elite, the Commonwealth is a bit like a grandfather clock that has been in the family for generations. It hasn't told the right time for decades, but no one has the heart to take such a treasured heirloom to the tip. All the same, Britain's mainstream parties had become increasingly reluctant in recent years to place significant weight on the Commonwealth as an instrument of the UK's diplomatic, economic or even overseas aid policy. Then, in June 2016, a seismic shock was delivered to the UK's sense of its place in the world when the majority of voters in that month's referendum opted to leave the EU. Suddenly, people started to talk about the Commonwealth again.

Even more frequently, particularly among disappointed Remain voters, they spoke of the role in the referendum of 'imperial nostalgia'. Hull, the city where I grew up, voted to leave by one of the largest margins in the country: 67.6% to 32.4% (against a national total of 52% to 48%). Apparently, when asked to choose between a pan-European identity and one supposedly inflected by imperial nostalgia based on the UK's identity at the centre of an inter-continental network, Hull had opted, in Churchill's phrase, for the 'open sea'. This was despite the city's strong trading links with major European ports like Zeebrugge and Rotterdam, and the fact that, as recently as November 2014, the decision by German manufacturer Siemens to produce North Sea wind farm blades in Hull had given a huge boost to the local economy. It was an investment the city—the UK's third most deprived local authority—badly needed. So had I been missing something? Were those subliminal messages about Britain's essentially imperial identity more profound and long-lasting than I had imagined?

The following chapters will attempt to make sense of the complexities and contradictions of Britain's relationships both to the Commonwealth and to its own imperial past. They do so by considering a series of questions: why has the organization evolved as it has? Why has it survived for so long, and what value has been attached to membership of it? What has been the role of the monarchy in holding it together? How does it fit into debates about the legacy of Empire? How successful has it been in defining itself as a 'principles-based' organization, and how did someone who appeared not to observe them come to hold its highest political office? Finally, what role did it play in the Brexit debate, and where does it stand in the aftermath of that political earthquake? In seeking to answer these questions, *The Empire's New Clothes* examines how the myth of the Commonwealth has evolved. Ultimately, it seeks to understand why something as seemingly insubstantial as an invisible suit, offered to a foolish fairytale emperor, continues to exert such a hold on the minds of British policy-makers.

MEET THE FAMILY

Whose Commonwealth?

A familiar analysis of the failure of the Commonwealth, and a common accusation made against the UK, is that the British, having created the organization, simply lost interest in it and allowed it to fall into disrepair. This is the argument at the heart of *The Rise, Decline and Future of the Commonwealth*, a history of the organization published in 2005 by Krishnan Srinivasan, who had observed the situation at close quarters as a senior official in the Commonwealth Secretariat. Commonwealth orthodoxy has it that, some time around 1949, the Commonwealth ceased to be focused on the UK and instead became an organization of which all its members had an equal sense of ownership. Srinivasan disputes that interpretation, arguing that the Commonwealth is essentially British in its origins and conception; and if the UK is not prepared to invest it with a special sense of ownership then, rather than being 'Everybody's Commonwealth', its fate is to be 'Nobody's Commonwealth'.

Srinivasan was reflecting the frustration of many overseas observers who have viewed British policy from the vantage point of the Secretariat. David McDowell, a former New Zealand diplomat and special adviser to the first Commonwealth secretary-general, recalled:

> Time and again, I used to think, "What the hell are the British up to?" I mean, the Indian government was doing this so-called 'tilt' towards Russia at one point, and you'd sit down with a bunch of officials and Indian diplomats and they were still pretty pro-British under the skin. They sounded British, their argumentation was British, [and] a lot of them were British-educated. This was a huge asset, and the British would ignore them! To me, it's one of the enduring mysteries of British foreign policy over those years. Why didn't they use this institution, the Commonwealth, much more effectively than they did? And I've got no final answer. We could not understand that.[1]

One clue to this mystery might lie in the question of whether and to what extent the Commonwealth really was a British invention. While this may seem self-evidently the case, there is another way of looking at the organization's evolution. One could argue that it occurred more in spite of British designs than because of them. In this sense, it is hardly surprising that UK governments should have found the Commonwealth difficult to mobilize in its interests, and that the result was a growing sense of disillusionment.

Breaking this down further, it is possible to identify three distinct phases in British engagement with the Commonwealth. The first, which lasted until the mid-1960s, was one in which the British struggled to contain the centrifugal forces that were robbing the Commonwealth of much of its practical value. To put it another way, in seeking to ensure that the Commonwealth should mean 'something', the British were forced to make major concessions to those members who wished it to mean virtually 'nothing'.

From the mid-1960s onwards, there was a period of institution-building within the organization. But in that process the

British were, at best, grudging participants. It began during a period of profound dislocation for British foreign policy. On the one hand, the UK government was beginning to come to terms with the fact that the Commonwealth had lost much of its former significance. On the other, however, it was recovering from the shock of the failure in 1963 to join the European Economic Community (EEC) at the first attempt. As such, it felt unable to block developments that might reinvigorate the Commonwealth, while being uneasy with the form that these took. What followed was a period when the Commonwealth agenda was dominated by the related issues of the settler regimes in Southern Rhodesia and South Africa. While these questions gave the Commonwealth a sense of mission and purpose, the British government frequently found itself in a small minority opposing policies proposed by most Commonwealth members.

The final phase saw the British government in the early 1990s seeking to play an uncharacteristically proactive role in re-orienting the Commonwealth as a vehicle to promote democracy, good governance and market reforms. Yet this new approach was so at odds with the nature of the organization's operation hitherto that the tangible results were meagre. The government shifted its focus to other areas and institutions where it could hope to exert greater influence.

This story begins, as all stories about the Commonwealth must begin, with the phrase 'In the beginning was an Empire.' Having had its fingers badly burned by the fractious colonists of North America in the 1770s and '80s, British governments of the following period realized that trying to maintain direct control over the remaining settler colonies was likely to be counterproductive. Instead, they were gradually allowed to develop their own self-governing institutions. Speaking in Adelaide in 1884, the British statesman Lord Rosebery recognized this new dispensation when he envisaged the British Empire's development into a 'Commonwealth of Nations'. As Mark Mazower has noted, this notion became a particularly powerful one as political leaders searched for some basis on which to reconstruct international order in the wake of the First World War.[2] It found a perhaps unlikely champion in Jan Smuts, who went from being Britain's most brilliant adversary during the Second Boer War to a key member of the British Imperial War Cabinet and a future prime minister of the Union of South Africa. As the First World War neared its end, Smuts suggested that the British Commonwealth model—combining as it did effective cooperation between members with the greatest autonomy for each—was one that could be followed on a larger scale by a future League of Nations, another idea he championed.

Certainly, during the inter-war period, the Commonwealth appeared to prove itself capable of both promoting cooperation and safeguarding the autonomy of its members. Perhaps the defining moment in the genesis of the modern organization came with the report of a committee chaired by former British prime minister Arthur Balfour, presented to the Imperial Conference of 1926. The report offered a definition of the relationship between Britain and what were then commonly referred to as the Dominions—the self-governing countries of the Commonwealth. It identified them as "autonomous communities within the British Empire, equal in status, in no way subordinate one to another in any aspect of their domestic or external affairs, though united by a common allegiance to the Crown, and freely associated in the British Commonwealth of Nations."

This formulation, which has remained a central tenet of Commonwealth orthodoxy ever since, found legislative expression in the 1931 Statute of Westminster, which at that point related to the governments of the UK, Canada, Australia, New Zealand, South Africa (which left the Commonwealth in 1961), the Irish Free State (which left in 1949) and Newfoundland (which became a province of Canada in 1949). In particular, it made clear that the legislative competence of Commonwealth member states' parliaments was not restricted by acts of the British parliament, and that they also had the power to legislate with extra-territorial effect. The following year, at the 1932 Imperial Economic Conference in Ottawa, there was agreement for tariff reductions between Commonwealth members—apparently opening the door to the creation of a vast imperial trading bloc. Yet even in these apparently positive developments one can already identify the seeds of future problems.

The 1932 Ottawa agreements were far less extensive than many imperial enthusiasts had hoped. As one recent account of the Conference notes, the negotiations were characterized "by intensive, often bad-tempered bilateral deal-making, in a fashion quite at odds with rhetoric about an underlying commonality of interests."[3] In a sign of things to come, individual members were unwilling to subordinate their own individual interests to some supposedly greater good. As to the Balfour Report's precise formulations of 'equality of status' and 'free association', these had a very specific purpose for British policy-makers in 1926—they were intended to head off a demand from the South African prime minister, J.B.M. Hertzog, for formal recognition of his country's independence.

The term 'independence' was anathema to British policy-makers well into the 1950s, striking as it did at the cohesion of the British Empire/Commonwealth. Far from an argument for independence, then, the notion of equality was an important means of maintaining what many in Britain saw as an essential prop of British great-power status. At the same time, however, 'equality' suggested at least in theory that member states would not automatically accept or welcome British leadership of the organization. As the Commonwealth was augmented from the 1940s by India, Pakistan and Ceylon (Sri Lanka), and thereafter by developing countries from South East Asia, Africa, the Caribbean and the Pacific, it was increasingly important to disavow notions that the Commonwealth was being driven by British interests. More broadly, the UK wished to avoid a perception of the organization as driven by Western, white or neo-colonial interests, however defined.

Certainly the British government was anxious that India should remain in the organization after independence in 1947, and was prepared to sanction a radical change to the basis of Commonwealth membership to that end. It did so in the mistaken belief that India's huge standing army would continue to underwrite British great-power status. Previously, the defining feature of Commonwealth members was that all recognized the sovereignty of a single monarch. India, however, would be allowed to remain part of the organization on becoming a republic in 1950. To achieve this, a new, separate and purely personal role was created for the British monarch, as head of the Commonwealth. The London Declaration of 1949 acknowledged India's "acceptance of the King as the symbol of the free association of its independent member nations and as such Head of the Commonwealth".

The irony was that, although this concession allowed the organization to embrace a hugely greater land-mass and population than would otherwise have been the case, it was made in order to accommodate a government determined that the practical implications of Commonwealth membership should be virtually nil. It was another step in the direction of 'nothingness'. In his regular letters to the chief ministers of India's provincial governments, Prime Minister Jawaharal Nehru made a point of stressing how little membership of the Commonwealth would actually imply in terms of the obligations upon his country. In January 1949, he told them, "People who have criticized the possibility of our having some future relationship with the United

Kingdom and the Commonwealth must realize now that even if there is such a relationship it cannot affect our foreign policy. That would not mean lining up with any particular group of nations."[4] He continued to reiterate this point after terms had been agreed for India's future membership, and as his familiarity with the organization increased. In June 1952, he told the chief ministers that India's association with the Commonwealth posed no threat to the country's independence:

> It is completely informal and there are no commitments. It brings us certain advantages and there is no reason whatever, so far as I can see, why we should give it up ... In international affairs our association with the UK and the Commonwealth has led far more to us influencing them in a particular direction than their influencing us.[5]

In the years that followed the 1949 London Declaration, the British government became markedly less enthusiastic about the Commonwealth expanding further. In the 1950s, Kwame Nkrumah, leader of the principal nationalist movement in the Gold Coast (now Ghana), caused some dismay in Whitehall by demanding dominion status for his country. It was one thing to accommodate the old Harrovian Nehru. But was the Commonwealth really ready to accept into its councils a radical African nationalist prime minister?

Even greater hand-wringing was occasioned by the prospect of Cyprus joining the Commonwealth. Talks in 1959 promised an end to the brutal armed struggle that had been waged on the island since 1955, and provided a pathway to full independence. But would Commonwealth membership be the logical outcome? Senior British officials initially hoped not. Well aware that the majority of its existing dependencies were so small as to be barely viable as independent states, and certainly unlikely to serve the UK as useful strategic or economic partners, Whitehall had toyed with devising forms of association short of full Commonwealth membership.[6] But these had largely foundered on the fact that such second-class citizenship was unlikely to be attractive to the states concerned.

This was certainly the case with Cyprus. But the island raised other questions about the nature of the Commonwealth association. Surely some important components were the shared use of the English language and at least a residual sense of identification with and affection for the UK? Cyprus hardly seemed to qualify. Indeed, the leader of the Greek Cypriot community and first prime minister of Cyprus, Archbishop Makarios, was widely believed to have been directing the insurgency devoted, until very recently, to attempting to eject the British. As Cypriot independence neared, British Cabinet Secretary Norman Brook was hardly alone in suggesting that Cyprus would be "much more of a liability than an asset to the Commonwealth".[7]

As the Commonwealth grew in size, it continued, as Lorna Lloyd has noted, to lose much of what had previously invested it with particular value from a British perspective.[8] As we have already seen, with the decision in 1949 to allow India to remain in the Commonwealth as a republic, common allegiance to the monarch ceased to be the constitutional bond holding the organization together. Meanwhile, the notion of a shared Commonwealth citizenship—based on member-state populations' status as British subjects—had been shattered by the Canadian Citizenship Act of 1946. From 1962 onwards, UK legislation steadily eroded the universal right of all UK and Commonwealth subjects[9] to migrate to Britain.

The idea that the Commonwealth as an important military resource would automatically take Britain's side in any major conflict had already been dealt a blow by the Irish Free State's neutrality during the Second World War and the reluctance with which South Africa joined the conflict. In the post-war era it was further called into question by lukewarm Indian and Pakistani support for the British position in the Korean War, and undermined by Indian non-alignment. The death-blow came with the deep divisions within the Commonwealth caused by the Suez Crisis of 1956. Similarly, the National Party victory in South Africa in 1948 and the imposition of military rule in Pakistan in 1958 made it difficult to speak of the Commonwealth as united by common political characteristics inherited from Britain itself.

Finally, the Sterling Area arrangement, under which most of the Commonwealth member states had fixed their own exchange rates to the pound and held their exchange reserves in sterling, had once seemed a source of strength for the UK. In the post-war period, however, it increasingly became seen as more of a millstone, with international confidence in the currency threatened by massive sterling balances outside British control (effectively debts to other Area members accumulated during the Second World War). Nevertheless, the defence of sterling's value and with it the Sterling Area itself was a major British policy objective until devaluation in 1967 spelled the beginning of the end for the system. At a special Economic Conference convened by Churchill's second administration in 1952, any hopes that ministers might have entertained of reviving the Commonwealth as a protected trading bloc were brutally dispelled by other Commonwealth members.

Faced with these changes, senior British policy-makers naturally began to ask fundamental questions about the utility of a heterogeneous and rapidly expanding Commonwealth, its numbers swelled by rapid decolonization. Submitting to the prime minister a report by officials on the future of the Commonwealth, Cabinet Secretary Norman Brook framed the problem in April 1962 in terms that recognized the shifts underway. He asked:

> What is the significance and purpose of the Commonwealth in the years ahead? What function and value will this new Commonwealth have in the modern world? What are the links that bind its members together? There was a time when they were united by their allegiance

to a common Crown. In the 'thirties after the Ottawa Conference, there was a period when it seemed possible that they could form an interdependent economic unit; but this possibility has been progressively eroded, not by the United Kingdom but by the economic development of the other members. Later, it could be said for a time that they all had in common a way of life based on Parliamentary democracy and the common law; but the logic of events in Pakistan and in Ghana and the possible course of constitutional development elsewhere have made it necessary to mute this claim. Now it is difficult to find any factor common to them all save the use of the English language and the fact that all were once parts of the British Empire.[10]

The British comic song-writing duo, Flanders and Swann, translated this dilemma into music. They included in their mid-1960s stage shows a number called 'Commonwealth Fair', set to the tune of the English folk-song 'Widecombe Fair'. It included the lines:

> The Commonwealth hasn't much meaning today,
> All-about, turn-about, round-about, lee,
> Except for the few who're still willing to play,
> Like Australia, New Zealand and Canada:
> Well, that's about the lot, really....
> The others may still wear the Commonwealth coat,
> Though there's practically nothing on which we agree,
> What does Commonwealth mean, when it comes to the vote...[?]

What indeed?

The Birth of the Secretariat

Ironically, however, as the British government itself was agonizing about what, if anything, the organization continued to represent, high-level meetings between Commonwealth leaders were becoming more frequent, encouraged by improved long-distance transport and communications. During the first decades of the twentieth century, Commonwealth leaders had met together in London at a number of imperial conferences and great state occasions. Towards the end of the Second World War, Commonwealth prime ministers' conferences were instituted, and they became regular gatherings in the immediate post-war period. Thirteen took place between 1944 and 1964. As a result of these meetings, Commonwealth leaders began to forge their own agenda, particularly around the issues of development and the ending of white minority rule in Southern Africa. They also began to demand the creation of more formal structures to facilitate consultation.

Indeed, the present-day administrative architecture of the Commonwealth was devised as much in spite of the wishes of London as because of it. There was certainly a brief period in the 1960s when British governments from both major parties suddenly rediscovered an interest in the Commonwealth. The catalyst seems to have been General de Gaulle's decision early in 1963 to veto Britain's first application for membership of the EEC. The shock of having what seemed to be an almost inevitable move towards Europe stopped in its tracks prompted a renewed interest in the Commonwealth. As Trevor Reese noted, "For the first time in three-quarters of a century people in England, besides editors of the Beaverbrook press and members of certain societies, thought seriously about the Commonwealth".[11] There was certainly a new openness in Whitehall to ideas for turning the Commonwealth into a more effective and meaningful association. Yet ahead of the Commonwealth prime ministers' meeting of July 1964, the proposals put forward by London largely were not about political cohesion but focused instead on development, education and training. It also proposed an idea, ultimately adopted, for a Commonwealth Foundation to promote contacts across the non-governmental Commonwealth.[12]

At the meeting itself, however, the UK was taken by surprise when the president of Ghana, Kwame Nkrumah, proposed the creation of a 'central clearing house' in London to coordinate the Commonwealth's activities. Proposals for the establishment of some sort of Commonwealth secretariat had been raised periodically over the decades, most notably by Australian prime ministers. Indeed, in 1959, it had been announced that the Queen was making one of her royal palaces, Marlborough House, available as a venue for Commonwealth activities.[13] Yet it was novel to hear this proposal from one of Africa's most radical nationalist leaders. Nkrumah won immediate backing from Uganda's leader, Milton Obote, and from Eric Williams of Trinidad. The creation of a secretariat would, of course, remove from Britain the coordinating role in the Commonwealth, which had been exercised through the Dominions Office and subsequently the Commonwealth Relations Office. But since Whitehall was already considering the possibility of merging the Commonwealth and Foreign Offices, the proposal had an added attraction from the UK's perspective. Since the idea seemed to have momentum behind it, the British government decided not to reject it.[14]

The British general election of October 1964 was narrowly won by Harold Wilson's Labour Party. Under Wilson's predecessor as Labour leader, the party had fiercely opposed Britain's first attempt to join the EEC, and Labour's manifesto in 1964 included a forthright statement of support for the Commonwealth. As such, Wilson's government had no desire to reverse the progress made under the previous administration. Nevertheless, senior British officials worried that the secretariat might achieve too much influence and autonomy. An official committee meeting in January 1965 concluded that it "should not arrogate to itself executive functions ... it should operate on a modest footing; and its staff and functions should be left to expand pragmatically in the light of experience, subject always to the approval of Governments."[15]

A determination that any secretariat should remain a relatively weak body was not confined to Whitehall. Australian Prime

Minister Sir Robert Menzies, a firm believer in the values and style of the 'old Commonwealth', told Wilson of his fears that the new body might want to start 'pushing governments around'. India was also cautious, and the prime minister of New Zealand expressed the hope that the secretariat would not weaken Britain's 'old Commonwealth' links.[16] Nevertheless, the plan was accepted by Commonwealth prime ministers when they met in June 1965. The meeting also endorsed the proposal that Arnold Smith, a senior Canadian diplomat, should become the Commonwealth's first secretary-general. An interesting footnote to this appointment was that the other front-runner for the post, Alister McIntosh from New Zealand, had been ruled out because security sources apparently reported that he was homosexual.[17] At this stage, of course, all forms of male homosexual activity were illegal in both Britain and New Zealand (where decriminalization only occurred in 1986). It seems difficult to believe that an openly gay candidate would have any chance of being elected secretary-general even today, given that the majority of member states still criminalize homosexuality.

Arnold Smith served as secretary-general for ten years until 1975. He has had five successors: Shridath 'Sonny' Ramphal from Guyana (1975–90), Chief Emeka Anyaoku from Nigeria (1990–2000), Don McKinnon from New Zealand (2000–8), Kamalesh Sharma from India (2008–16) and Baroness Patricia Scotland, who has joint British and Dominican citizenship (2016–). Each has had a unique style of leadership, and has operated against a distinct geopolitical backdrop.

David McDowell, a New Zealand diplomat who worked as Smith's special assistant in 1969–72, remembers that his former boss approached his new responsibilities pragmatically, and was keen for the Commonwealth to be seen in similarly practical terms: 'Not as some romantic hangover from Empire, obviously, but as a practical means where there are so few networks like this existing in the world today.'[18] In the light of the ambivalence to the Secretariat's creation among some of the Commonwealth's leading members—including Britain—Smith realized that he himself would have to take the initiative if the organization was to make a mark on the international scene. He could not simply wait around until a consensus magically appeared among its heads of government. Tony Eggleton, who worked as director of communications under Smith, recalls,

> Arnold taught me some useful lessons: i.e. don't call a meeting unless you can be fairly certain of its outcome; write the draft minutes before the meeting and try to ensure the final communiqué is a fair reflection of the draft! I found these tactics of value in my later political career!![19]

In terms of institution-building, Smith's major legacy was the 1971 creation of the Commonwealth Fund for Technical Cooperation (CFTC). Its defining feature was that it sought to move away from the bilateral provision of aid from the First to the Third World, instead offering expert assistance at the request of developing countries on a swift and flexible basis. Crucially, this could include South-South assistance, with developing nations sharing knowledge and experience. Like the Secretariat itself, the idea was not universally welcomed. As McDowell remembers,

> It was still a pretty hard sell at the beginning. People kept on saying, "Oh, well, we've got the World Bank and the IMF and the regional development banks starting to be set up and we've got the UNDP and the UN specialized agencies ...What is the point of the Commonwealth one?" Arnold argued very persuasively ... that this was a unique global association and it could draw quickly and accurately on a whole range of expertise, which wasn't necessarily easily available to huge outfits like the UNDP and the World Bank.[20]

Indeed, as demonstrated by a recent detailed study of the CFTC's early years, Britain, Australia and Canada—as major donor nations of the Commonwealth—were all distinctly ambivalent about the new agency.[21] International aid, after all, was a significant tool of diplomacy. By serving as an intermediary, the CFTC threatened to dilute the influence donors could exert over recipients. India, too, was sceptical about the idea. Nevertheless, as we shall see in Chapter 3, the CFTC did demonstrate its value on a number of occasions, although its meagre budget continued to constrain what it was able to achieve.

Smith's successor as secretary-general was Shridath Surendranath 'Sonny' Ramphal. Trained in Law at King's College London and London Gray's Inn, Ramphal had served as Guyana's foreign minister before taking up the post. A charismatic figure with finely tuned political antennae, Ramphal presided over the Commonwealth in a period (1975–90) when it and its secretary-general were seldom out of the news. The organization played a significant role in Rhodesia's peaceful transition to majority rule and formal independence as Zimbabwe. It launched major initiatives aimed at bringing an end to apartheid, such as the 1977 Gleneagles Declaration on sporting links with South Africa and the 1986 mission there by a Commonwealth Eminent Persons Group. The Commonwealth continued to develop a reputation as an innovative actor in the area of development and aid. Ramphal himself served as a member of the Brandt Commission on International Development and the Palme Commission on Disarmament and Security.

This is not to suggest that Ramphal himself or his style of operating were universally popular. Under his leadership, Britain frequently found itself isolated within the Commonwealth, particularly over its reluctance to support sanctions against South Africa. He certainly made enemies among members of Mrs Thatcher's government from 1979. Lord Carrington, her first foreign secretary, never forgave him for what he regarded as Ramphal's unhelpful interference in Zimbabwe's independence negotiations. In his memoirs, Ramphal recalls Carrington's remark that he would "swim the Atlantic twice" to frustrate Ramphal's ambition to become UN secretary-general.[22] Douglas Hurd, one of Carrington's successors as British foreign secretary, recalled, "Ramphal was what I would call, in the nicest possible way, a loud mouth'. He talked a lot. He blew his own trumpet anywhere he could and in a way I think that reduced the total of good that he did."[23]

It could be argued that even the animosity Ramphal aroused could, in a sense, be taken as proof of his success in confirming the Commonwealth as an organization to be reckoned with. In retrospect, it might seem that he was fortunate in serving when he did. His time in office coincided with a period of optimism and solidarity within the developing world, and one in which the Commonwealth was seen by many as a useful corrective to the divisive geopolitics of the Cold War. There was also the key rallying point of the campaign against Southern African white minority rule. The point, however, was that the Commonwealth under Ramphal rose to those challenges and used them to lend momentum and purpose to the organization.

But those on the right of the British political spectrum who call for a reinvigoration of the Commonwealth tend to forget that during this 'golden age' it was sometimes an uncomfortable presence for UK policy-makers, and a frequent target for attacks by the popular press. For instance, Lord Howell, the current guru-in-chief of London's Commonwealth true-believers, chairs the Royal Commonwealth Society (RCS), which regularly boasts of the organization's success in ending apartheid and lionizes the memory of Nelson Mandela. At the time, he took a rather different view. At a press conference concluding the Vancouver Commonwealth Heads of Government Meeting (CHOGM) in October 1987, Mrs Thatcher claimed that a reported threat by the ANC to target British firms showed "what a typical terrorist organization it is."

The remark was widely criticized and served to heighten the impression that the British government, which had continued to resist calls for tougher sanctions against South Africa, was isolated within the Commonwealth. Yet Howell, then a loyal government backbencher, leapt to her defence in the Commons:

> Was not my right hon. friend at Vancouver entirely right to condemn and criticize the role of the African National Congress? Was not the ANC an organization which notably failed to condemn the monstrous atrocity of necklace burning? Would not the Opposition and others who want to see the apartheid problem defeated and overcome do better to listen to the voice of the Inkatha movement which represents millions of black South Africans who want more prosperity and more investment rather than sanctions and lectures?[24]

The 1990s witnessed a further change in the UK's relations with the Commonwealth. It was heralded in 1990 by the departure from the scene of both Ramphal and Thatcher, seasoned antagonists who had crossed swords so frequently over the issue of South Africa. In their place appeared two much more emollient figures: respectively the Nigerian career diplomat, Chief Emeka Anyaoku, and Prime Minister John Major. The Major government (1990–7) witnessed a brief proactive role for the UK in shaping the Commonwealth's mission and institutions. By the time of the 1991 CHOGM in Harare, not only were Ramphal and Thatcher gone, but the international scene was witnessing profound change. The Iron Curtain had fallen. Nelson Mandela had been released from jail in South Africa, and was now actively involved in negotiating the terms for a transition to majority rule.

The British government recognized the chance to turn the tables on those Commonwealth members who had been vocal in condemning the denial of democracy and human rights in South Africa, while showing little respect for such values in their own countries. The British cabinet secretary Sir Robert Armitage played a leading role in the drafting of a set of principles agreed by heads at the Summit. These placed particular emphasis on "democracy, democratic processes and institutions which reflect national circumstances, the rule of law and the independence of the judiciary, just and honest government" and "fundamental human rights, including equal rights and opportunities for all citizens regardless of race, colour, creed or political belief".

The 1991 Harare Declaration led four years later to the creation of a new institution dedicated to monitoring and enforcing adherence to these principles: the Commonwealth Ministerial Action Group (CMAG). This was established at the 1995 CHOGM in Auckland as part of the so-called Millbrook Commonwealth Action Plan to deal with "serious or persistent violations" of the Harare principles. A major impetus for this initiative was the sense of shock and anger felt by Commonwealth leaders at the execution of Ken Saro Wiwa and nine fellow activists by the military government of Sani Abacha, at the very moment when Commonwealth heads of government were meeting. While Anyaoku had already been canvassing support for a body to monitor compliance with the Harare principles, it is questionable whether he would have been able to obtain agreement on the matter had it not been for the outrage generated by the executions.

CMAG originally consisted of eight Commonwealth foreign ministers, increased to nine in 2003 with the addition of the foreign minister of whichever state held the post of chair-in-office. Although CMAG's remit was potentially broad, the Millbrook statement specifically mentioned that the Commonwealth would not tolerate the "unconstitutional overthrow of a democratically elected government". It also stipulated that CMAG would recommend measures "aimed at the speedy restoration of democracy and constitutional rule." Both carried an expectation that CMAG's principal focus would be on countries where the government had been unconstitutionally overthrown.

Indeed, with the exception of Zimbabwe, this has been the common feature of those states that have appeared on its agenda. CMAG was given the power to suspend a country from participation in Commonwealth meetings, without reference to Commonwealth heads of government. Beyond that, it can ultimately recommend the full suspension or expulsion of states, although this does require the consent and cooperation of other heads of government.

The 1995 founding of CMAG was a fundamental departure from the past evolution of the Commonwealth. Arguably, the whole idea of a watchdog monitoring the internal behaviour of member states was fundamentally at odds with the spirit of the organization; the logistics of bringing eight Commonwealth foreign ministers together have added to the problems. Since its creation, CMAG has met on average fewer than three times a year, for relatively short periods; most meetings coincide with other international gatherings in London and New York. With such limited opportunity for discussions, it is hardly surprising that CMAG has confined its attentions to the worst offenders—namely, countries where the government had been forcibly removed. Perhaps more importantly, it lacks a permanent staff tasked with gathering evidence on violations of Commonwealth principles. As such, it is highly dependent on the Secretariat itself for information-gathering; as we will see later in the case of Sri Lanka, the flow of information between the two has not always been satisfactory.

Perhaps the fundamental criticism of the CMAG system is that, in many cases, the Commonwealth simply lacks sufficient leverage to bring recalcitrant member states into line. The case of the Gambia is an example of this weakness. The country, one of the first states to appear on CMAG's agenda, should have been a fairly easy target—a relatively weak nation heavily dependent on the West for development aid. Yet President Yahya Jammeh, who had seized power in a 1994 coup, was able to resist pressure from the Commonwealth for a number of years, partly by cultivating alternative donors such as China and Libya. While his country's heavy indebtedness finally forced Jammeh into an accommodation, the form of democracy he introduced was of a highly limited nature. Oil-rich Nigeria, another early target of CMAG, proved even more capable of resisting Commonwealth pressure. The end of military rule there was ultimately the result of the sudden death of General Abacha in 1998. Unless the grim reaper was an ex officio CMAG member, then, there was little evidence that CMAG really made any appreciable impact. Conversely, there have been far more powerful organizations, such as the World Bank and the IMF, that have been putting pressure on Commonwealth member states to make democratic reforms.

It fell to Secretary-General Don McKinnon (2000–8) to try and operate the system put in place by his predecessor. It was an unenviable task, one he undertook with energy and determination—but successes proved to be elusive. Perhaps his single largest problem was the unravelling of one of the Commonwealth's great success stories: the peaceful transfer of power in Zimbabwe. The sort of pan-African solidarity which had previously aided the Commonwealth's efforts in minority-rule Southern Africa now became a hindrance in the organization's new-found mission to promote democracy and good governance. There had been growing concern at the authoritarian and economically disastrous policies of Zimbabwe's ageing president, Robert Mugabe. This came to a head following the presidential elections of March 2002. While Mugabe claimed to have won 56.2 per cent of the vote, a result endorsed by the Organization of African Unity, the Commonwealth's own election monitors—in common with many other international observers—maintained that it had been undermined by irregularities and violence.

A judicial investigation commissioned by South African President Thabo Mbeki endorsed the Commonwealth's verdict, but was suppressed by the South African government for twelve years.[25] Commonwealth heads had been meeting in Coolum, Australia, just a few days before the election took place, and Zimbabwe had featured prominently in discussions. It was agreed that a troika, composed of the last, present and next Commonwealth chair-in-office—Mbeki, Australian Prime Minister John Howard and President Olesegun Obasanjo of Nigeria—would await the monitoring team's report and then take action. On 19 March, Howard announced that Zimbabwe would be temporarily suspended from the councils of the Commonwealth—a move that fell short of full suspension, which both Howard himself and his counterparts in Britain and New Zealand would have favoured. It was clear at Coolum that the Commonwealth was split on the matter, with many African members proving sympathetic towards Mugabe.

These divisions, both within the Commonwealth itself and between Howard, Mbeki and Obasanjo, hindered attempts to use the troika to pressure Mugabe. While some African members blamed the failure of the troika's efforts on Howard for his supposed intransigence and insensitivity, Howard himself told my colleague Sue Onslow that the initiative "just died in the sand because frankly the southern African states' sense of fraternity they felt towards the Zimbabwean leadership was greater than anything else."[26] Divisions were also apparent at the next CHOGM, held in Abuja, Nigeria in December 2003, with some members actually pressing for Zimbabwe's membership to be reinstated. Instead, it was decided that its suspension should be made permanent, and Mugabe responded by withdrawing his country from the organization. It was a depressing outcome for the Commonwealth: a great deal of high-level diplomatic energy had been expended to no constructive end. Of even greater concern, perhaps, was the spectacle of the organization dividing on racial and economic lines over the defence of supposedly core shared values: democracy, human rights and the rule of law.

If McKinnon's period in office provided relatively few tangible achievements, he did at least maintain a fairly high public profile and he could certainly not be accused of evading difficult decisions. His successor, Kamalesh Sharma (2008–16), achieved even less without even giving the impression that he was trying very hard. A shy, cautious Indian career diplomat, Sharma struck an uncertain note on the public stage from the very start. As he later recalled,

> A couple of hours after I was elected, I was dragged before the media to say something but the bulk of the media had been detained for security reasons. Most of them were not there, it was just a handful of people. So it was a very short press conference, but they did ask me the same question as you did, and I said something to the effect that, "As for the roadmap, it is best to devise it after you have been on the road and seen where you are on it. But as for the orientation, I want to make it clear that I'm certain about one thing: that as SG I will not allow the Commonwealth to be seen as a boutique organization, and work for the Commonwealth as the great global good, which it is." This phrase was unrehearsed, unprepared; it just came out from the heart, in what I said. That's how I looked at the Commonwealth. It is a great global good and I thought as SG it would be my task to advance it as a great global good. So, if you like, my vision was that the Commonwealth should not be a niche player in global affairs but a mainstream contributor to global action and wisdom.[27]

It is unimaginable that McKinnon or Sonny Ramphal would ever have described themselves as having been "dragged" before the media. As seasoned politicians, they were more than comfortable in the limelight, and understood that it was their duty to provide the Commonwealth with a recognizable public face. Sharma, by contrast, never seemed at ease with journalists; nor was he a great orator or a natural communicator of any kind. Perhaps because of his diplomatic—not political—background, he was arguably too willing to defer to the senior ministers he encountered. From the start, the status and role of the Commonwealth secretary-general had been poorly defined. In a famous put-down, the New Zealand premier Robert Muldoon once told Ramphal to stop talking and concentrate on taking the minutes. Ramphal and Smith had worked hard in the 1970s and '80s to establish the secretary-general as more than a secretary, and had pushed at the boundaries of what was acceptable in order to signal the autonomy of the position. Sharma, by contrast, too often seemed to conform to the original conception of the secretary-general: essentially the servant of Commonwealth governments. McKinnon, not unnaturally, had believed that it was a post better suited to a politician than an official:

> To me, it is a political job, because as a senior politician you are treating the leaders as equals, and they see you as close to one of them ... You have got to be their equal. I have noticed that those who come from the civil service will always defer to ministers, presidents and prime ministers.[28]

Another problem exposed by Sharma's account of his initial press conference was his insistence that the Commonwealth should not be seen as a "boutique" organization but as a "great global good". Although the sentiment might seem laudable, previous leaders of the Commonwealth had had to grapple with the limited budget at their disposal—a tiny fraction of that of many other international organizations. As such, the Commonwealth needed to be nimble and innovative in its use of those resources, and could only hope to be successful if it concentrated on a relatively small number of issues. Sharma, however, seemed to willing to buy into the myth of the Commonwealth as an organization of almost unbounded potential. The consequence was an apparently endless series of well-meaning pronouncements from the Secretariat, unsupported by meaningful action. And we shall see that when the organization did face significant challenges—largely internal ones—Sharma's handling of them was far from confident.

If the Commonwealth is beset by nostalgia, it is not for Empire, but for a supposedly golden 'Camelot'-style era when it seemed to be at the forefront of radical change and, in particular, was guided with courage and wisdom from the court of King Sonny. Indeed, during episodes such as the clumsy handling of the 2011 Commonwealth Eminent Persons Group report, or the disastrous 2013 CHOGM, direct criticism of Sharma was muted, but apprehensive Commonwealth supporters invoked memories of Ramphal's strong and decisive leadership. The barely hidden message was that Sonny would never have allowed things to reach such a pass. These mutterings tended to be heard most clearly from members of the Commonwealth's extensive network of affiliated organizations. And it is to these that we now turn.

The Other 'Commonwealths'

For anyone encountering the Commonwealth 'family' for the first time, perhaps its most perplexing feature is the vast array of associated so-called 'civil-society' organizations, over seventy of which are recognized by the Secretariat as affiliates., Covering a bewilderingly broad sweep of professions and causes, and dating from a variety of different eras, these add Rococo embellishments to an already-elaborate institutional architecture. To give a few random examples: the Conference of Commonwealth Meteorologists (established in 1929), the Conference of Commonwealth Postal Administrators (1971), the Commonwealth Association of Architects (1965), the Commonwealth Forestry Association (1921), the Commonwealth Medical Association (1952), and the Commonwealth Veterinary Association (1967). The remit of these organizations, at least, was fairly self-explanatory. But there were also some puzzlingly esoteric-sounding outliers, such as the Commonwealth Human Ecology Council.

Many of the bigger beasts in this particular Commonwealth ecosystem were survivals of organizations that had grown up to promote or celebrate Empire and imperial linkages. Their gradual adaption to changing geopolitical conditions gives the lie to the notion—vigorously promoted by the Secretariat—that the Commonwealth emerged new and fully-formed in 1949. An associated myth is that its birth was marked by the decision to refer to it not as 'the British Commonwealth', but simply as 'the Commonwealth'. In fact, there were few attempts to synchronize any change in terminology. Following the 1948 Commonwealth prime ministers' meeting, speculation had arisen that its final communique had deliberately dropped the word 'British' before 'Commonwealth'. But, in a Cabinet memorandum circulated at the end of December that year, Prime Minister Clement Attlee denied that there was any great significance in this. He suggested that—while 'Commonwealth' was probably a safer term in view of the sensibilities of the organization's new Asian members—it might still be appropriate in certain circumstances to speak of the 'British Commonwealth'. The only firm rule was that the old word 'Dominion' was no longer suitable in official communications.[29]

The rather haphazard way in which 'Imperial' became 'Commonwealth' over time is nicely illustrated by the changing names of some of the more prominent affiliated organizations. The Royal Commonwealth Society, for example, began life in 1868 as the 'Colonial Society'. Having received a royal charter in 1882, it became the Royal Colonial Institute and three years later moved into a large purpose-built home on Northumberland Avenue, just off Trafalgar Square. The name changed again in 1928 to the 'Royal Empire Society', before the decision was made in 1958 to move with the times and re-christen the organization with its current name. Likewise, the organization now called the CPU (Commonwealth Press Union) Media Trust owes its origins to the Imperial Press Conference of 1909. This spawned the Empire Press Union, which in turn adopted the name CPU in 1950. The Association of Commonwealth

Universities (ACU) began with a congress at the University of London in 1912, which led, the following year, to the establishment of the Universities Bureau of the British Empire. This was renamed the Association of Universities of the British Commonwealth in 1948, and then the Association of Commonwealth Universities in 1963.

The Round Table, which continues to be the principal academic journal devoted exclusively to Commonwealth affairs, can trace its origins back to 1909. The 'Round Table' group, established that year, consisted of a committed band of imperial enthusiasts. At its core was the 'Milner Kindergarten', a group of Oxford-educated officials and intellectuals gathered together by Lord Milner, the British high commissioner for Southern Africa at the time of the Second Boer War (1899–1902). Gatherings of the Round Table were, and still are, described by members as 'The Moot', an Anglo-Saxon term that reflected Milner's faith in British racial superiority. The group's avowed aim, as it put it in 1913, was "to bring about the closer union of the British Empire".[30] First published in 1910, the journal's original subtitle was *A Quarterly Review of the Politics of the British Empire*. Until 1966, all its articles were published anonymously, conveying the sense that they represented the collective wisdom of the group, rather than of any particular individual.

It is notable, although probably not surprising, that sports organizations were considerably behind the curve in shedding old imperial terminology. In terms of visibility, perhaps the most high-profile event associated with the Commonwealth is the sporting competition organized every four years by the Commonwealth Games Federation. When the Commonwealth Games began in 1930, they were then called the British Empire Games. This evolved name into the British Empire and Commonwealth Games in 1954, and 'the British Commonwealth Games' in 1970; it was only in 1978, after the blazer-clad panjandrums of the

Federation finally reconciled themselves to the new global dispensation, that the competition announced itself as 'the Commonwealth Games'. Similarly, what began in 1909 as the Imperial Cricket Conference did not substitute 'International' for 'Imperial' until 1965—notably declining to include 'Commonwealth'. Perhaps this can be explained by the ICC's supposedly broader remit; a number of countries, including the US, took up the offer of associate membership from 1965, not posing much threat to Britain or other Commonwealth stalwarts. Had the US been allowed to compete in the Commonwealth Games, that would have been quite a different matter.

My own institution, the Institute of Commonwealth Studies, has survived without any name changes for nearly seventy years. Yet its roots were undeniably imperial. They can be traced back to a letter sent in May 1943 by the secretary of state for India, L. S. Amery, to the vice-chancellor and the acting principal of the University of London. Amery suggested a meeting about the part the University might play "in the Empire and in the world after the War", claiming that even if New York should displace it as the world's commercial centre in peacetime, London had the chance "of becoming, in a sense never realised before, the intellectual and cultural centre of the world."[31] Action was delayed while the University considered plans for other ventures connected to colonial administration and education. The University of London Senate finally decided to create an Institute of Empire Studies in October 1948. A few months later, however, the University's Special Advisory Board in Colonial Studies "decided that in view of recent developments in the political sphere it would be more appropriate if the title of the proposed Institute were 'Institute of Commonwealth Studies' [ICwS] instead of 'Institute of Empire Studies'". Professor W. K. Hancock was appointed its first director in June 1949 with the title of 'Professor of Commonwealth Studies in the University of London'.

As Hancock's latest successor in 2009, for me this network of Commonwealth-related organizations was more than just a matter of historical and anthropological interest. Clearly it made sense to try to collaborate with some of them. But which ones? There seemed to be a particularly crowded field of those specializing in education, from the Commonwealth Education Trust and Association of Commonwealth Universities to the Commonwealth Council for Education Administration and Management and the Commonwealth of Learning, an inter-governmental organization created in 1987 to focus on open and distance education and training.

On paper this supposedly globally-oriented array offered further proof of David Howell's dictum: that the Commonwealth was the ultimate network in an increasingly networked world. Indeed, one of my predecessors as director of the ICwS maintained that instead of 'the Commonwealth', we should speak of 'the Commonwealths' in order to encompass this rich, associational universe.[32] The problem was that, as I began to explore the potential for collaboration with these and other affiliated groups, I discovered—very much through a process of trial-and-error—that they varied greatly in terms of their level of funding, scale of operation, reach, and quality of personnel and leadership.

I certainly came to admire some of these groups, and not only the ones with the greatest capacity. The Commonwealth Parliamentary Association, for example, which can trace its origins back to 1911, is genuinely impressive. It has an authentically Commonwealth-wide reach, with around 175 branches in national and regional legislatures around the world. Its UK branch is relatively well-resourced, with annual funding of around £1.8 million from the British Parliament. And, conceptually, the CPA makes sense. The British Westminster Model was not adopted root and branch across the Commonwealth. There are many hybrid forms of legislature drawing on other national models, so no one can claim to have a universally applicable instruction manual. But there is, at least, a strong family resemblance across many Commonwealth legislatures, and it makes sense to bring together parliamentarians from across its member states to compare notes and discuss common problems.

By the same token, given the widespread adoption of British common law across the Commonwealth, it makes sense to encourage a dialogue between legal scholars and practitioners. The Commonwealth Magistrates' and Judges' Association, under the able leadership of its director-general Dr Karen Brewer, is an example of an organization that has played an important role in this respect, and in defending its members in their clashes with powerful state and non-state interest groups. Even in cases where an organization had a less obvious geographical rationale and far fewer resources, many achieved important results, partly through sheer force of personality among their leadership. A good example was the Commonwealth Journalists' Association (CJA) under the presidency of Rita Payne, a tireless friend to journalists across the Commonwealth in their sometimes dangerous struggles to report freely.

Yet I was far less impressed by many other affiliated organizations. As I was beginning to make sense of the London Commonwealth 'scene', the Royal Commonwealth Society was conducting a major survey on public perceptions of the Commonwealth, partly funded by the FCO. Its report, 'The Commonwealth Conversation', was published in 2010. This noted that most of the Commonwealth's associated and accredited organizations were small, and "we estimate that around a third have no employed staff".[33] This lack of capacity tended to limit their ability to be genuinely representative of their supposed constituencies. As the report went on to note,

> too many Commonwealth civil society organizations are staffed solely by longstanding volunteers. This is not to diminish their work or

their commitment. Rather, as one civil society representative said during the Conversation, "Commonwealth civil society and professional bodies are too aged, too male and too white. They are also too UK based. They are not representative of the young Commonwealth. But they are devoted to it."[34]

This 'devotion' to the Commonwealth was something I had certainly encountered. Indeed, when I was interviewed for the directorship, I was told by a panel member from the Secretariat, "You must be a *true believer*." Though I didn't fall at that particular hurdle in the appointment process, I had realized fairly early on in life that I wasn't one. Even as a child, it was clear to me that the world was divided between gang members and loners, and I wasn't much older before it became apparent that this translated into the distinction between people of faith and sceptics. In both cases I definitely belonged to the latter group.

Nevertheless, certainly within a mile radius of Trafalgar Square, there were plenty of people who wanted to be orthodox members of the Commonwealth gang. They seemed to be most closely concentrated in something called the Commonwealth Association, an affiliated organization made up specifically of former staff from the Secretariat, the Foundation and the Commonwealth of Learning. Many of the stalwarts of other parts of the London Commonwealth community came from a similar background. Often they seemed closely associated with a particular point in the Secretariat's history, generally the Ramphal or Anyaoku eras. As such, their passionate commitment to the organization sometimes seemed to be tinged with a nostalgia for their own 'glory days', and a sense that the contemporary Commonwealth fell short of those achievements.

These Commonwealth devotees were deeply versed in the arcane law and language of the organization: terms like CHOGM, CMAG (also a verb: 'to CMAG') and, my favourite, the COW (Committee of the Whole) tripped easily off their tongues. In short, this felt very much like a kind of sect. Whatever their doubts about the way in which the organization was currently being led, they clung to a belief that the Commonwealth was an idea that would triumph in the end. Their reaction to each new setback—and as we shall see, there have been many in recent years—was rather like that of the cult members in the famous 'Beyond the Fringe' sketch, eagerly expecting the end of the world. When the end doesn't come at the appointed hour, their leader is reassuring: "Well, it's not quite the conflagration I'd been banking on. Never mind, lads, same time tomorrow ... we must get a winner one day." This attitude, as we shall see in Chapter 3, contrasts sharply with that of Commonwealth member governments, which tend to have a far more hard-headed and pragmatic view of the organization's value.

The comments in the Commonwealth Conversation report about many bodies' lack of resources also rang true. Within the educational sphere, the Association of Commonwealth Universities is—rather like its Parliamentary counterpart—a serious and well-funded organization with a Commonwealth-wide reach. It has close links with an equally valuable body, the British branch of the Commonwealth Scholarship Commission, which is directly funded by the Department of International Development to provide UK scholarships for talented students across the Commonwealth. Many other education-related bodies, however, seemed under-funded and under-staffed. This created obvious dilemmas in trying to forge relationships with them. In meetings aimed at exploring projects for collaboration, as a rule of thumb I found that everyone assumed someone else in the room had money.

The Commonwealth Foundation, established at the same time as the Secretariat, should have acted as a focus and mentor for civil society organizations. Certainly, according to seasoned Commonwealth observer Richard Bourne, in the 1970s and '80s it nurtured new affiliated bodies such as the Commonwealth Lawyers Association and the Commonwealth Journalists Association.[35] Yet the Foundation itself had very limited funding, and from the end of the 1980s seems to have been keen to develop links with more 'grassroots' NGOs. This made for a potentially tense relationship between an under-resourced Foundation and the under-resourced Commonwealth civil society organizations that looked to it as an obvious source of funding.

As it turned out, it was not only the minnows in the Commonwealth civil society pond that were struggling. After wrestling for years with the issue of how to remain financially viable, in February 2013 the RCS announced that it was having to sell the premises it had occupied on Northumberland Avenue since the 1920s. Thereafter, it had a somewhat nomadic existence, briefly sharing an office with the Duke of Edinburgh's International Award Foundation before moving in 2016 to Commonwealth House on Pall Mall, shared with the Commonwealth Games Foundation and the Commonwealth Local Government Forum. With this move, Commonwealth House (previously Quadrant House, an additional office space for the Secretariat) was designated an exciting new 'Commonwealth Hub', its launch marked by a visit from the Queen.

But none of the fanfare could disguise the fact that financial difficulties had compromised the RCS's ability to sustain itself as a fully independent organization. Also compromised by the time of the move were the Society's non-partisan credentials. In December 2015 it had merged with the Commonwealth Exchange (established in 2013), which had strong links to the Conservative Party and to prominent 'Eurosceptics'. Tim Hewish, the Exchange's executive director, now became director of policy research at the RCS. He had previously served for a number of years as a parliamentary researcher for the Eurosceptic Conservative MP Steve Baker, who played an active part in the

2016 Leave campaign as co-chair of the pressure group Conservatives for Britain.

Aside from their individual sustainability, there is a deeper problem with the notion that these affiliated organizations somehow represent 'civil society' across the Commonwealth. In recent years, the Secretariat has been keen to portray itself not simply as an inter-governmental organization, but as a body accountable to 'the people' of the Commonwealth. Yet it still relies, at least in practice, on an oddly corporatist model, in which a variety of profession- or even sports-based groups (such as the Commonwealth Boxing Council) are supposedly represented by their corresponding affiliated organizations. 'Civil society' consultations are usually dominated by these groups. However, there is a stark disjuncture between their putative remit and their actual visibility and reach across the fifty-two Commonwealth countries. Early on in my directorship of the ICwS, I was contacted by someone from a Commonwealth organization of whose existence, I must confess, I had been unaware. He claimed that this organization was "the official voice of over a billion young people in the Commonwealth". I couldn't help wondering precisely what proportion of those billion young people shared my own—unforgiveable—ignorance of the body concerned. I had a similar experience at the 2011 CHOGM at Perth, as an accredited representative of the ICwS. I was invited to meet Commonwealth foreign ministers in a 'civil society consultation session'. I'd have been reluctant even to put myself forward as a representative of 'Professors of Commonwealth History'; the notion that I was in any way a suitable representative of 'the people' of the Commonwealth in a meeting of this kind was completely surreal. I politely declined.

As with the funding situation, this incoherent structure of representation leads to a tense and sometimes dysfunctional relationship between the 'official' Commonwealth and the 'civil society' bodies. For the latter, lacking serious resources, their best hope of exerting influence is through the inter-governmental Commonwealth. This in turn leads to a 'process-' rather than 'outcome-focused' approach. Seemingly, the affiliated organizations often regard the adoption or even mere mention of part of their agenda in Commonwealth meetings or communiques as a valuable achievement in its own right, irrespective of the longer-term impact.

This sort of lobbying has occasionally achieved things of some substance. In 1998, for example, the Commonwealth Parliamentary, Lawyers, Magistrates and Judges, and Legal Education Associations agreed the so-called Latimer House Principles on the separation of powers between the Commonwealth's legislative, executive and judicial branches. They eventually succeeded in having these adopted by the 2005 CHOGM.[36] Though, as we shall see, the Secretariat has sometimes been less than vigorous in enforcing them, the Latimer House Principles have become a particularly useful measure of encroachments on the judiciary's powers. Too often, however, this kind of lobbying simply adds to the impression that the Commonwealth community in London is something of a bubble, with its civil society elements pressing official bodies for the adoption of statements and resolutions that ultimately go nowhere, and to which the rest of the world seems largely deaf.

The consultation process also makes it more difficult for the official Commonwealth to focus its own limited resources on a relatively small number of areas where it has some prospect of making a difference. It is a commonplace that the organization should prioritize more. But any 'civil society' consultation on what those priorities should be is likely to come up with dozens of different priorities. The influence of so many competing agendas helps to explain why CHOGM communiques are so often characterized as seemingly endless shopping lists of good intentions. As the RCS's 2010 'Commonwealth Conversation' noted,

The communiqué issued from the 2009 CHOGM is an interminable list of largely unrelated topics running to 117 paragraphs. The subjects it addresses are endless—disarmament and arms control, terrorism, migration, human rights, the economy, trade, investment, climate change, food security, energy security, education, youth, the digital divide ... to name but a few. None is given prominence over another and there is no indication of a workable agenda for the Secretariat for the coming two years. And this communiqué does not stand alone. There were five other statements produced by leaders at CHOGM, adding another 69 paragraphs to the mêlée. "Commonwealth communiqués include everything except the kitchen sink", one senior official at a consultation event told us.[37]

As we have already seen, and will explore further in Chapter 3, the key to the Commonwealth's success under Smith and Ramphal in the 1960s–90s owed much to their willingness and ability to exert genuine leadership. That meant exercising their own judgement about where the Commonwealth could best make a difference, and acting quickly and imaginatively to achieve those ends. The more recent tendency to pronounce on all of the world's ills is a constant barrier to the careful targeting of energy and resources.

In some ways then, the network of Commonwealth-associated organizations can sometimes resemble a rather closed and esoteric sect, within which it is unthinkable that anyone would question the broader value of the organization. Outside that 'bubble', on the other hand, leaders of the member states have often taken a far more pragmatic view. So for what reasons have they valued the Commonwealth, and why has it lasted for so long?

3

"WHAT IS IT GOOD FOR?"

As we have seen, of the various accusations levelled against the Commonwealth, perhaps the easiest to refute is that the British government masterminded its post-war expansion as part of a grand geopolitical strategy. That view of the organization conforms nicely with the British myth of a seamless mission to guide the Empire's dependencies towards self-government in a spirit of friendship, as well as with more radical theories of neo-colonialism. In fact, however, the way the modern Commonwealth developed owed more to 'consumer demand' on the part of Britain's former colonies than to any template devised in London. Indeed, its current organizational infrastructure emerged in no small part due to conscious efforts to loosen, not enhance, the UK's coordinating role and influence.

Once we appreciate this reality, it becomes easier to understand why, with only a small handful of exceptions, the Commonwealth member states have chosen to remain within the organization over the many decades since independence. Nevertheless, it is not in itself a sufficient explanation for such an extraordinary phenomenon. Why, in 2018, do fifty-two states—the vast majority of them former colonial dependencies—continue to adhere to an organization that maps so neatly onto the former British Empire, an entity of which few but their oldest inhabitants can have any personal memory? We need to consider a more varied set of explanations—some of them ephemeral, others resonating with some but not all members—but collectively enough to have got us where we are today.

Quite aside from the chronological remoteness of Empire, we might have expected even those who do remember those days to be hostile to the Commonwealth. From a twenty-first-century perspective, this might be the most puzzling question. The member states had been governed after independence by generations of colonial nationalist leaders, whose lives had been devoted to freeing their countries from British imperial rule and who had often suffered prosecution and imprisonment as a result—why, then, have they voluntarily retained this apparently neo-colonial bond with the UK?

Historical Raisons d'Être

The first point to note is that during the decades immediately following the Second World War, the Commonwealth was still dominated by leaders who felt a strong sense of cultural attachment to Britain and British institutions. Sandra Pepera, a political scientist who worked in the Commonwealth Secretariat and DfID notes, "They might have been coloniser and colonised, but to a certain extent, they did have the same worldview. They'd read the same books. Some of them had been to the same colleges ... There was this commonality of understanding and it carried the Commonwealth a long way."[1]

The importance of these personal ties to the UK—rather than to the broader Commonwealth idea—was also underlined by the influential Uganda businessman and politician Martin Aliker, who fled into exile after General Amin seized power and returned to his country as a senior advisor to President Museveni. For the political elites of newly independent countries like Uganda, "our sense of belonging to the Commonwealth was not really that strong. Our tie was mostly to the United Kingdom—because of obvious reasons, the most important being education. Many of us came to this country for university education."[2]

The UK higher education system is sometimes described as a form of 'soft power', precisely because so many future world leaders have passed through it. Yet the repercussions of this were complex and not always to Britain's immediate advantage. Many of those from imperial territories who were educated in the UK in the first half of the twentieth century absorbed political and philosophical ideas that they then turned on their colonial masters in the struggle for independence. Yet they still in some cases associated Britain, and by extension the Commonwealth, with ideas and values they had come to cherish. The Indian official K. Shankar Bajpai spoke about this from a particularly informed perspective. The son of the first Ministry of External Affairs general secretary following independence in 1947, he studied Modern History at Merton College, Oxford and would eventually follow in his father's footsteps, rising through the ranks of the Indian foreign service to become foreign secretary himself under Indira Gandhi in the 1980s. He recalls that, for his father, the Commonwealth represented

> the extension of the Enlightenment to the great, wide world and it enabled the values of the Enlightenment to be practiced—in the British tradition, but with local colour—and that it would enable the local colour, in a sense, to be able to shape a new multicultural and multiracial organization.[3]

The British educational experience of future Commonwealth leaders also brought them into contact with contemporaries from other parts of the world, leading to stronger regional and internationalist ties and identifications. Joe Clarke, who served as prime minister of Canada in 1979–80, suggests,

> A lot of talented young Canadians who went away to school in the 1920s and 1930s came to the UK, so all sorts of personal bonds were formed—not just with Brits but with others who had been drawn to Britain as well. Many of those Canadian students came home to join the Foreign Service, and often brought with them a view that was more internationalist.[4]

While this may have enhanced their enthusiasm for the Commonwealth, it also encouraged them to work with a variety of other regional and international organizations; it did not necessary make them more sympathetic to the UK's position.

For instance, alongside this sense of internationalism was a growing intolerance of racial discrimination, something that sat uneasily with what many regarded as the British government's excessively lenient attitude towards white minority rule in Southern Rhodesia and South Africa. While Australia had also tended to be sympathetic towards at least white settlers of Southern Africa, this changed markedly following the election of Gough Whitlam's Labor government in 1972. Whitlam adopted a more hostile stance towards South Africa, one which, perhaps surprisingly, survived his ejection from office in 1975 and the installation of a centre-right administration under Malcolm Fraser. Bob Hawke, who succeeded Fraser as prime minister, explained his predecessor's loathing for apartheid in terms of his experiences as a student in England:

> [H]e came from a very wealthy family—a 'squattocracy'—and he had private education at home and then he went to boarding school at Melbourne Grammar School, one of those lead schools in Australia. And then he went straight from Melbourne Grammar to Oxford. And he would have been a very lonely person, and I think he probably met a lot of black students there who were also probably lonely.

I think he formed friendships with them, which established his judgement about the question of colour.[5]

More recently, however, such trajectories have become less common, which is a longer-term problem for the Commonwealth: as these sorts of bilateral cultural and educational ties between member states and the UK diminish, so does the enthusiasm of member state leaders for what is still perceived as an essentially UK-centred organization. In 2015 Rashleigh Jackson, who served as Guyana's foreign minister between 1978 and 1990, identified in the current crop of Caribbean leaders a streak of parochialism that distinguishes them from their predecessors, diminishing their interest not only in the Commonwealth but also in regional organizations such as CARICOM:

I think you have to look at what is happening within member countries of the Commonwealth and ask yourself whether you are getting new generations of leaders and what their values are ... Speaking from the perspective of the Caribbean, I think now we have a generation of leaders in the Caribbean who don't have either the regional view or the world view of the generation of Eric Williams, Michael Manley, Burnham and Errol Barrow. Therefore, what will be possible for CARICOM is not predictable now.[6]

In any case, it would be dangerous to place too much weight on the argument that cultural affinities naturally encourage Commonwealth heads to take the organization seriously. Throughout the period since 1947, there have been strong links between the Indian political elite and the British university system. Indeed, for most of that period, India was governed by four long-serving, Oxbridge-educated prime ministers: Jawaharlal Nehru (Trinity College, Cambridge, 1907–10), his daughter Indira Gandhi (Somerville College, Oxford, 1937–40), her son, Rajiv Gandhi (Trinity College, Cambridge, 1961–4) and, more recently, Manmohan Singh (St John's College, Cambridge, 1955–7). Yet although Nehru certainly acted as one of the founders of the modern

Commonwealth, and his daughter and grandson both played significant roles in its deliberations, the Indian government's approach to the Commonwealth since independence has been distinctly ambivalent. Muchkund Dubey, another Oxford graduate who served as India's foreign secretary in the early 1990s, recalls his interview to join the foreign service in 1957:

> In those days it used to be the practice that the individual interview [was] followed by [a] group interview. So some six or seven candidates would be interviewed individually and then together to discuss a particular subject. So in my group the subject they put for discussion was 'Should India leave the Commonwealth'?[7]

As Dubey notes, the context for this was partly the aftermath of the 1956 Suez campaign, during which the Indian government was highly critical of the Anglo-French assault on Nasser's Egypt. In many respects, Suez put an end to the illusion that the Commonwealth could serve to underwrite Britain's great-power status in the post-war era. This was also a period when India was breaking free of the orbit of the Sterling Area and beginning to take control of its own reserves. Diplomatically and financially, it was beginning to emerge as a major regional and global actor in its own right. Nehru firmly embraced a non-aligned position in the Cold War, and under his daughter there was a notable tilt away from the West and towards closer relations with the Soviet Union. Increasingly, the Commonwealth took a marginal role in Indian external affairs. Indeed, in the key histories of Indian foreign policy, one finds only the most fleeting references to the organization. Whatever vestigial cultural bonds remained with the UK, India had moved on.

India wasn't the only country to strike out on its own. By its nature, the old imperial dispensation—whereby much of the world was divided into possessions of competing European powers—did little to encourage ties between neighbouring territories, particularly if they had belonged to different colonial systems. The key connection, politically and often economically, was between the individual territory and its colonial overlord. Even between adjacent British states, economic relations and even basic infrastructure were often under-developed. It was only towards the end of the colonial period that the British sought to develop regional groupings of its territories, with ill-fated federations in the Caribbean, Central Africa and South Asia. By 1965, all three had dissolved in acrimony. In the post-colonial period, newly independent states began to develop regional ties on their own terms, inevitably weakening links with London in the process. At the same time, the UK itself began to re-imagine its own political and economic geography, forging closer links with its immediate neighbours in continental Europe.

There is something of a myth circulating in Brexit Britain that, if the UK suddenly decides to take a renewed interest in the Commonwealth after decades of concentrating on European relations, her traditional Commonwealth partners will embrace her like a prodigal mother. This is a highly questionable assumption even when it comes to those Commonwealth states with which the UK appears to have the closest 'cultural affinities'. One of the guilty secrets of London's Commonwealth relations is that there has always been an 'inner' and an 'outer' Commonwealth, the former consisting of the old 'Dominions' of Australia, New Zealand and Canada. Certainly strong links remain, particularly in the areas of diplomacy and military/intelligence liaison, encouraged by their sharing of a common sovereign. Characteristically, the plain-speaking John Howard, who served as Liberal prime minister of Australia from 1996 to 2007, was prepared to spell out the ongoing distinction between the 'old' and 'new' Commonwealths:

> I always looked at the Commonwealth in a sense separately from our bilateral relations with the old Commonwealth. Let's be realistic: there is a difference. Those countries that belong to what is called 'the

old Commonwealth' have a closer affinity with each other than with those countries that do not. That's always been my feeling. And it's true. We're bound by obviously the common sharing of a monarch, our institutions and customs and—this is particularly relevant in the modern world—the close intelligence co-operation which is one of the strongest bonds of the lot ... Not that we were indifferent to the broader Commonwealth, but it's almost unmanageably large. You talk about leadership. Well, it's very, very difficult for the Secretary General because it's so big; it's 53 countries and they range from very big to very small. It's valuable but it can't be very cohesive...[8]

This is a sensitive subject, since it also hints at a degree of racial solidarity between Britain and member states dominated by populations of European settler origin. However, as we shall see in Chapter 8, in recent years British politicians—particularly those on the right—have become less shy about invoking this 'special relationship' with members of the 'old' Commonwealth as a possible basis for future diplomatic and economic relations. Yet it is important to remember that these countries have themselves moved on, in a process that has been described as 'de-dominionization', forging new senses of national and regional identity. In the case of Australia and New Zealand, this radical re-imagining of political and economic geography famously involved reconciling themselves to the fact that the 'Far East' was in fact the 'Near North'. Although acknowledging the value of the Commonwealth in its various forms, John Howard is keen to emphasize that it is Australia's bilateral relations which now matter most:

I am not a fervent multilateralist I have to tell you. I'm not saying this just in the context of the Commonwealth; broadly I think the thing that's important about the foreign relations with my country are the accumulated bilateral relationships we have and they matter. There's no such thing as an Asian foreign policy; there's a foreign policy in Australia towards Indonesia and Japan and China and India and

Malaysia and Singapore. There are bilateral, regional associations which are helpful, but we still live in a world of nation states.[9]

Former prime minister of New Zealand Jim Bolger makes a similar point, with particular reference to his country's economic relations:

> When I was Prime Minister in the 1990s, the Commonwealth was 'modestly important'—not overwhelmingly important—in shaping foreign policy. As a country like New Zealand moved trade more into Asia, we were dealing with more and more countries that don't have Commonwealth links. Many, of course, have strong links to the Commonwealth because, in most cases, they were at one time colonies of the former British Empire. World politics and world trading links are in a period of rapid change, and this of course has an impact on New Zealand's focus. If we go back to 1965, before Britain started negotiating entry into the EEC, then New Zealand's trade focus was almost entirely on Britain in terms of markets. The United Kingdom is now a relatively minor market for New Zealand, and that change in importance has inevitably changed perspective. [sic][10]

This growing sense of regional identity among Commonwealth states partly explains what, to many outsiders, seems to be one of the more puzzling aspects of its recent history: that it has expanded to include states with no direct historical links with the United Kingdom. The accession of Mozambique, a former Portuguese territory, in 1995 began the process. This owed much to the influence of Nelson Mandela, who had brought South Africa back into the Commonwealth following its first free elections in 1994. For Mandela, Mozambique had played a key role among the 'frontline states' supporting the ANC's campaign against the apartheid regime. Thus, as it emerged from a long period of conflict, Mozambique appeared particularly deserving of whatever support the Commonwealth could provide. Geographically if not historically, its membership appeared entirely logical. Mozambique was surrounded at that time by no fewer than six Commonwealth neighbours: Tanzania, Malawi, Zambia, Swaziland, South Africa and Zimbabwe (which was to leave the organization in 2003).

Equally perplexing to many was the accession of Rwanda in 2007. Here again, however, the artificial colonial borders that had demarcated the state cut across ethnic and linguistic boundaries that reached into neighbouring Commonwealth states. The leaders of those states had a strong interest in encouraging peace and stability in Rwanda, and when they engaged with their Rwandan counterparts, even during periods of tension, they discovered they had much in common. Martin Aliker recalls,

> Uganda was very happy for Rwanda to join the Commonwealth because Rwanda and Uganda are basically the same country. They are different, but the same country, and Uganda has always provided the safety valve for Rwanda's population. There are about two million Rwandese living in Uganda. At the time when the government of Rwanda and the government of Uganda were about to go to war against one another [in 2001], the population didn't see what was the problem. And I can also tell you that I was in the delegation that came to London. While President Kagame and President Museveni were with Prime Minister Blair at Number 10 Downing Street, the rest of us were left in [Marlborough House] ... and we were sitting around the same table and speaking in Luganda—not even in English! And I remember very vividly talking to the Chief of Security of Rwanda and I asked him, I said, "Where did you do your medicine?" He said "Makerere." And I said, "Which school did you go to?" He said, "I went to Kings College, Budo." Which is where I went! And he said, "I'm hoping that my son will get into Budo next year." Now, here is a country with which we are about to go to war, and he wants his son to come and be in foreign and enemy territory? It didn't make sense.[11]

In terms of dealing both with close geographical neighbours and more distant countries, there is clearly some intrinsic symbolic value in the fact that fifty-two different states treat each other not as foreigners but as members of a kind of international family. This assumption finds expression in the fact that Commonwealth members exchange not ambassadors but high commissioners. This has not, of course, prevented intense rivalry or even occasional armed conflict between member states, most notably in the case of the fraught relationship between India and Pakistan. Yet one can underestimate the importance of the 'mood music' against which diplomatic relations are exercised, and in the case of the Commonwealth, this is relentlessly soothing. Kamal Hossain, who served as foreign minister of Bangladesh shortly after it achieved formal statehood, remembers this as being particularly important in his country's efforts to define its maritime boundaries with India:

> If you are doing maritime boundaries and getting Commonwealth support, India could not perceive this as something opposed to it because they are also members of the Commonwealth. Therefore it was not a question that the Commonwealth would not be doing something that would be basically prejudicial against the interests of another Commonwealth country. The concept of a cooperative endeavour in these matters helped.[12]

In the context of the Cold War, these relationships took on a particular importance. For Kwame Nkrumah of Ghana and other leading figures in the 1960s Commonwealth, the organization appeared an important instrument for solidarity across various parts of the developing world, at a time when newly independent countries were coming under pressure to line up behind either the US or the USSR. For the UK, which was firmly in the former camp, the Commonwealth provided an important means to foster and maintain close relations with countries that might prove receptive to Soviet overtures.

Neville Linton, a senior official in the Political Division of the Commonwealth Secretariat in the 1980s and '90s, suggests that the Cold War also provided an opportunity for the organization itself. He notes that, whereas other international bodies found themselves stymied by superpower rivalries, the Commonwealth was able to maintain its freedom of action. It was, he argues, a situation that Sonny Ramphal skilfully exploited to the organization's advantage:

> The Cold War and the Secretary General gave the Commonwealth a particular significance and importance. Ramphal was an extraordinary individual at a unique time. The right people could exploit the opportunities, and the unique dynamics of international relations at this time. Ramphal could use that atmosphere and environment which his successors have not been able to. It was a very flexible era, exactly because of the two extremes in the Cold War, and the floating group which was being wooed in the middle. And in the floating group, there were the states whose leaders wanted to make a difference; hence the Scandinavians spent large sums in foreign aid, development on different lines of the programmes of the established powers. Their approach to aid was quite different: Ramphal was able to operate in this arena.[13]

Along with the Cold War, the issue that gave purpose and momentum to the Commonwealth between the 1960s and the 1990s was that of the continuation of white settler rule in Southern Rhodesia and South Africa. Although technically a 'Crown Colony', Southern Rhodesia had, from the 1920s, enjoyed something close to dominion status, with its prime minister regularly attending the meetings of Commonwealth premiers in London. From 1953, it was the dominant political partner in a federation formed with Northern Rhodesia (Zambia) and Nyasaland (Malawi). After the federation was dissolved in 1963, its two other members moved rapidly to independence under black majority rule. Southern Rhodesia also demanded its own independence—there, however, black Africans remained largely excluded from the franchise. The British government's lengthy negotiations failed to persuade Southern Rhodesian leadership to liberalize the constitution enough for independence to be acceptable to and recognized by the Commonwealth, and the wider international community. Indeed, most Commonwealth states maintained that nothing short of full black majority rule would be an adequate precondition.

Negotiations finally broke down in November 1965, when the government of Rhodesia (as it was by then commonly called) made a unilateral declaration of independence (UDI). Attempts by the British to hold fresh negotiations in 1966 and again in 1968 proved abortive. Meanwhile the UK came under intense pressure from its Commonwealth partners to take decisive action, including the use of military force, to break the defiance of the Rhodesian settler regime. By the end of the 1960s, the country was in the grip of a full-scale civil war. Resistance to the white minority government was led by two separate factions: the militant organization ZANU, which drew its support largely from the Shona-speaking communities, and the Ndebele-dominated ZAPU. Robert Mugabe eventually assumed leadership of ZANU's armed wing, while ZAPU's was led by the veteran nationalist, Joshua Nkomo.

Meanwhile, the Union of South Africa had been a reluctant Dominion since its creation in 1910, forced into the British sphere of influence by the Second Boer War of 1899–1902. Between the two World Wars, partly in an effort to reconcile the competing ambitions of the English- and Afrikaans-speaking white communities, the government of South Africa had consistently pressed for the maximum possible recognition of its autonomy and independence within the Commonwealth framework. It narrowly voted to enter the Second World War on the Allied side, but with ongoing opposition from within the Afrikaner community. With the electoral victory of the Afrikaner-dominated National Party in 1948, relations with the UK were placed under further strain.

The 1957 Commonwealth accession of Ghana, its first black African member state, pointed to the difficulties of reconciling an influx of new members from tropical Africa with a National Party-ruled South Africa, which was gradually augmenting the legal mechanisms enforcing white minority rule and racial segregation. The efforts of the Macmillan government to maintain this balancing act were scuppered in 1960, when South Africa voted to become a republic. By convention, it was required to re-apply for Commonwealth membership, and when, the following year, it became clear that this would be opposed by some existing and prospective members, South Africa withdrew its application. In the decades that followed, global abhorrence of the chilling theory and brutal reality of apartheid made South Africa a pariah state with few rivals.

The apartheid regime in South Africa, and its highly dependent client state of Rhodesia to the north, became the main focus of Commonwealth attention and activism from the mid-1960s onwards. There were two reasons for this. The first was that these white-minority-ruled states represented the antithesis of the Commonwealth ideal as it had developed by that stage. They were the areas of Africa where decolonization and the dismantling of racial oppression had stalled. In the process, South Africa had officially left the Commonwealth, while the Rhodesian regime had illegally frustrated the ambitions of the country's African majority to join it as a properly independent state. There was therefore something visceral about the campaigns waged by the Commonwealth—as though it was seeking to recover two lost limbs. Secondly, the Commonwealth could clearly play a direct role in solving the problem. Bringing together many of the key neighbouring states of Central and Southern Africa, it was an ideal forum for coordinating diplomatic solutions. If one wants to understand the continuing importance of the Commonwealth to Britain in the late 1970s and the '80s, one need only look at the Cabinet minutes released to the National Archives in recent years. During this period Rhodesia and later South Africa provided staple agenda items.

No speech about the value of the Commonwealth is complete without paying tribute to the organization's contributions to the path to independence for what became Zimbabwe in 1980, and to the final end of apartheid, with Nelson Mandela's swearing in as South Africa's first black president in 1994. The problem is that an organization in decline can only survive on its glorious memories for so long before the dysfunctional present starts to shape perceptions of that cherished past. From our current perspective, it becomes increasingly tempting to identify in the Rhodesia and South Africa campaigns the weaknesses of the Commonwealth as well as its strengths. After all, fifteen years separated the Rhodesian UDI and the independence of Zimbabwe, and a full thirty-three between South Africa's departure from the Commonwealth and Mandela's accession to the presidency. During that intervening time, if not exactly divided, the Commonwealth faced a situation in which the UK, the country most members believed had a moral duty to take the lead, seemed out of step and lacking much sense of urgency.

Yet the Commonwealth also proved that it was capable of acting as an instrument for resolving these issues. In the case of Rhodesia, the Lusaka Heads of Government Meeting (CHOGM) in August 1979 helped to persuade Mrs Thatcher that her government could not simply accept the results of the flawed general election that had been carried out in April that year under the white-minority regime. The summit provided the framework for a constructive transfer of power based on fresh elections. In a unique initiative, the organization also provided a Commonwealth Monitoring Force to supervise a cease-fire by the country's guerrilla armies ahead of those elections, held in February 1980.

In the case of South Africa, a Commonwealth Eminent Persons Group that visited the country in March 1986 had come tantalizingly close to establishing the basis for negotiated political change, before South African military strikes against the front-line capitals of Lusaka, Gaborone and Harare scuppered the initiative. The visit had been supported by Thatcher as a means of buying time, in the face of fierce pressure from the Common-wealth for tougher sanctions against South Africa. She had clearly hoped, by appointing former Conservative chancellor Anthony Barber to the Group, to ensure that its recommenda-tions were acceptable to her own government. Yet by all accounts, Barber proved quite able to form his own judgement on the situ-ation. The Group held wide-ranging talks including three visits to Mandela in Pollsmoor Prison. According to the then South African foreign minister, Pik Botha, "The EPG came closer to success than most people realise ... The 'Negotiating Concept' was a prophetic document. It embodied all the elements which formed the basis of the negotiations between the South African Government and the ANC four years later."[14] Nevertheless, it was clearly unacceptable at the time to the government of P. W. Botha. In light of this, Barber displayed his independence by putting his signature to the EPG's recommendations for fresh economic and financial sanctions.

Indeed, it was in the area of financial sanctions that the Commonwealth arguably made its most effective and concrete contribution to ending apartheid. By the time Commonwealth heads met for their summit in Vancouver in 1987, it was clear that conventional economic sanctions based on trade embargoes were not having the desired impact. For Mrs Thatcher, this was an argument for simply discontinuing them. But for other Commonwealth members it was evidence of the need for an approach concentrated instead on the South African financial system. In retrospect, a number of Commonwealth premiers have been keen to claim a share of the credit for its success. Edward Seaga, then prime minister of Jamaica, recalls,

I found in the United Nations that there was an organization that was particularly concerned with trading with South Africa—the United Nations Centre on Transnational Corporations—and what had been done in sanctions. I used the data to expose the fact that the imposition of sanctions was in the wrong area. Instead of trying to create trade barriers which largely did not work, we should turn to attacking the South African rand. Once the rand started to fall in value, all that had been built up over the decades by the elite of South Africa would start to fall with it. Trade would be dislocated because South African goods would be cheaper for exports, but far more expensive for imports, and a dislocation of trade and investment would result in adverse movement of the exchange rate. This, they couldn't deal with. That's exactly what happened.[15]

Meanwhile, Seaga's then counterpart in Australia, Bob Hawke, remembers,

I rang my friend Jim Wolfensohn, who was then running a private commercial bank in New York. I said, "Come up to Vancouver", and he did. I put my proposition to him. He said, "I think it could work." I said, "Will you help us?" He said, "Yes." So, I set aside senior people in our treasury and they worked with Wolfensohn and the investment sanctions were applied. And that's what brought the regime down. The last South African Finance Minister, Barend du Plessis, went on record as saying that it was the investment sanctions that put the final nail in the coffin of apartheid.[16]

It is safe to say that the jury is still out on the significance of the Commonwealth's role in bringing the South African government to the negotiating table. First, as Mrs Thatcher herself proudly boasted at the end of the summit, the final communique of the Vancouver CHOGM announced no additional economic or financial sanctions against South Africa. Secondly, while fears of divestment may well have been important, it is not clear that these resulted directly from international pressure by organizations such as the Commonwealth. As R. W. Johnson notes, throughout its history the South African state had been heavily dependent on foreign investment. Yet the pressure on this front was already mounting well before 1987. By the mid-1980s, a steady fall in the price of gold was already beginning to squeeze the South African economy. When, in August 1985, P. W. Botha's widely-heralded 'Rubicon' speech in Durban failed to announce an anticipated liberalization, the financial markets drew their own conclusions about the viability of his regime, and the US bank Chase Manhattan swiftly called in a major loan.[17] In short, although the Commonwealth may well have helped to promote the idea of the efficacy of financial sanctions, its specific role in using these as a lever to end minority rule in South Africa remains unclear.

Purposelessness

What is more clear is that the transition to an ANC-governed South Africa in 1994 was a bittersweet victory for the Commonwealth. While it was able to draw on some of Mandela's moral capital as South Africa rejoined the organization, it was now effectively deprived of the issue that had given it purpose and momentum for three decades. The end of the Cold War served further to undermine its value and significance, as did other geopolitical developments. One was the proliferation of new international organizations that provided alternative diplomatic frameworks for its member states. Particularly striking has been the increasing role and influence of regional organizations, which bring together countries with often widely differing historical formations and links to European colonialism. Among the oldest is the Organization of American States, established in 1948, which links Canada and the US to thirty-three other countries. Its membership overlaps with that of the Caribbean Community, a diplomatic, developmental and trading bloc established in 1973. In Africa, regional organizations include the Economic Community of West African States (ECOWAS, est. 1975). India, Bangladesh and Pakistan are members of the South Asian Association for Regional Cooperation, founded in 1985 to facilitate improved economic and political relations. 1999 witnessed the establishment of the Pacific Islands Forum, which seeks to develop inter-governmental cooperation in the region.

These bodies increasingly provide the sort of support—such as helping to negotiate international trade deals and representing the interests of small states—that members might formerly have sought from the Commonwealth. This was noted in the Royal Commonwealth Society's 2010 survey 'The Commonwealth Conversation'. The Commonwealth boasts that it has a particular role in representing the interests of small states; thirty-four of its fifty-two members can be classified as such. Yet even here, the RCS pointed out, it was facing challenges from newer groupings of states:

> Take the example of AOSIS, the Alliance of Small Island States. This coalition of small island and low-lying countries now has 42 members who have grouped together because they share similar development challenges and concerns about the environment, especially in terms of their vulnerability to the adverse effects of global climate change. It seems that AOSIS has displaced the Commonwealth as the pre-eminent forum and voice for small island states. This impression was reinforced by our consultations with relevant member governments, especially those who had seen the work of AOSIS at the Copenhagen Climate Conference in December 2009. It is crucial that the Commonwealth does not assume that it continues to have a monopoly over the unique roles it once played. In many cases, it has been left behind.[18]

Against this background, the unique selling point of the Commonwealth is that it associates a large and varied group of developing countries with some relatively powerful states such as the UK, Canada and Australia, which lend the organization added economic and diplomatic weight without dominating it. Yet the regional organizations have certainly a greater coherence, and arguably a greater legitimacy.

One instructive indication of this is the recent case of the Gambia. For over two decades, this former British colony had been governed by Yahya Jammeh, who first seized power in a military coup in 1994 and subsequently transformed himself into an elected president. Jammeh's idiosyncratic version of democracy, which provided little space for political opponents, ensured his return in successive general elections, seeing him gain around 72% of the popular vote in 2011. The Commonwealth appeared to take none-too-close an interest in reports of human rights abuses in the Gambia, and its election observer groups issued a succession of mealy-mouthed reports each time Jammeh gained a new mandate. The one following his 2011 victory recorded features that might well lead one to question whether the election had been free and fair, including the use of government resources and personnel by Jammeh's party, and the intimidation of opponents and journalists. Yet its ultimate conclusion was blandly and cheerily upbeat, rather like a poor school report which ends with a confident prediction that the student will do better next year: "The results of this election show that the Government of The Gambia has the mandate of its people to embark on the necessary democratic reforms which will guarantee sustainable economic development. The Commonwealth stands ready to assist in such reforms."[19]

Given that he had hardly been hounded by the Commonwealth, there was widespread surprise when, in October 2013, Jammeh announced that he was withdrawing his country from the organization. The trigger seems to have been not so much the Commonwealth itself but the British government, which earlier in the year had published some trenchant criticisms of

The Gambia's human rights record. The president turned his wrath on the Commonwealth, denouncing it as a "neo-colonial institution". Then, in 2016, something even more surprising happened: he lost that December's presidential election. After some initial indications that he might go quietly, Jammeh instead made it clear that he would not concede power to the winning candidate, Adama Barrow. The patience of his regional neighbours in ECOWAS snapped. They gave him until 19 January to surrender power peacefully; when he still refused to go, an ECOWAS-backed Senegalese force crossed into the Gambia, and Jammeh fled into exile.

It would have been inconceivable for the Commonwealth to be involved in any way in an operation of this kind. It would have set a dangerous precedent for too many other member states with poor records on democracy and human rights. And any Commonwealth initiative involving the UK would have aroused the standard accusations of 'neo-colonialism', not just from Jammeh himself but internationally and within Britain itself. As it was, ECOWAS, which had both the capacity and legitimacy to do so, acted quickly. There were no significant international protests, no 'Stop the War' marches outside Senegalese diplomatic missions. This was widely regarded as a case of West African states setting their own house in order.

In some important respects, then, the Commonwealth is less well-equipped than more recently established regional organizations to deal with serious breakdowns in democracy, human rights and the rule of law. Nevertheless, at its best, it is valued by members for its capacity to offer specialist technical advice and assistance of a sort not easily available locally. Particularly under Smith and Ramphal in the 1960s–'80s, it established a reputation for nimble and extremely innovative assistance. Former Bangladeshi foreign minister Kamal Hossain recalls the Secretariat's role in the 1970s in offering Bangladesh support from Professor Daniel

Patrick O'Connell, a leading expert in state succession law, during negotiations over the new country's maritime borders:

> The great advantage of the Commonwealth as a source of technical cooperation was how non-bureaucratic it is. I identified Professor O'Connell—it's not that you're going through and people had written long notes and sent it up to the Secretary-General. We just made a request. "Look, we want O'Connell," and they said, "Fine." They got on the phone, O'Connell agreed and within a week he was in Bangladesh...[20]

In other words, the Commonwealth was a 'smart' organization, able to out-think and out-pace the bigger beasts of the international community, precisely because of the small-scale and informal way in which it worked. It was also prepared to throw its weight behind developing countries in their often unequal negotiations with major international corporations. David McDowell, a New Zealand diplomat who served as special advisor to Secretary-General Smith, recalls an urgent request for advice from Seretse Khama, president of Botswana, on a mineral concessions agreement soon to be signed with the Anglo-American Corporation. Within a week, the Commonwealth Fund for Technical Cooperation had a team on the ground led by its own head, the development economist Gordon Goundrey:

> We had a specialist on royalties and minerals from the New Zealand Treasury. We had a development lawyer from Mauritius, who had worked on many Concession Agreements, and we had a smart Brit from Sussex, whose name I can't remember. Anyway, they sat down and they negotiated—in constant consultation with the Botswanans—on behalf of the Botswana Government. At the end, two things happened. First, the De Beers people [a subsidiary of Anglo-American] were grumbling away in their beers and Seretse invited us over for a weekend at his place and said, "My people tell me that you've got us three times what we would have got if we'd done it ourselves." The other thing was that Harry Oppenheimer

rang Gordon Goundrey and said, "Goundrey, if you'll join us [Anglo-American], tell me what your salary is and I'll quadruple it." Gordon just laughed. He said, "Harry, I'm a multis-basher. I always was and I always will be."[21]

At the same time, for all the intellectual firepower the Commonwealth brought to bear on behalf of its members, its effectiveness has always been hampered by its relatively meagre funding. The CFTC currently operates on a budget of only around £30 million per annum. Kaliapote Tavula, Fiji's former foreign minister (2000–6), acknowledges the importance of some Commonwealth initiatives in the Pacific region, but adds, "The Commonwealth is long on ideas, but very short in terms of resources to back up those ideas".[22] Speaking from a Ugandan perspective, Martin Aliker agrees with this diagnosis: "Our needs and requirements are of a monetary nature, and the Commonwealth Secretariat, as such, doesn't have the funds. So, we tend to go directly to the individual Commonwealth countries for assistance, rather than go to the Secretariat."[23]

While it is within the power of the Secretariat to revive the Commonwealth's reputation as a 'smart' organization, incubating new ideas subsequently taken up by other parts of the international community, there is no realistic prospect for its own initiatives receiving better financial backing in years to come. Indeed, as we shall see in Chapter 8, the UK and other major sponsors have recently threatened to cut funding if the Secretariat does not improve its performance. It is caught in a vicious circle, lacking the funds necessary to achieve much impact, but unable to persuade its backers to increase their contributions without it doing so.

Keeping On Keeping On

When we strip away some of the more questionable claims about what the Commonwealth has achieved in the past or might be capable of in the future, we are left with a couple of factors that help to maintain a degree of member engagement. The first is the very heterogeneity that makes it so difficult to focus the organization on achievable concrete aims. At a witness seminar I attended some years ago, the former British chancellor of the exchequer, Sir Geoffrey Howe, spoke warmly of the insights he gained from meetings of Commonwealth finance ministers into the problems faced by his counterparts in the developing world. Such serendipity is always a likely benefit of interactions between leaders of such a diverse group of states. Perhaps unintentionally invoking the spirit of Flanders and Swann, Douglas Hurd, who served as foreign secretary under John Major, recalled,

> My general feeling about the Commonwealth is that it is a great big meeting place. It is a sort of fair: a medieval fair, and you wander round and you visit one booth and then another, and all the time you are actually meeting, you are learning, you are absorbing other people's ideas, but you are not in a forum where you immediately have to respond. The Commonwealth, like the UN, but in a more intimate and jokey way, provides such a useful forum.[24]

On the other side, for members of the Commonwealth's smaller and more vulnerable states, this opportunity to interact with and lobby the richer and more powerful members is particularly valuable. It was also a powerful draw for the government of South Africa, which rejoined the Commonwealth shortly after the elections of 1994. Aziz Pahad, who served as South Africa's deputy foreign minister from 1994 to 2008, explains that the newcomer ANC was keen to build up broader networks on the international scene:

> we knew that members of the Commonwealth were in many other organizations, whether it was the UN or the OAU and other multilateral structures. We saw it as a platform where we could interact and where our leadership in the breakaways could informally interact without the presence of any bureaucracy and [we could] really discuss

issues that mostly never see the light of day, and to really 'find themselves' ... and, of course, Madiba [Mandela] had just come out of prison a few years earlier, and for him meeting so many leaders at that level formally and informally was quite an experience.[25]

But is serendipity enough to encourage heads of government to invest their time in attending the lengthy biennial CHOGM? Certainly, in recent years there has been a tendency for heads to skip them altogether, sending their deputy or foreign minister to represent them. Sandra Pepera, who served in the Political Affairs Division of the Secretariat in the late 1990s and subsequently worked for the UK's Department of International Development, worries that the tangible benefits to members states are not sufficiently obvious:

the Secretariat is an inter-governmental organ and it has to understand that, and if it's not engaged with the governments of the Commonwealth, then actually it has no constituency. I think that is something that has to be addressed. In engaging with the governments of the Commonwealth, you have to show what's in it for them, and I think—both politically and in terms of the development agenda—this has not been clear to the governments of the Commonwealth.[26]

In the end, it is probably reasonable to suggest that what currently holds the Commonwealth together more than anything else is a certain sort of inertia. When I asked K. Shankar Bajpai, former Indian foreign minister, what he saw as the greatest achievement of the Commonwealth, his response was amusing but astute:

Its great achievement is its survival. [*Laughter*] I'm afraid I'm not joking. You know, the very fact that people want to keep it going ...They will not think about it every day of their lives, but when the time comes, nobody is saying, "Let's get out of it" ... So, what is the bond? I can't think of anything else. If you're in a club, why leave it?[27]

Why indeed? No one is going to restore their domestic finances to health by dropping the modest subscription fee. Nor does the organization place any very onerous demands on its members. It is difficult to imagine a movement in any member state urging voters to 'get their country back' by leaving the Commonwealth. Certainly, the domestic and international controversy involved in leaving or demanding the break-up of the Commonwealth is likely to be more troublesome than could be justified by any corresponding benefits. As veteran Indian foreign correspondent Surendra Nihal-Singh noted, "dismantling something is a very difficult operation and requires a large amount of willpower, and that is difficult to gather at the best of times." At the back of leaders' minds is probably the vague suspicion that the Commonwealth might, at some unforeseen time and in some obscure way, come in handy. As Douglas Hurd suggests, with no great sense of enthusiasm, "I think it is there, it is useful, it is a tool, it is worth keeping it, and keeping it in reasonably good shape. Keeping it serviced, as it were."[28]

4

LONG TO REIGN OVER US?

Crowns: Divided and Subtracted

In Chapter 3, we considered a number of reasons why member states have historically seen, and continue to see, value in belonging to the Commonwealth, and why the organization has survived far beyond what many British officials in the 1960s would have regarded as its natural lifespan. There is one important factor that we have not yet considered: the role of monarchy, both in terms of the 'Crown' as a form of sovereignty, and the personal role of the monarch herself.

As we have seen, viewing the Commonwealth as a conscious creation of the British government is a deeply flawed assumption. It has evolved in ways that the UK has found undesirable or positively unhelpful, and the UK's control over this process has been relatively weak and intermittent. If this is true of the elements we have already considered, it is all the more so in the case of the monarchy. If the UK were to decide in the future to 'Brexit' from the Commonwealth as an organization, it would be a remarkably easy procedure. Arguably (to judge by the precedent set by other states that have withdrawn in recent years), it would involve little more than a letter to the secretary-general on 10 Downing Street-headed notepaper. But even then, Britain would still be one of sixteen Commonwealth Realms recognizing the Queen (or her successors) as sovereign. Short of abolishing the monarchy, there is absolutely nothing the UK can do about this—despite the fact that, as we shall see, it sometimes places the government in an awkward position.

Up to 1949, the basic definition of the Commonwealth was of a group of countries under a common sovereign. Since then, with India allowed to remain in the organization as a republic (see Chapter 1), the monarch has had a rather separate, personal role as 'head of the Commonwealth'; the organization now consists overwhelmingly of states of which she is not sovereign. As we shall see, the headship is a role that Queen Elizabeth II (1952–) has taken extremely seriously. Indeed, her commitment to and enthusiasm for the Commonwealth has often exceeded that of British prime ministers. This has certainly been a factor in helping to bind Britain and other countries to the organization, and in recent years her patronage has been increasingly important to the Commonwealth itself. The Queen's involvement in its events is now virtually the only thing about the organization that media outlets consider newsworthy.

Although the headship of the Commonwealth is generally considered not to be hereditary, there are clear signs that the Queen wishes it to pass to her successor as monarch. In an article written in the run-up to the disastrous 2013 CHOGM in Sri Lanka, I made a little joke that was not well received by the Commonwealth's true-believers: "A former prime minister of New Zealand once famously described the Queen as 'the bit of glue that somehow manages to hold the whole thing together'. Increasingly, however, the Commonwealth resembles a dead parrot which relies on that glue to keep it upright on its perch." The organization's defenders indignantly maintained that the parrot was 'just resting'. But five years on, it still shows few signs of life. A consideration of the role of the glue therefore seems as germane as ever to the Commonwealth story.

That story is complex and contentious. But there is one thing that monarchists and republicans can readily agree upon: it is fiendishly difficult to understand. The nineteenth-century British prime minister Palmerston famously said of the Schleswig-Holstein affair: "Only three people have ever really understood [it]—the Prince Consort, who is dead—a German professor, who has gone mad—and I, who have forgotten all about it." Similarly, I would imagine that only a handful of the Commonwealth's 2.3 billion citizens are fully conversant with the ins-and-outs of the Queen's position in relation to the headship, the Commonwealth and the Commonwealth Realms. One would be the Queen herself. After more than six decades on the throne, she probably has a deeper knowledge of the Commonwealth, its issues and personalities than anyone else alive. In terms of academic expertise, I would always defer to the refreshingly sane Australian professor Anne Twomey, whose detailed grasp of the constitutional and legal intricacies of the Realms is never less than astonishing. As to myself, having written a book on the Queen and the Commonwealth, I would claim to have a fair working knowledge of the subject. But I would feel nervous having to take an exam on the subject, particularly if Anne were sitting at the desk in front of me.

This might seem like a rather discouraging way of introducing a chapter that seeks to explore the Queen's relationship with the Commonwealth. It is, however, a useful starting point. The United Kingdom is closely connected to fifteen other Commonwealth Realms through the sovereignty of the Queen, and more loosely connected to another thirty-six member states under her headship; but the nature of those links is very poorly understood. Effective diplomacy relies, to some extent, on everyone knowing the 'rules of the game'. Otherwise, damage may be caused by misunderstanding, either innocent or willful. But in the case of the monarch's role, virtually no one knows the rules, nor is there even a rule book to consult. This goes a long way to explain why, from the dawn of rapid decolonization, many senior figures in Whitehall regarded the monarchy's place in the Commonwealth as more of a hindrance than a help in Britain's relations with its former dependent territories.

There is nothing new about a monarch reigning over a series of geographically scattered territories with their own distinct laws and traditions. Indeed, this was a prominent feature of the dynastic power structure of medieval and early modern Europe. Yet the reluctant acceptance by the UK government in the mid-twentieth century that it was merely one part of a divisible monarchy represented a break with a centuries-old process, in which the direction of travel within the British Isles had been in the opposite direction: towards the uniting of distinct kingdoms under a single, indivisible Crown.

The process had been a slow one. The conquests under Edward I in the thirteenth century ended the autonomy of the Principality of Wales, but it was not until the Laws in Wales Acts (1535–42) that Wales was formally absorbed into the Tudor state. When James VI of Scotland succeeded Elizabeth I as King of England in 1603, the two kingdoms both came under his personal rule. Yet they remained separate until the Act of Union in 1707. In the case of Ireland, the process stretched over an even longer period of time. English kings adopted the title 'Lord of Ireland' in the twelfth century. In 1542, Henry VIII proclaimed himself king of the island. Again, however, Ireland remained a separate kingdom with its own Parliament until the Acts of Union of 1800–1. Even then, the United Kingdom's sovereign was—and had been since 1714—a member of the Hanoverian dynasty. It was not until the 1837 accession of Queen Victoria—who, as a woman, could not succeed to the Electorate of Hanover—that the UK's dynastic link to mainland Europe was broken.

Even today, vestiges of a pre-modern 'divisible monarchy' still remain within the United Kingdom. In the Isle of Man, the Queen is known as the Lord of Man, and in the Bailiwicks of Guernsey and Jersey as the Duke of Normandy. Each of these three Crown dependencies has its own legislative body, and a lieutenant governor who serves as the Queen's representative. These details aside, however, by the middle of the nineteenth century, the UK had arrived at the point where its own monarchy was united. Thereafter, the government began to insist that the principle of unity of the Crown should apply to its growing Empire. This was at least feasible—if ultimately doomed—in those areas under the formal jurisdiction of the Crown. Elsewhere, there was never any prospect of achieving such a seamless blanket of imperial sovereignty. For instance, even after Victoria was declared Empress of India in 1876 in the wake of the 'Indian Mutiny', she was sovereign only of those areas designated as 'British India'. Right up until independence in 1947, there remained hundreds of Indian Princely States, which technically enjoyed protectorate status under the suzerainty of the British Crown. Their local rulers exercised a considerable amount of legal autonomy.

Much of the rest of what we commonly refer to as the 'British Empire' was a constitutional patchwork, composed of Crown colonies, protectorates, protected states, and latterly League of Nations mandates and United Nations Trusteeship territories. Even some individual British 'colonies', such as the Gold Coast, actually consisted of a jumble of these different forms of jurisdiction. This, of course, proved a nightmare for anyone responsible for determining protocol or precedence on important royal occasions, and regularly caused confusion even within the Colonial Office. While policy-makers in London were keen to promote the monarchy as a symbol of unity, in reality the numerous distinct relationships with the Crown of particular peoples and regions across the Empire represented, instead, an important marker of difference.

Running alongside this was a more profound issue: how could the concept of a united Imperial Crown be maintained as, from the mid-nineteenth century, the British government began to allow its older 'settler' colonies (the Dominions) an increasing measure of political autonomy? Within the Austro-Hungarian Empire, the rising force of nationalism had led in 1867 to a formal division: the so-called 'dual monarchy', under which the Habsburg monarch was designated, quite separately, as both Emperor of Austria and King of Hungary. The government in London resisted such fissiparous tendencies. It was buttressed in this by an imperial ideology maintaining that the Dominions shared with the UK, in effect, a common nationality; that they were proud outposts of a 'Greater Britain', and that their reverence for the British monarchy was a natural by-product of this. This already ignored the substantial French-speaking population of Canada. Then, as the Afrikaners of South Africa and the Catholic nationalists of the Irish Free State were corralled unwillingly into this happy imperial family in 1910 and 1922 respectively, the notion of a shared loyalty to the 'British' Crown was stretched to breaking point.

At the same time, the logic of constitutional monarchy also pointed in the direction of divisibility. At a national level, the monarch was represented in each of the Dominions by a governor-general, who discharged the prerogative powers of the Crown. With the devolution of political power to the law-making bodies of the Dominions, the governor-general became, in effect, a sort of contracted-out constitutional monarch, acting in all important respects on the advice of local ministers. As we have seen, the 1926 Balfour Report described the Dominions as "autonomous Communities within the British Empire, equal in status, in no way subordinate one to another in any aspect of their domestic or external affairs". As such, the government of each Dominion should have the right to advise the Crown "in all matters relating to its own affairs". At the Imperial Conference of 1930, bringing together the Dominion premiers in London, the principle was established that this included the right to advise the sovereign on the selection of their governor-general.

So, by the end of the inter-war period, despite the official British insistence that there was one unified 'Crown', sovereign over the whole of the Empire and Commonwealth, there was already a de facto divisible monarchy. The government of South Africa was particularly keen to emphasize that principle whenever the chance arose. As the coronation of Elizabeth II approached in 1953, the UK government effectively had to concede this point, passing a Royal Style and Titles Bill that allowed each of the Commonwealth Realms to recognize their monarch with a distinct title for her. She was, in law and in practice, Queen of New Zealand, and separately Queen of Ceylon, and so on. In those various capacities, which are quite distinct from her role as monarch of the UK, the British government has no right to advise her. If she is invited to visit Canada by her Canadian prime minister, the British government has no say. And when she is there, she speaks and acts on the advice of her Canadian government. It is also entirely up to the governments—and in some cases the peoples—of these Realms whether to retain or abolish the monarchy. The British government has absolutely no control over the matter.

Time Come?

It is equally important to recognize that over the last fifty years neither the British government nor the Palace has been inclined to put any pressure on the Realms to retain the Queen as their sovereign. One would not realize this on the basis of some of the press coverage of the issue. To take one example, in 2012, the Jamaican judge Patrick Robinson gave a lecture to the Institute of Commonwealth Studies on the twin movements in his country to establish a republic and to end appeals from there to the UK Privy Council. He subsequently published a version of the lecture in *The Round Table* under the arresting title 'The Enduring Cry for Freedom'. It rehearsed the long history of British oppression in the West Indies: "Born in bloodshed and sustained in bloodshed, the relationship between England and Jamaica was marked by atrocity upon atrocity against the enslaved". Moving on to the monarchical system that had survived independence, Robinson delivered the punchline: "Jamaica is a post-oppression society and its people should not be asked to have as its Head of State a person who symbolizes the oppression inflicted on their enslaved and other ancestors".[1]

All this went down extremely well with his audience, a large section of which was drawn from London's expatriate West Indian Community. But it did pose an obvious question: who precisely was holding Jamaica back from this? In the course of the 1960s, a series of recently-decolonized African countries had made the rapid transition from monarchical to republican status. The first was Ghana, which became independent in 1957 and a republic in 1960, followed by Tanganyika (now Tanzania), which waited only a matter of months after independence in 1961 to establish a republic. Nigeria followed in 1963, then Kenya (1964), Malawi (1966) and the Gambia (1970). The British government did not seek to impede this process; indeed, by the end it was actively cheering on the republican reforms. And there is no indication that British governments of the twenty-first century would be any less relaxed. So my question to Robinson at the end of his speech was, essentially: "That's all fine. But what kept you so long?"

This mystery is certainly one that deserves some consideration, particularly given the conspicuous lack of Commonwealth countries turning republican in recent years. Again, this is not something one would necessary pick up on by following the news. Prime ministers from the Caribbean Realms regularly make headlines by announcing their intention to drop the monarchy. At her swearing-in in January 2012, the new prime minister of Jamaica, Portia Simpson-Miller, declared: "I love the Queen, she is a beautiful lady, and apart from being a beautiful lady, she is a wise lady and a wonderful lady.... But I think time come."[2] In March 2015, Barbadian Prime Minister Freundel Stuart told his followers, "we have to move from a monarchical system to a republican form of government in the very near future."[3] Indeed, he raised the prospect of a ceremonial presidency by the following year, the country's fiftieth independence anniversary. From this rhetoric, one might have supposed that Realms were dropping like flies. Yet in neither case has anything actually happened. Nor were such calls unprecedented: in 1975, Michael Manley had announced on the BBC that a republican form of government was more suited to Jamaica; in 2003, P. J. Patterson had called for Jamaica to abolish the monarchy by 2007.

If this was not enough, looking at the broader picture also leaves one sceptical about Simpson-Miller's prediction that "time come". Since Trinidad and Tobago became a republic in 1976, only one other former Commonwealth Realm—Mauritius in 1992—has made the transition by constitutional means (Fiji became a republic in 1987 after General Rabuka staged a coup there). Even in the case of Mauritius, the government used its commanding parliamentary majority to push through the necessary legislation. To find a precedent for a Commonwealth Realm rejecting the monarchy by popular referendum, one has to go right back to apartheid South Africa in 1960.

Even some of those Realms that have dropped the monarchy have done so at an extremely slow pace. In 1956, for example, Prime Minister S. W. R. D. Bandaranaike of Ceylon informed the Commonwealth prime ministers' meeting that his country intended to become a republic. The following year, a Joint Parliamentary Select Committee on constitutional reform was established to consider the process for achieving republic status. Yet it was not until 1967 that Prime Minister Sananayake announced the preparation of legislation to put it into effect, and it took a further change of government before Ceylon finally made the transition under Mrs Bandaranaike, adopting the new name of Sri Lanka in 1972.

The main question, then, is why what many would see as a natural process of shedding a colonial legacy has been so slow and faltering. The answer is certainly not to be found in the attitude or actions of the British government, which historically has kept aloof from these matters. Indeed, if the Whitehall 'official mind' has had a preference, it has generally been in favour of the transition to republican status, precisely because it serves to clarify relations with the UK's former dependencies. Of course, an 'official mind' is not the same as an 'official memory'. Anyone who has dealt with the contemporary Foreign and Commonwealth Office will know that the latter can be fairly short. As such, it has sometimes been necessary for the FCO to learn the value of neutrality from first principles. But the outcome has been the same.

In essence, this attitude took shape in the early 1960s. In Ghana and Tanganyika, the newly independent governments' rapid moves to implement republican constitutions seemed to many British officials firm evidence of the way the wind was blowing. They reasoned that the 'British' monarchy had relatively shallow historical roots in Africa. In some cases, the association had lasted no more than a few decades. The intricacies of

constitutional monarchy were not expected to be properly understood there, and with many of their neighbours adopting presidential rule, African leaders who merely had the status of prime
minister under an absentee monarch were likely to see themselves
as second-class citizens at international gatherings. British ministers and officials were generally less than optimistic about the
prospect of stable government surviving for very long in their
former African dependencies, and they were nervous about the
Queen being associated with or even drawn into any future crises
there. Furthermore, the prospect of independence celebrations
being followed rapidly by republic day celebrations looked like a
double slap in the face for the Queen personally and the UK
generally. Better, London thought, to get the whole ghastly
business over in a single night. So it was that, by 1963, the
British government was actively encouraging its remaining
African colonies to become republics on independence.

At the same time, Whitehall regarded the Caribbean as a very
different matter. Here, links with the monarchy dated back, in
some cases, to the earliest days of English expansionism overseas.
And, indeed, the survival of constitutional monarchies among
the Commonwealth's Caribbean members has been a remarkable
feature of their post-colonial history. Jamaica and Trinidad led
the process of decolonization, becoming independent in 1962
following the break-up of the West Indies Federation. Of the ten
island states that followed in the '60s, '70s and '80s, only
Dominica achieved independence as a republic (1978), and at the
time of writing only two—Guyana and Trinidad and Tobago—
have subsequently transitioned. In Grenada, the monarchy even
survived a Marxist coup in 1979. Nevertheless, when Trinidad
and Tobago did choose the republican path, the British attitude
was largely one of relief. The British High Commissioner,
C. E. Diggines, predicted that the move would "have the advantage of defining more clearly the relationship which was becom-

ing increasingly blurred", and suggested that "if anything, I believe that, with this final severance of even a symbolic colonial umbilical cord ... there is every possibility that the relationship, already generally good, could even become better."[4]

The attitude of the Palace has been equally relaxed. It has consistently maintained the view that the future status of Commonwealth countries was entirely a matter for themselves. As a constitutional monarch, the Queen could only be embarrassed if the transition to independence was made by unconstitutional means. This sentiment recurs in British government records. But it was also famously spelled out publicly by the Duke of Edinburgh, in characteristically forthright terms at a press conference during a visit to Ottawa in October 1969. Clearly irritated by attempts to draw him into the debate about the monarchy's future in Canada, Prince Philip told journalists,

> If at any stage any nation decides that the system is unacceptable then it's up to them to change it. I think it's a complete misconception to imagine that the Monarchy exists in the interests of the Monarch—it doesn't. It exists in the interests of the people: in a sense—we don't come here for our health, so to speak ... I think that the important thing about it is that if, at any stage, people feel that it has no further part to play, then for goodness sake let's end the thing on amicable terms without having a row about it.[5]

Overall, then, the survival of the Commonwealth realms owes almost nothing to pressure from the British political establishment. In fact, it is undoubtedly the case that republican movements across the Commonwealth have been impeded from within, by a sense of respect and even genuine affection for Queen Elizabeth II—including in Britain itself. So long as she remains alive, there will be many politicians inclined to keep their republican sentiments to themselves. What happens after that, however, may be an entirely different matter.

Rather, the endurance of the British monarch as shared sovereign is virtually entirely down to local factors. Each Realm is different, and in each, at any one time, there have been historical, social and political circumstances either encouraging or hampering the progress of republicanism. In New Zealand, for example, as Peter Boyce has noted, the debate has been overshadowed by the political legacy of the 1840 Treaty of Waitangi between Maori chiefs and the British Crown, leading to fears that the move towards a republic might have implications for indigenous rights.[6] Canada's proximity to the US, and its desire to differentiate itself from its southern neighbour, is sometimes cited as a reason for the monarchy's resilience there. But the Realms also share many conditions that have impeded republicanism.

First, in many cases their independence constitutions contained quite significant legal impediments to the creation of republics. Generally, however, these came about because of disagreement between local parties as to the desirability of shedding the monarchy. In the case of Trinidad and Tobago, for example, the position of the Crown was entrenched in the constitution agreed at the 1962 Marlborough House conference. Yet this was essentially a concession to the Democratic Labour Party (DLP) opposition by the country's prime minister, Eric Williams, who agreed that any move to a republic would require a three-quarters majority vote in the lower house and a two-thirds majority in the upper house. In Jamaica, changes to the executive authority of the Queen require a two-thirds majority in both houses, plus a referendum.

In early 1980s Canada, afraid that controversy around the future of the Crown would hijack the debate about broader constitutional reforms, Prime Minister Pierre Trudeau effectively ring-fenced the issue, in the process erecting an almost insurmountable constitutional barrier to republicanism. Section 41 (a) of the 1982 Constitution made provision for amendments relating to "the office of the Queen, the Governor General and the Lieutenant Governor of a province". Yet as the consequence of Trudeau's negotiations with the provincial premiers in November 1981, any such amendments would require resolutions from the Canadian Senate and House of Commons, as well as the unanimous backing of all the provincial legislative assemblies.[7] In Australia, meanwhile, any move to a republic has to be approved in a referendum. To succeed, the motion requires the support of 50 per cent of the national vote, and majorities in at least four of the six Australian states. The 1999 referendum on a republic came nowhere near this. Only 45.3 per cent of Australian voters supported the motion for a republic, while 54.7 per cent rejected it. Of the six states, there was a narrow majority for the motion in only one: Victoria.[8]

As UK governments have recently learned to their cost, a referendum can be an unpredictable thing. One factor is the precise nature of the proposal itself. It is broadly accepted that the monarchy survived in Australia in 1999, not because the Australian electorate was hostile to a republic in principle, but because the motion specifically provided for a nominated president. This effectively split republican voters, many of whom favoured a directly-elected presidency. Referenda can also very easily turn into a means for voters to express general lack of confidence in the government or in politicians more generally. It is striking that in Australia, of the eighty-three simple Yes/No referenda held since 1906, the motion has only been carried in eight cases. There seems to be a general suspicion of proposals that appear to enhance the power of the political class and of the federal government in particular.

Some of the Commonwealth's smaller Realms have also seen referendum motions defeated. The tiny Polynesian island state of Tuvalu has already held two on the republican question. In both cases, voters opted to retain the monarchy, most recently by

65 per cent, in 2008. A 2009 referendum in the Caribbean state of St Vincent and the Grenadines produced a similar result, with 56 per cent rejecting a republic. One notable feature of these two votes is that both took place after the 2007 CHOGM had agreed changes to the criteria for Commonwealth membership. This meant that countries transitioning to republican status no longer had formally to reapply for Commonwealth membership. Yet, even though the anti-republican camps could no longer posit the (always remote) possibility that dropping the monarchy might risk future membership, they still won handsomely.

It might well be suggested that, in contrast to the heady days of the 1960s and '70s, voters have begun to adopt a more 'bread and butter' approach to constitutional reform, asking how, in practical terms, it would actually make their lives better. Meanwhile, supporters of the Crown have been striving to shift this profit-and-loss audit further in their favour, by stressing how little a republican settlement would add, even in constitutional terms. This has involved 'depersonalizing' the system by stressing the significance of the 'Crown' rather than the monarchy. As Peter Boyce puts it, "An underlying theme of the Crown's evolutionary process in Canada through the past half century has been the ever widening separation of the person of the monarch from the concept of the Crown itself, a theme also evident in the Australian and New Zealand experience."[9]

The corollary of this displaced emphasis has been to beef up the role of the Queen's local representative in the Realms, the governor-general. A standard complaint of Commonwealth republicans has been that they suffer from having an absentee head of state, particularly in the sphere of international relations. When the Queen visits the United States, for example, she is routinely referred to in the American press as the "Queen of England". Only an extremely sharp-eyed reporter might mention that she was also the Queen of Canada, and it is unlikely in the extreme that anyone would call her the Queen of Tuvalu. As such, monarchists have been keen to enhance the role of the governor-general as the effective 'head of state', particularly on foreign engagements, and the preferred term for the Queen has been the 'sovereign'. In the run-up to the 1999 Australian referendum, Buckingham Palace duly obliged by removing from its website a statement that the Queen was "head of state" in her overseas realms.[10]

This tactic promises to assist in preserving the Commonwealth Realms in two respects. Firstly, it allows monarchists to claim that, in a sense, the Realms are essentially 'Crowned Republics'. A formal move to republican status would do nothing more than replace a ceremonial governor-general with a ceremonial president. Secondly, it serves to insulate the institution of the monarchy from the inevitable disruption that will follow the Queen's death. It is well known that Prince Charles is far less popular than the Queen around the Commonwealth. By depersonalizing 'the Crown', monarchists can hope with some reason that Charles' own character will be less of an issue if and when he inherits his mother's various Commonwealth titles.

Head of the Commonwealth

If the UK government long ago lost any control or even influence over the system of the Commonwealth Realms, it has also sometimes seemed uncomfortable with its monarch's second role as head of the Commonwealth. This is despite the fact that the title, if not the role, was in large part a British invention. At the Commonwealth prime ministers' meeting that opened on 22 April 1949, the British had seized upon the idea of the King as a symbol of Commonwealth association when seeking to construct a formula under which India could recognize him in some Commonwealth capacity, and thus remain within the organization as a republic. The declaration that emerged from the meeting spoke of India's "acceptance of the King as the symbol of the free association of its independent member nations and as such Head of the Commonwealth". This was enough to persuade the other premiers to accept India's continued membership.

The title 'Head of the Commonwealth' was simply that: a form of words. It was not conceived as a particular formal role by the British or any of the other participants at the 1949 meeting. Indeed, the declaration made clear that the King would not exercise any constitutional function by virtue of the headship.[11] The reason for this was spelled out by the Queen's private secretary, Michael Adeane, in September 1959: "No constitutional function was attached to it [at the time of the declaration] and none can belong to it now because no Head of the Commonwealth could act in a commonwealth [sic] sense without constitutional advisers and no such commonwealth advisers exist."[12] The defining feature of a constitutional monarchy is that, except in very limited circumstances, the sovereign only acts in a political capacity on the advice of their ministers. This both ensures that policy is determined by elected representatives and shields the monarch from political criticism. Yet there were no ministers capable of advising the monarch on a Commonwealth-wide basis.

Despite this minimalist conception of the headship, however, the role has been given substance over the decades through a series of regular commitments on the part of the Queen. These include her Christmas and Commonwealth Day messages and her support for and regular attendance at events such as the Commonwealth Games and the Commonwealth Day Multi-Faith Service at Westminster Abbey. She has also placed particular importance on being present at the biennial CHOGM. Although she only obtained a formal role in these summits in 1997, she had previously made a point of receiving the Commonwealth representatives outside the main sessions and hosting a banquet for them. Before 2013, in sixty years of headship she had only missed one: the CHOGM in Singapore in January 1971, which her British prime minister Edward Heath had formally advised her not to attend.[13] She has also visited all but two of the fifty-two Commonwealth member states, many on multiple occasions. Indeed, the headquarters of the Commonwealth Secretariat is itself a royal palace, made available rent-free by the Queen.

In effect, since the beginning of her reign in 1952, the Queen has taken a title, and by a series of ceremonial accretions turned it into a role. Nevertheless, the original objection to the headship as a suitable role for a constitutional monarch still stands, and remains an area in which the standard theory of the institution fails to operate. When she addresses the Commonwealth at Christmas, on Commonwealth Day or at the opening ceremony of the CHOGM, she does so as head of the Commonwealth, and as such neither solicits nor expects to receive advice from her ministers, in the UK or elsewhere. While no one would claim that the Queen has ever used those occasions to make challenging or controversial personal statements, there is no guarantee that a less circumspect future monarch would not take greater licence with the platform the headship provides.

What the Queen has managed to do is to help keep the myth of the Commonwealth alive. It is her project; and she gives generously of her time to promote its interests. By contrast, her oldest son and heir, Prince Charles, has spread his restless energies over a fairly wide range of issues including architecture, education, complementary medicine and the environment. For decades, his letters to ministers on these and many other policy questions have caused headaches to civil servants and proved difficult to reconcile with the notion that the monarchy should steer clear of political controversy. The Queen's approach to the exercise of political influence has been far more subtle, and arguably more effective.

The key to this is repetition. It's such an obvious point that we often lose sight of it. The Queen never gives interviews and never departs from the texts of her cautiously-worded speeches. Essentially, we only know what she thinks because of what she does, and particularly what she does repeatedly. On that basis we can, for example, safely infer that she likes (in no particular order) horses, Scotland, the armed forces, the Church and the Commonwealth. In her public utterances, she frequently speaks of the importance of her Christian faith and of the value of the Commonwealth. Perhaps the greatest mark of her success in negotiating all the pitfalls of constitutional monarchy is that, over decades in which British adherence to Christianity has been in steady decline, and the Commonwealth has come under fire from senior politicians and the press, she has presented both as somehow 'above' any sort of controversy. An extremely long-reigning monarch can shape the political landscape like an iceberg: by steadily maintaining the same course, they can exert a powerful influence on our collective values. Arguably, the Queen's greatest contribution to the myth of the Commonwealth has been to reinforce the impression that it remains a powerful and constructive force in the world, and that feeling part of that broader family is a natural and logical feature of British national identity. The British monarch's highly visible status as head of the Commonwealth is a powerful incentive to the UK government to continue engaging with the organization, whatever doubts it might have about the effectiveness of the Secretariat.

No doubt with this in mind, there have been increasing signs in recent years that the Palace is determined for Prince Charles to inherit this role. The problem is that little thought was given to this question in 1949, and there is no body competent to pass a succession law for the Commonwealth as a whole; the 2013 Commonwealth Charter notwithstanding, the organization does not operate according to a formal constitution. Instead, the

Palace has sought to encourage the assumption that Charles would automatically succeed to the headship. He represented the Queen at the 2013 CHOGM in Sri Lanka, and at the 2015 Malta CHOGM he joined her on stage for the opening ceremony. In case anyone should miss this clear signal of intent by the Palace, the Queen took the opportunity to state for the record that she could not "have been better supported and represented in the Commonwealth than by The Prince of Wales who continues to give so much to it with great distinction."

We also recently had some hard evidence of manoeuvring behind the scenes. Speaking in London in October 2016, as a visiting professorial fellow at the Menzies Centre, King's College London, former Australian prime minister Julia Gillard provided an important insight into the Palace's tactics.[14] Between the CHOGMs in Perth in 2011 and in Colombo in 2013, Gillard occupied the role of chair-in-office. In that capacity, she was the recipient of Palace lobbying around the headship. She recalled,

> In early 2013, I was advised that Sir Christopher Geidt, the Queen's private secretary, wanted half an hour of my time in my capacity as Chair of the Commonwealth, an office the host holds until the next meeting. He would fly to Australia to anywhere I was in order to get it. The upshot of our meeting, which took place in Adelaide … on 21 February 2013, was a clearly worded statement for the public record about how succession works for the role of the Head of Commonwealth. In the Australian Parliament on 20 March, I duly gave the statement and sent it to all Commonwealth countries.

The statement came in the wake of the signing of the new Commonwealth Charter. Gillard stated,

> As I table this charter today we also pay tribute to the distinguished service of Queen Elizabeth as Head of the Commonwealth over these many decades. The institution of the Head of the Commonwealth, standing as it does above individual governments, has been an asset

of the Commonwealth since its foundation, and we need not be reticent about its future. For Australia's part, I am sure the Queen's successor as monarch will one day serve as Head of the Commonwealth with the same distinction as Her Majesty has done.

The statement was not widely reported across the Commonwealth, and its wording was so low-key that its significance was generally missed at the time. But the Palace had succeeded in putting down an important marker. It may well be continuing to apply pressure behind the scenes. Certainly it seems highly, not to say mysteriously, confident that some sort of agreement will be in place by the time of the Queen's death.

In this it can certainly rely on the support of other influential figures within the Commonwealth. There has been a growing recognition of the important role that the Queen, and by extension the headship, plays in keeping the organization in the public eye. It is instructive to compare photographs taken at Commonwealth prime ministers' meetings and subsequent CHOGMs over the course of her reign. The Queen, of course, is always at the centre of the formal group photograph. But during the early decades of her reign she was surrounded by some genuinely remarkable figures of twentieth-century history: Nehru, Nkrumah, Menzies, Makarios, Lee Kuan Yew and Nyerere. Even without her, these gatherings would have been events of note. Increasingly, however, and particularly since Nelson Mandela left the political stage, she has become by far the most notable and distinguished figure in the room, and it is on her that international media attention tends to focus. Whereas in the 1960s and '70s, there was a feeling in some quarters that the monarchy was something of an anachronism—not to say an embarrassment for an international organization rapidly establishing its radical credentials—now it is perhaps the only aspect of the Commonwealth that commands widespread public interest.

This has been noticeably reflected in recent Commonwealth initiatives' focus on the Queen. A major new scheme announced at the 2011 CHOGM in Perth was the launch of the Queen Elizabeth Diamond Jubilee Trust, chaired by the former British prime minister Sir John Major. Aimed at supporting charitable causes across the Commonwealth, it was promised a contribution of up to £50 million from the British government.[15] Meanwhile, the Royal Commonwealth Society has increasingly been living up to its name. Many of its most high-profile initiatives are currently centred on the Queen or in her honour. In addition to the Queen's Commonwealth Essay Competition, which has been on the go since 1883, we have recently seen the introduction of the Queen's Young Leaders Award and the Queen's Commonwealth Canopy, established in 2015 "to create a network of forest conser-vation initiatives throughout the 52 nations of the Commonwealth to mark Her Majesty The Queen's service and dedication as Head of the Commonwealth." The RCS marked the Queen's Jubilee year of 2012 with the launch of its virtual 'Jubilee Time Capsule'. Citizens from around the Commonwealth were invited to "Share your story with the Queen" on a dedicated website.

The extent to which attitudes to the monarchy have changed can also be gauged by comparing the arrangements for the 1977 CHOGM—the last time the summit was held in London—with the preparations for the April 2018 CHOGM, when the UK hosts again. The idea of holding the 1977 CHOGM in London, in the year of her Silver Jubilee celebrations, was the Queen's own. However, the idea of conflating the two raised fears that the Commonwealth summit might be perceived as some sort of neo-colonial 'Durbar', and the then secretary-general, Sonny Ramphal, personally warned the FCO of the sensitivities sur-rounding the monarchy.[16] Today, it is difficult to detect similar scruples from within the organization about plans for 2018. Tim Hitchins, a former deputy private secretary to the Queen, has been appointed by the government as chief executive with overall responsibility for planning the summit, which is due to have a distinctively royal flavour, involving Buckingham Palace, Windsor Castle, and the royal family prominently on show. It will certainly provide a further opportunity to reinforce the impression that Prince Charles stands in 'natural' succession to the headship, and may offer chances for some more discreet lobbying of Commonwealth Heads on this count.

The monarchy provides a dilemma for the Commonwealth. It has undoubtedly become its most important life-support mechanism. Yet the more the organization embraces this association, the less chance it has of escaping the perception that it is simply a relic of British imperialism. And, as we shall see in Chapter 5, the spectre of Empire, far from receding, has returned to haunt the corridors of power in the UK.

5

GUILT

"The last place you would want to see the Commonwealth appear is in the history curriculum."

Danny Sriskandarajah, director of the Royal Commonwealth Society, giving evidence in April 2012 to the House of Commons Select Committee on Foreign Affairs inquiry into the Commonwealth

We are nearing a time when the dissolution of the Empire is so remote that no one living will actually recall it. One might have imagined that this would lead to a more 'dispassionate' approach to the subject, and that was probably the expectation of many of my generation of historians as we began our doctoral research in the late 1980s. Documents were beginning to flow into the Public Record Office (now the National Archives). Soon, the thinking behind Macmillan's 1960 'Wind of Change' decolonisation policy for Africa, would be as open to conventional archival analysis as the 'Scramble for Africa' or the origins of the First World War. We then expected the morally-infused questions that seemingly obsessed older generations to fall away: "Was Empire a good or a bad thing?" "Did we do a good job?" Instead, the new task for historians would be to gain a detailed, nuanced understanding of

105

how the imperial system of government operated and why it came to an end.

This assumption, as we shall see, turned out to be incorrect. On the contrary, we have witnessed a familiar process, in which major events—severed from the messy, compromised reality of personal experience and memory—are reified into something totemic, often drawing on the myths woven around them by propagandists at the time. Soldiers rarely return from any battlefield confident that they have been the untarnished instruments of a great moral victory. More often, what binds them together is a shared sense of trauma, guilt and complicity. As such, it has probably required the gradual falling away of the Second World War's veterans for that conflict to assume its current incarnation: as the great sacred myth of British national identity, the UK taking the lead in history's one genuinely just war. As we know, particularly from the late nineteenth century, the rickety, unstable structures of the British Empire were dressed in a shimmering cloak of mythology. As memories of the less-glamorous reality fade, a version of that myth lingers in the collective consciousness. Yet, in the deeply polarized context of 'Brexit' Britain, there is also a counter-narrative. This sees imperialism as the nation's collective original sin, for which it has yet to perform proper penance.

For decades, opposition to British imperialism was a shibboleth for the UK far left, and its record in this area a matter of great pride. The Labour Party, particularly under the post-1945 Attlee administration, undoubtedly compromised its values to accommodate what Herbert Morrison, one of its leading ministers, glibly called the "jolly old Empire". Nationalists from Britain's colonies generally found more stalwart friends in the Communist Party of Great Britain and other Marxist factions. This old Leninist and Trotskyite left has now been largely displaced by a new politics of intersectionality, which seeks to replace proletarian solidarity with an alliance of groups marginalized by factors such as class, race, religion and gender. But, for this new manifestation of the left, hostility to the notion of Empire—characterized by the supposed fetishization of white, masculine Judeo-Christian power and privilege—remains a key unifying principle. Indeed, it sometimes seems that for those keen to import a version of US-style identity politics, the legacy of the Empire is analogous to that of pre-Civil War American slavery, animating and legitimating a home-grown form of black political consciousness.

So, the question of whether the British Empire was a 'good' or 'bad' thing hardly seems to have lost its urgency. And violence was indeed a central underlying feature of British colonial rule. Debates tend to focus upon the more notorious cases of imperial brutality and neglect: the ruthless response to the 1857 Indian uprising; the Amritsar Massacre of 1919; the Bengal Famine during the Second World War; and the bloody counter-insurgency campaigns in Malaya, Kenya and Cyprus in the late 1940s and 1950s. But even in less extreme cases, the implicit threat of racially-inflected violence by the colonial authorities was ever present. The ultimate recourse to overwhelming physical force was always available to British representatives, albeit in the knowledge that this might damage their careers—such calling in of muscle being seen in London as evidence that they had lost control of the situation.

At the heart of this bloody aspect of imperialism was a vacuum of legitimacy. The British struggled to establish a genuine basis of consent for their own authority, while also denying the legitimacy of those who claimed to speak for proto- or fully-fledged nationalist movements. The issue of colonial violence was clearly not something that UK imperial governments were keen to highlight. Then, in the independence period, the Commonwealth's boost to the UK's international image was obvious: being on friendly terms with former colonies sent a powerful signal that, in spite of all that had happened, Britain was essentially one of the good guys. There is no escaping this reality of the decolonizing context in which the Commonwealth was established.

Cover-up?

This 'forgetfulness', which greased the wheels of post-independence Commonwealth relations, was itself facilitated by the British government's conscious efforts to destroy or hide evidence of the darker elements of colonial rule. A powerful reminder of this came in April 2011, when *The Times* ran a story with potentially huge implications for the whole history of British withdrawal from Empire. Ben Macintyre, who broke it, claimed that

> Government efforts to cover up one of the worst episodes in British colonial history have been revealed by the discovery of a vast cache of documents relating to the bloody Mau Mau rebellion in Kenya ... The papers, documenting efforts to put down insurgency, were spirited out of Africa on the eve of Kenya's independence and have been held in secret government archives for half a century.[1]

We have subsequently learned far more about the background to this revelation.[2] The story is a labyrinthine one, open to multiple interpretations, but the basic outline is fairly clear. In June 2009, the London solicitors' firm Leigh Day & Co had issued a compensation claim against the British government on behalf of five elderly Kenyans who had been detained and, they claimed, tortured during the campaign against the Mau Mau rebellion, a conflict also known as the Kenya Emergency. At a preliminary hearing, the court ordered the Foreign and Commonwealth Office—which had inherited responsibility for the Colonial Office's files—to make a full disclosure of all relevant documents in its possession. Edward Inglett, head of the Kenya desk at the FCO, conducted a search, and in the process secured the release of several files at the National Archives in Kew that had previously been closed to researchers. In November 2010, however, he submitted a witness statement to the court claiming that no additional materials had been discovered. The following month, the court received another witness statement, this time from the historian and Kenya expert David Anderson, alleging that the British government was withholding no fewer than 1,500 files in 300 boxes, which had been removed from Kenya on independence in 1963.

This was a very precise claim. An archaeologist might have an informed hunch that somewhere in a field in Norfolk there is likely to be an Anglo-Saxon burial site containing precious metals. One would not, however, expect them to predict that it included seven large urns containing precisely 185 gold coins. Did Anderson have paranormal abilities? We will return to this intriguing question in a moment. Of more immediate relevance is that his submission stirred something deep within the FCO's apparently sieve-like institutional memory: "Ah—*those* secret files!" The following month, the files were 'discovered' in a government repository at Hanslope Park, Buckinghamshire, a site that had for many years been an outpost of the British intelligence community. By February 2011, the legal team representing the former Kenyan detainees had begun working its way through the newly disclosed material. As the court case opened in April of that year, the existence of the files was officially confirmed. They included not only the material that Anderson had uncannily predicted would be there, but thousands of additional files relating to dozens of other former British colonies. In June 2011, the government appointed the Cambridge historian Tony Badger to oversee the declassification of the Hanslope Park material and its gradual transfer to the National Archives.

So is David Anderson really the Uri Geller of the historical profession? No—he merely applied a trick of the trade: when seeking to get a sense of what the government is hiding, you work sideways from files that are already in the public domain. Ironically, the British had left behind incriminating evidence in the Kenyan archives: papers that detailed arrangements for the files' removal. In 1967, only four years after independence, Kenya demanded their return. The UK government rebuffed the Kenyan approach, but, again, it recorded the exchanges in an FCO file, which Anderson had discovered at Kew. The file made it clear that government officials were aware both of the extent of the 'migrated' files—around 1,500 of them in over 300 boxes, taking up around 100 linear feet of storage space—and that they contained potentially embarrassing material relating to abuses carried out during the Emergency.

The issue of the Kenyan files periodically resurfaced over the subsequent decades. In 1971, the Labour MP Andrew Faulds asked a parliamentary question about material missing from the Kenyan archives, and received a thoroughly evasive reply. Further direct approaches by the Kenyan government in 1974 and in 1982 were again brushed aside. While civil servants in Whitehall appeared to have had few qualms about dismissing the Kenyan claims, there was a related question that did vex the official mind: if the files had been legitimately removed from Kenya in 1963, and not merely stolen, surely that implied that they were British records? If so, under the terms of the 1958 Public Record Act they should be deposited in Kew and eventually made available to the public. Yet when the National Archives was asked on a number of occasions—most recently in 2009—whether it was prepared to take them, it refused, on the strictly technical basis that it did not believe the 'migrated archives' were indeed UK public records as defined by the 1958 Act. They had, after all been generated by a separate jurisdiction—that of the Crown Colony and Protectorate of Kenya—and not by the British government. But if they weren't UK records, by what right was Britain holding onto them?

Of course, legal opinion can be disputed and can change; in the event, shortly before the Kenyan compensation case was due to open in 2011, the National Archives decided—on grounds that remain unclear—that the migrated archives did indeed include UK public records that might be transferred to Kew. Yet a central part of the British government's defence in court rested on the argument that the colonial government of Kenya was a separate jurisdiction. As such, even if the claimants could prove that they had been mistreated by colonial officials or troops, responsibility had legally passed to the new government of Kenya at independence in December 1963. But surely, then, this implied that the current Kenyan government was also the legal owner of the records?

Of course, it was not the ownership of the documents that was on trial. With these legal loose ends hanging uneasily in the air, the compensation case opened in the High Court in London in April 2011. I attended a couple of sessions, my first time in a court of law. It was a strange mixture of harrowing detail and esoteric legal argument. In its submission to the court, Leigh Day had included claims that detainees suspected of involvement in the Mau Mau movement had been subjected to "sodomy, the insertion of sand into men's anuses and the insertion of glass bottles filled with hot liquid into women's vaginas". Yet, for the reasons explained above, the first session I attended was largely taken up with a deeply theoretical disquisition on the principle of the divisibility of the Crown.

Throughout all of this, the elderly claimants sat unobtrusively and patiently awaiting the court's decision. Ultimately, they secured a series of victories: in July 2011 they were granted leave to sue the British government; in October the following year, the judge ruled that the case could go to a full trial. In the meantime, the British government came under international pressure to ensure a just resolution of the claims against it. Finally, in

June 2013, Foreign Secretary William Hague announced an out-of-court settlement of nearly £20 million, paid to 5,228 alleged victims of abuse. Meanwhile, between April 2012 and November 2013, the so-called 'Hanslope Park' files were released at the National Archives. But if the government was hoping that a line had been drawn under the whole affair, it was to be disappointed. In October 2013, *The Guardian* ran a story by investigative reporter Ian Cobain, claiming that the FCO had retained a further 1.2 million files, in contravention of the Public Record Act. To date, the nature and ultimate fate of these records remains the subject of heated debate.

In the wake of the Hanslope case there was much soul-searching among historians, and a fair amount of mutual recrimination. Had they simply been hoodwinked by the British government into believing the standard 'Commonwealth' narrative of a global happy family that had weathered an amicable divorce and become all the closer for it? Had they acted as passive consumers in the great historical supermarket of the National Archives in Kew, oblivious to the fact that the devious proprietors had been watering down the goods, or hiding the best stuff away in the back of the shop? This was certainly an accusation levelled by the Harvard historian Caroline Elkins, who had supported the Kenyan claimants in the Hanslope case. Her own controversial account of the Mau Mau Emergency, *Britain's Gulag: The Brutal End of Empire in Kenya* (2005), had certainly raised the stakes in the colonial violence debate. Its introduction claimed, "I now believe there was in late colonial Kenya a murderous campaign to eliminate Kikuyu people, a campaign that left tens of thousands, perhaps hundreds of thousands, dead."[3]

Although the basis of this particular claim has been vigorously disputed, if the British government was, indeed, withholding significant quantities of documentary evidence, then who knew how many mass graves waited to be discovered in Kenya and across the former Empire? And, some asked whether, in colluding with official silence over colonial violence, historians had enabled the British public to remain complacent about their country's murderous role in world history. After all, a YouGov poll conducted in the UK, published in January 2016, found that 44 per cent of respondents claimed to be "proud" of their country's colonial record, while only 21 per cent regretted it and 23 per cent held neither view.

A discussion of this broader debate would not get us much further in our consideration of the Commonwealth. But one point does deserve to be made: whether or not there were—or are—attempts at a state cover-up of colonial abuses, in reality such British official secrecy has not been particularly effective. For instance, historians of Africa were already putting the pieces together long before the FCO was forced to come clean about its 'forgotten' files on the Mau Mau Emergency. As far back as the late 1980s and early 1990s, books had shed fresh light on the Emergency and highlighted the brutal repression employed by the authorities.[4] This earlier scholarship, and Elkins's own book, drew partly on official files in the National Archives that contained a considerable amount of information about brutal acts of violence by security forces and colonial officials. Of course, there were gaps in the record where the official censor had obviously been at work. But plenty of incriminating evidence remained. Certainly the Hanslope papers seem to contain little to substantiate Elkins's claim that deaths in Kenya resulting from British counter-insurgency might have run into the hundreds of thousands.

Penance

The Hanslope 'revelations', then, did not prompt a major re-evaluation of the role of colonial violence—neither among the historical community, nor in broader British society. The predominant view among those who have studied the new material in any depth is rather that, particularly in the case of Kenya, they provide some interesting additional evidence, but contain nothing to cause a major paradigm-shift in our understanding. Indeed, they emerged at a time when there was already a renewed focus on the negative impacts of British imperial expansion. The British government's handling of the Hanslope affair simply reinforced already widespread perceptions that it was continuing to evade moral responsibility for that past. This could be seen in the wider conversation about the Hanslope case, which included suggestions that the British colonial authorities' atrocities matched those of Nazi Germany.

As part of that broader critique of the UK's colonial record, a series of campaigns demanding reparations for colonialism and slavery were also gaining in momentum and prominence in the 2010s. The debate related to Africa and the African diaspora drew inspiration from the well-established US movement around the legacy of the trans-Atlantic slave trade, as well as the increasing attention given to historical treatment of indigenous peoples in both North America and Australia. The reparations issue was a complex one: to what extent should such a campaign focus specifically on how black Africans were affected? Should it concentrate solely on the impact of the slave trade, or also encompass the continent's formal colonization? Indeed, should it extend to the global legacy of colonialism?

Nevertheless, the movement had been gathering steam since the early 1990s, when conferences were held in Nigeria to explore the possibility of seeking reparations from the former colonial powers. In 1993, the African Reparations Movement was established in London, headed by the Labour MP Bernie Grant. In 2006, the British prime minister, Tony Blair, made at least a partial apology for Britain's role in the slave trade. More recently,

Caribbean states taking the lead have provided fresh momentum. In 2012, Jamaica reconvened a commission on reparations and Barbados established one of its own. The following year, the regional organization CARICOM established a separate commission chaired by Sir Hilary Beckles. Its remit was "to prepare the case for reparatory justice for the region's indigenous and African descendant communities who are the victims of Crimes against Humanity in the forms of genocide, slavery, slave trading, and racial apartheid."

In March 2014, the fifteen CARICOM member states unanimously adopted a ten-point plan drafted by Beckles's committee. This called for a full formal apology from European states for their role in the slave trade, a repatriation programme for Caribbean people of African descent who wished to 'return' to the continent, and European contributions to improving conditions in the Caribbean, in areas such as health, education and debt relief. Advising CARICOM on the plan's implementation was Leigh Day, the legal firm that had already secured victory in the Mau Mau compensation case. Meanwhile, a major historical research project based at University College London was giving the campaign a fresh contemporary resonance: a searchable digital database of the government compensation extended to British slave owners when slavery was abolished throughout the Empire in 1833. The total compensation for loss of this 'property' was around £20 million—a figure that accounted for about 40 per cent of the Treasury's annual spending at the time, and is the equivalent of around £16.5 billion today.

While that figure had long been known, the publicity surrounding the launch of the database helped to bring it to the attention of a broader readership, and it was inevitably written up in the press in the context of the contemporary reparations campaign. If the British government had been prepared to compensate so handsomely those who benefited from the institution of slavery, why could they apparently find nothing to address its dire consequences? The project also gave further impetus to the campaign by allowing researchers to map out the full extent of slave ownership in the UK, and to identify living figures whose ancestors had profited from the slave trade. One of them, it turned out, was the then British prime minister, David Cameron. When Cameron made a visit to Jamaica at the end of September 2015, he was keen to emphasize that he would be "talking about the future". Yet his Jamaican counterpart, Portia Simpson-Miller, explicitly raised the reparations issue, which very much overshadowed coverage of the visit.

More recently, Dr Shashi Tharoor, a former Indian government minister, has published *Inglorious Empire: What the British Did to India* (2017), which lays responsibility for the deaths of around 35 million Indians at the door of the British colonial administration. In a charismatic performance at the Oxford Union shortly before the book's publication—which went viral on YouTube—Tharoor argued that the UK government owed symbolic reparations to India as a moral acknowledgement of the economic damage inflicted by British rule. It also opened a wider debate about how Empire should be taught and remembered in the UK.

Alongside the campaign for reparations, another movement was developing in the Commonwealth nations, aimed at drawing attention to the continued memorialization of figures associated with imperialism and the slave trade. Again, this echoed protests that been going on for some years on US university campuses, seeking to erase the symbolic legacy of slavery and segregation. The strand of this campaign that has attracted the greatest attention in the British press took as its target a famous—or rather notorious—Oxford alumnus, Cecil Rhodes.

Rhodes was perhaps the most emblematic and controversial figure in the history of the late-nineteenth-century 'scramble for

Africa'. An arch-imperialist who dreamed of a British colonial presence that would stretch in Africa from Cairo to the Cape of Good Hope, Rhodes had grown fantastically wealthy on the proceeds of his South Africa gold and diamond mines. He served as prime minister of the Cape Colony in 1890–6, and his company's activities played a significant part in drawing Britain into the Second Boer War (1899–1902), to subdue South Africa's two Afrikaner-ruled republics. His British South Africa Company colonized and, until 1923, administered two territories that would bear his name until their formal independence: Northern Rhodesia (now Zambia) and Southern Rhodesia (now Zimbabwe).

Early in 2015, a movement led by students and staff at South Africa's University of Cape Town (UCT) demanded the removal of a Rhodes statue, which since its unveiling in 1934 had occupied a prominent position in front of the main university buildings. UCT had close associations with Rhodes—he had donated the land on which the main campus was built, and not far away his architect, Herbert Baker, had constructed an imposing memorial to the man. Within weeks, the self-styled 'Rhodes Must Fall' campaign had achieved its initial objective: the UCT Senate voted to recommend the statue's removal to the local council, and a month later iconic images spread across the global media of a large crane hoisting Rhodes away. Similar movements spread to other South African campuses, including Stellenbosch, Rhodes, Pretoria and the Orange Free State. As at UCT, these focused not merely on the physical environment, but upon the nature of the curriculum and the racial composition of the staff and student bodies. The overarching demand was for the universities to be 'decolonized'.

Inspired by the success of the South African movement, a British version of 'Rhodes Must Fall' launched a campaign in Oxford. In his will, Rhodes left £100,000 to his old college, Oriel—a staggeringly generous bequest at the time. The money funded the construction of the Rhodes Building, completed in 1911, which now forms the main façade of the college, overlooking the High Street. In pride of place is a statue of Rhodes himself. Late in 2015, protests were launched to demand its removal, and on 20 January 2016 the famous Oxford Union debating society passed a motion of support.

The reaction of Oriel College serves as an object lesson in precisely how not to respond to such controversies. In the middle of December 2015, it had announced its decision to launch "a structured six-month listening exercise on the statue, running from early February 2016, seeking the views and ideas of students and staff of the College and the wider University, alumni, heritage bodies, Oxford City Council, residents of Oxford, and other members of the public, as we seek a positive way forward." Yet before Oriel's 'listening exercise' was even due to begin, the college announced that, after "careful consideration", Rhodes would stay. *The Daily Telegraph*—which is rarely wrong when it comes to the internal politics of Oxbridge colleges—reported, based on leaked minutes, that Oriel's Development Office had warned the college's governing body that it had already lost £1.5 million in cancelled donations, and was likely to lose more if the protesters' demands were not firmly rebuffed.

Through its mishandling of the affair, Oriel ended up with the worst of all possible worlds. It was derided by opponents of the protests for its initial willingness to give ground, while its rapid volte-face left it perilously exposed to accusations that it had privileged the sentiments of wealthy white donors over those of black student protesters. But the wind had undoubtedly gone out of the campaign's sails. In March 2016, 'Rhodes Must Fall' organized a 'mass' protest against Oriel's decision, a walking tour of Oxford sites associated with colonialism and slavery, including the Rhodes Building and the former Indian Institute. Yet, according to some reports, only about 100 people turned out, on a particularly cold and wet winter's day.

The march also took in Rhodes House, a slightly unnerving mixture of mausoleum and colonial club house designed by Herbert Baker, which currently acts as the headquarters of the Rhodes-Mandela Trust and was, until recently, the repository for the Bodleian's collections on imperial history. Rhodes House was a second home to me during my time as a graduate student, as it was to many anti-apartheid scholars, Marxists and other anti-imperialists. In those days, with battles yet to be lost or won, the pressing objectives of overthrowing capitalism, white minority rule in Southern Africa or both left little time or inclination for identity politics. I only took notice of the building's echoing, now largely unnoticed imperial grandeur to the extent of mild amusement at its sheer hubris. For me, this and all the other statues and monuments to Britain's heroes of Empire might as well have taken Shelley's words for their inscription:

My name is Ozymandias, king of kings:
Look on my works, ye Mighty, and despair!
Nothing beside remains....

But there is no room for wry humour or irony at the extremes of the new politics of the left, where memory and victimhood are the order of the day. It is probably fair to say that campaigns like 'Rhodes Must Fall' set their face not only against those with a more positive view of Empire, but also against an older generation of radicals, from some of whom one could sense a slight bemusement. They could remember a time when politics still seemed to be capable of promising a better future, rather than simply a better past. In the good old days, you held the revolution first, and then pulled down the statues.

It would be tempting to suggest that one of the explanations for the new power of this debate is a mundane one: the large-scale cleaning of such monuments in recent decades. This process has both made statues and buildings more visible in public space, and, given this, has been seen by some as an institutional relegitimization—it was one thing simply to leave in place existing memorials to imperial figures, and another to respond to their datedness by sprucing them up rather than removing them. Back in the 1970s, the heyday of the older activist generation, all stone statues in Britain seemed to be covered in a thick coating of anonymizing soot. Unless one was dealing with Queen Victoria, it was difficult to identify the figure concerned; this, at the very least, served as a reminder that the monument dated back to an era more distant than the Clean Air Acts. Now that so many statues have been scrubbed clean by local councils, it seems easier to believe that their celebration of distant imperial victories comes with some form of modern institutional endorsement.

From where else has this debate on the legacy and guilt of Empire come? One of the key intellectual foundations of campaigns to topple statues 'glorifying' the imperial past and 'decolonize' university campuses is *The Racial Contract*, published in 1997 by the Caribbean philosopher Charles W. Mills. Rather than being a social ill that governments around the world have striven and are striving to eradicate, white racism is, according to Mills, "*itself* a political system, a particular power structure of formal or informal rule, socioeconomic privilege, and norms for the differential distribution of material wealth and opportunities, benefits and burdens, rights and duties".[5] Mills conceptualizes this in terms of a social contract between whites dating back centuries, which manifests itself today in a global system of white domination.

One can see the power of this theory, for instance, for the younger generation of political activists in South Africa. More than twenty years after the ANC took power, racial divisions within the country still map depressingly neatly onto the main indexes of inequality and deprivation. These sorts of figures suggest why there is so much disillusionment with the ANC's record in government, and may explain the attraction of an approach to politics focused directly on challenging white power, as opposed to the conventional political ideology of national liberation and reform. It is on the back of this sort of frustration that we have seen the rise of opposition politician Julius Malema and his Economic Freedom Fighters.

There are other possible reasons why the Empire has made such a comeback in recent years as a subject of debate and activism. Some have suggested that it arises from a crisis within 'progressive' politics over the past quarter-century. In an important study of the politics of remembrance and reparation, John Torpey argues that the collapse of Communism in Central and Eastern Europe from 1989 had more than simply practical implications: it delivered a formidable blow to the very notion of bringing about a radical transformation of society. And, as Torpey succinctly puts it, "When the future collapses, the past rushes in."[6] Now, he argues, unable to focus on a horizon pregnant with bright possibilities, 'progressives' have increasingly turned their attentions to the past, both as a source of apparently intractable political problems and as the battleground for a new kind of politics obsessed by gesture and symbolism. According to Torpey,

Efforts to rectify past wrongs have ... arisen in part as a substitute for expansive visions of an alternative human future of the kind that animated socialist movements of the preceding century, which have been overwhelmingly discredited since the fall of the Berlin Wall in 1989.[7]

What Torpey is articulating here is the idea that we have lost faith in the ability of conventional—particularly national—politics to effect meaningful change, and so have embraced a new form of politics, dominated by symbolism. Our ship may be heading inexorably towards a series of icebergs, but we can still occupy ourselves in heated debates about the arrangement of the deckchairs. The rise of 24-hour news and social media has made it possible to generate fierce controversy over the most apparently trivial of issues, so long as they can be represented as being of broader symbolic importance. Statues, memorials and other monuments to the past have increasingly been drawn into these sorts of debates.

In short, academics have suggested a weakening of what we might call a consensual 'national' memory, which allowed memorials and other historical sites to become places of reconciliation between conflicting contemporary points of view. Instead, they have become ideological battlegrounds. In the process, 'history' has increasingly been called upon to serve the interests of 'memory'. And, as David Rieff has recently argued in a lively polemic called *In Praise of Forgetting*, "The takeover of history by memory is also the takeover of history by politics ... [W]e have entered a world in which the essential function of collective memory is one of legitimizing a particular world-view and political and social agenda, and delegitimizing those of one's ideological opponents."[8]

Taken in this context, it seems unfair to equate the 'Rhodes Must Fall' campaign with puritan iconoclasm or the random cultural blitzkrieg of ISIS, as critics sometimes have. If memory is increasingly politicized, it's entirely reasonable that a new generation of radicals should choose this as one of their battlegrounds. But once we engage in the business of popular memory and memorialization, we enter a sphere of moral certainties, one that often fits uneasily with the professional historian's quest to challenge and subvert conventional moral judgements, and to find new areas of nuance and ambiguity. We risk a culture war, in which opposing sides are settled into deep ideological trenches, each operating in their own distinct—and often directly opposed—realities. This description will be familiar to all those who have been paying attention to the current deep polarization of left- and right-wing values in the wake of the Brexit vote—and we have already seen how debates around the legacy of Empire can be instrumentalized as proxy wars in this conflict.

In September 2017, the US-based political scientist Bruce Gilley published an article entitled 'The Case for Colonialism' in a special edition of the academic journal *Third World Quarterly*.[9] Down to its title, it was almost designed to court controversy. It made some fairly familiar arguments—at least, for those of us who have interacted with former Colonial Office personnel—about the positive benefits of colonial government and the history of state failure in post-colonial Africa. But, in a closing gambit that would perhaps have given pause even to the most Blimpish denizens of London club-land, Gilley appeared to argue that the Western powers might consider recolonizing parts of the African continent. He posited a scenario in which Guinea-Bissau might hand an offshore island to Portugal on a 99-year lease, allowing Portugal to focus its foreign aid budget on a small territory that, once transformed into a haven of good governance and prosperity, might eventually absorb the entire population of the country.

It doesn't take much logic to defeat this argument: what happens when the island's Liberation Front comes knocking in Lisbon and politely requests that the Portuguese withdraw? Those well-meaning neo-colonizers would then be in the same boat as the European imperial powers half a century ago, with a choice between accepting the 'popular will' or fighting it out. Regardless of whether or not colonial rule had any redeeming features, what cannot be in doubt is that it was not politically sustainable. But this was not the hole that Gilley's many critics chose to poke in his argument. Instead, they expressed moral outrage that the piece had ever appeared in print, particularly in a reputable journal like *Third World Quarterly*. Fifteen editorial board members resigned. The journal's publisher, Taylor and Francis, eventually took the article down, claiming that the journal editor had been subjected to "serious and credible threats of personal violence".[10]

The controversy over the Gilley article itself soon passed over. Its key relevance for debates within Britain and the Commonwealth about the legacy of empire was its exposure of a seemingly greater controversy—again one emerging out of the University of Oxford. Regius Professor of Moral and Pastoral Theology Nigel Biggar, who had partially defended Rhodes's reputation during the Oxford Union debate on 'Rhodes Must Fall', and who now defended Gilley's piece in a *Times* article entitled 'Don't feel guilty about our colonial history', claimed to be working on rather a similar project, 'The Ethics of Empire'.

This five-year interdisciplinary project was announced just days after Biggar's *Times* piece by the University of Oxford's McDonald Centre. The Centre, according to its website, "fosters conversation both between Christian theology and other disciplines, and between academia and those who shape public deliberation and policy."[11] Accordingly, one of the project's aims was "to develop a nuanced and historically intelligent Christian ethic of empire". But wasn't it a bit late to be doing this—around 250 years too late? Other stated aims were no less problematic. The project's intention "to enable a morally sophisticated negotiation of contemporary issues such as military intervention for humanitarian purposes in culturally foreign states, the cohesion of multicultural societies, and settling imperial pasts" more or less conceded the accuracy of critiques pointing to an attempted 'whitewash' of Britain's colonial past, in order to legitimize contemporary Western interventions in the developing world.

Biggar's combative stance and the strange timing of the various announcements on the project led to perhaps unwarranted suspicions that he was 'sexing up' a preexisting programme to surf the publicity wave generated by Gilley's article. This perception placed scholars already signed up to 'Ethics and Empire' in a difficult position. The social media reaction to the announcement of Biggar's project was predictably furious. Suggestions that Oxford University might actually be funding Biggar's project added fuel to the perennial accusation that it was simply a reactionary bastion of white upper-class privilege.

Unsurprisingly, many scholars based in Oxford and working in this field decided they needed to distance themselves from the whole enterprise. The project's co-leader, John Darwin, revealed that he was leaving the project,[12] and fifty-eight other scholars disowned the spirit of 'Ethics and Empire' in an open letter published on 19 December.[13] They argued that Biggar had created a straw man in suggesting that the prevailing academic orthodoxy held that imperialism was wicked: "We have never believed it is sufficient to dismiss imperialism as simply 'wicked'. Nor do we believe it can or should be rehabilitated because some of it was 'good'". They rather boldly pronounced that "Good and evil may be meaningful terms of analysis for theologians. They are useless to historians." As such, they suggested, Biggar's project "asks the wrong questions, using the wrong terms, and for the wrong purposes", and announced that they would not be engaging with it.

For anyone familiar with the sometimes vicious invective deployed in public disputes between academics, this all might have seemed fairly mild, not to say judicious, stuff. Perhaps the most serious charge that could be made against the signatories was that they had played into the hands of Biggar and his supporters in the press. Having gone out of his way to stoke controversy, Biggar was now able to complain—rather disingenuously—that he was being subjected to 'collective online bullying'. The right-wing tabloid press was not far behind. The entire affair was swept up in a wider media war. On one side were Twitter commentators such as the Cambridge scholar Priyamvada Gopal, who had responded to the announcement of 'Ethics and Empire' by denouncing Oxford and Cambridge as "the only places which still remain completely safe spaces for right-wing patrician white establishmentarians" and as "the intellectual arm of the British imperial establishment". On the other was a 'defensive' retort from the likes of *The Daily Mail*, which responded to the academics' open letter with a distinctly McCarthyite investigation into the signatories, caricatured as "loud mouthed, Tory-loathing, anti-Israel academics who believe only they should have freedom of expression". To the *Mail's* horror, "almost all the 58 Oxford academics who signed the letter appear to be card-carrying members of the Left."[14]

If you believed one camp, the University of Oxford was run by and for neo-imperialists; if you believed the other, it was in the hands of intolerant subversives. There are very few lessons to be drawn from this war of words that might advance our understanding of the complex historical issues involved. But what is clear is that ideas of Empire have been drawn into the highly polarized political environment we now inhabit. With a newly emboldened populist right wing, an academic community apparently intolerant of particular orthodoxies being questioned, and a history of 'willing forgetfulness' on the part of British governments, there is an urgent need for a candid yet nuanced resolution of the debate over Britain's colonial guilt.

Heads in the Sand

Unfortunately, such a settlement is unlikely to come from Britain's former colonies. The Commonwealth itself has, at best, an ambivalent attitude to its own history. Put simply, the organization is reluctant to admit that this reaches back before 1949. Indeed, if they had their way, member states wouldn't dwell too much on the period before the heady days of the 1980s anti-apartheid struggle. If possible, they would probably dispense with history altogether. But, to twist Trotsky's famous phrase, you might not be interested in history, but history is interested in you.

We have already seen that the mid-century UK itself had every reason to brush aside the imperial past and throw itself into the 'new dawn' of the Commonwealth. In the early decade of independence, Britain's former colonies likewise made relatively little play of any post-imperial 'debt', whether moral or financial; nor did they generally make the accusation, now increasingly frequent in Britain itself, of a systematic British attempt to sanitize the historical record. As such, Commonwealth membership might be viewed as part of a broad package of agreements dating from independence that, in some sense, drew colonial nationalist leaders into a relationship of complicity with what had gone before.

To make such an argument is not to criticize them—the first thing repressive regimes tend to steal from their victims is their innocence, and the British Empire was no exception. Everyone knew that few had emerged from the independence struggles with entirely clean hands. Nationalist failings and misdemeanours had no doubt been recorded faithfully in colonial Special Branch files, information that might remain available to the British. Violence had been a potent—if risky—strategy not only for those enforcing British rule, but also for those challenging it within the colonial territories. Demonstrating their potential to cause unrest and disrupt the colonial state—and their authority over their forces to stop the violence at will—was essential to the nationalist cause. Even famous proponents of non-violent resistance, like Kenneth Kaunda of Zambia, recognized the truth of this and used it, very effectively, to bring the British back to the negotiating table.

Furthermore, the most violent of those post-war struggles—in Kenya, Malaya and Cyprus—had exacerbated divisions between and within communities that, in the post-independence world, would have to live peacefully together. Dredging up this past of internal strife would serve the interests of nobody. Finally, an amicable deal with London would ensure the continuation of British aid and assistance, including training and advice for the security apparatus of the newly emerging states. Indeed, many of the colonial state's instruments of repression—the police and their intelligence units, the military, and forms of repressive legislation and emergency powers—might serve the new independent regime equally well. Under the circumstances, for independence leaders to raise uncomfortable questions about the methods used by the British might have raised equally uncomfortable ones about their use of that political inheritance.

The notion of 'moving on' was thus very much at the heart of the Commonwealth compact in the three decades after the end of the Second World War. It was not only implicit in colonial nationalists' promises of a bright new post-independence dawn; it was also increasingly prominent in the agenda of the Commonwealth itself. A proactive stance on 'development' was and remains a key expectation of the majority of members. Insofar as 'colonialism' was a focus for Commonwealth discussions in that period, it was largely in terms of its contemporary legacy in the white-minority-ruled states of Rhodesia and South Africa. Both the UK and its former dependencies had an interest in the Commonwealth achieving an 'exit velocity' in the popular imagination, which would allow it to break free of the gravitational pull of the British Empire.

For the Commonwealth, the great challenge was to break free of the memory of the British Empire and establish itself as something aiding rather than restricting the progressive ambitions of its members. It was aided in this by the sense of optimism and agency that inspired the leadership of so many Commonwealth states in the immediate post-independence period. Yet, even by the 1970s, the optimism had begun to sour. The change was partly ushered in by the disruption to the global economy that came with the 'oil shock' of 1973; by the 1980s, many Commonwealth states were grappling with the burden of unsustainable levels of debt. The ending of the Cold War not only helped to undermine the whole concept of state-led social and economic transformation; in a more immediate sense it removed from many developing states one of the few bargaining chips left to them in international affairs: their ability to play one superpower off against another. Instead they were increasingly at the mercy of the new free-market economic orthodoxy, with the World Bank stepping in to impose biting programmes of structural readjustment, and the West withdrawing support from heads of state who had previously seemed destined to keep going until they dropped off their presidential perches. At around the same time, the Commonwealth lost most of its remaining 'first-generation' independence leaders: those who had embodied the 'forgive and forget' principle.

These shifts provoked a reappraisal within the Commonwealth of how the economic 'take-off' predicted by many in the 1960s had been hindered by the legacies of colonialism: the colonial game of 'divide-and-rule' among ethnic and tribal lines; the lack of investment in basic transport infrastructure; unequal trading relationships and the extraction of mineral resources designed to benefit Europe rather the developing countries concerned; rudimentary education systems; repressive forms of policing and administration which had been inherited by the successor regimes; and, looking further back into the past, the dislocation and trauma inflicted on African societies by the brutal slave trade. Viewed in this light, Commonwealth gatherings might seem less like family reunions and more like support groups for the victims of a particularly brutal kidnapper. I'm reminded of this on a daily basis whenever I'm asked what my job is. The term 'Commonwealth' carries with it a very wide range of connotations, many of them negative particularly within the academic community.

Swan Song

Historians continue to debate when (if ever) the British Empire really came to an end. But I can at least claim to have been present for one imperial sunset, on 8 June 2017. By chance, this was also the date when voters failed to award British Prime Minister Theresa May the mandate for a "strong and stable" government that she had treated as nothing less than her natural right during the campaign. While British politics was experiencing its second upheaval in less than a year, the Overseas Service Pensioners Association (OSPA) was marking its formal dissolution at a reception and lunch in the De Vere Grand Connaught Rooms in London, a venue vaguely resembling a Las Vegas version of the Sistine Chapel.

OSPA was established in 1960 to defend the pension rights of members of the British Colonial Service (later Her Majesty's Overseas Civil Service). The Institute of Commonwealth Studies had worked with OSPA over a number of years to organize a series of witness seminars. Notwithstanding the understandable desire of OSPA members to portray Empire in a positive light, these seminars recorded and preserved many fascinating recollections on subjects such as the theory and practice of 'indirect rule', the Westminster system of government and development policy. It was a very useful historical exercise, and one that had earned me my invitation to OPSA's valedictory lunch.

The passage of time had greatly thinned OSPA's ranks—hence the decision formally to wind up the organization. But enough members had survived, at an average age of around eighty-four, for them and their families to fill the Connaught's vast dining room. They were seated at tables reflecting their former postings, and as the diners sought to locate their lunch partners at the preceding reception, there were calls of "Are you Nyasaland? Are you Northern Rhodesia?" The guest of honour, Prince Charles, worked the room with tireless good humour. He then gave a short speech from a lectern flanked by the flags of Great Britain and the Commonwealth. He told his audience: "I do so hope that you can all look back with immense pride that your tireless, selfless efforts very much laid the foundations for the modern Commonwealth; a family of 2.4 billion people in fifty-two Nations."[15] Concluding, he recalled the words of the first Commonwealth secretary-general, Arnold Smith,

> who wrote back in 1981 that "100 years from now, I suggest, historians will consider the Commonwealth the greatest of all Britain's contributions to Man's social and political history." And if that turns out to be the case, then it will be your legacy, ladies and gentlemen, for which we owe you an enduring debt of gratitude.

The lunch ended rather poignantly. Diners were invited to stand and sing 'God Save the Queen'. But the music, provided by a two-person mini steel band high up in a gallery, was initially so faint and indistinct that many in the audience seemed unaware that the national anthem had begun. Some began tentatively humming it, but it was only towards the end of the first verse that they really began to sing. A second verse—or rather a repeat of the first—was required before everyone felt they had done their patriotic duty. It brought to mind the final scene of Michael Cimino's 1978 war movie 'The Deer Hunter'. After the funeral of one of the trio of Vietnam veterans, a friend gathered in the bar begins to sing 'God Bless America'; the others join in, quietly at first and then with increasing vigour. "That's it," I thought. "End of Empire. Time for the closing credits."

Charles's remarks at the OSPA farewell lunch would have made uncomfortable reading for many contemporary Commonwealth leaders. The myth of the Commonwealth arose directly out of the myth of Empire. If the latter had been a great global family, then the Commonwealth was the product of natural generational movement within it. Two and a half years before the 'Wind of Change' speech, Macmillan told an audience in Mid Bedfordshire, "The pattern of the Commonwealth is changing and with it is changing Britain's position as the Mother Country. Our children are growing up." Implicit in the Prince of Wales's remarks was this old, paternalistic view of the Colonial Service as a gentle guide on the path to political maturity. To put it mildly, this is not how many Commonwealth states regard the struggle for national independence.

Charles's speech was carefully tailored for its intended audience, and made at what could be considered a private gathering (although Clarence House immediately made the text available online). There is no question, however, that if Theresa May or any other recent British prime minister had expressed similar sentiments in public, they would have been swooped upon by commentators in the UK and across the Commonwealth and cited as evidence of the UK's continuing state of denial about its history of imperial domination. Certainly, although a senior member of the Secretariat attended the reception, and Charles was speaking beside the organization's flag, Commonwealth high commissioners were notably thin on the ground. Even pointing out the links between the Empire and the contemporary Commonwealth is treading on very sensitive ground.

This book began by questioning the notion that the British people as a whole have, and depend on, some kind of ingrained nostalgia for Empire that has transferred itself to the Commonwealth. Yet this chapter has shown just how easily influential voices such as *The Daily Mail* can revive the idea of Empire as a sacred myth of post-Brexit national identity. If, as *The Daily Mail* clearly believes, pride in the record of the British Empire should be a key characteristic of any right-thinking English person—along with support for Brexit and the Conservative Party— this is not going to ease efforts to build new links with Commonwealth members in the wake of Britain's departure from the EU. Indeed, as Chapter 8 will show, suspicions that the UK might be seeking to rebuild its imperial networks have already begun to sour the process. We've also seen the growing power of movements opposed to any such glorification of the imperial past. The debate over Empire, its legacy and the UK's need to make reparations is clearly not going away.

So long as the Empire remains the proverbial elephant in the room, particularly in terms of how the Commonwealth is perceived, its phantom will continue to sabotage the organization's increasingly desperate efforts to rebrand itself as an exciting, contemporary geopolitical network. So far, there has been a personal commitment by those representing former colonies at the Commonwealth to uphold a collective amnesia; many of those who had posed for group photos with the Queen at Commonwealth premiers' meetings in the 1960s and '70s had previously been detained in her name. At the OPSA farewell lunch, Prince Charles recalled

> asking the wrong question to [Kenyan] President Jomo Kenyatta, 47 years ago, about whether he had ever visited Lake Rudolf, now Lake Turkana (where I had just been), only to be met by an ominous silence until he let out a roar of laughter and said, "Yes—I was a guest of your mother there for some time!"

Kenyatta had been held in Lokitaung, a prison by Lake Turkana notorious for its harsh conditions, after being sentenced in 1953 to seven years' hard labour followed by indefinite detention. His conviction for having managed the Mau Mau insurgency concluded an infamously flawed judicial process, heavily influenced by political considerations. Kenyatta's wry joke was a signal that, for him at least, times had moved on. As someone who had personally suffered at the hands of the imperial state, it was within his gift to offer forgiveness to his jailors.

But things had turned out all right for Kenyatta. After all, he had ended up in State House in Nairobi, a building designed by the quintessential imperial architect, Herbert Baker. Nor was he himself averse to taking harsh measures against political opponents to protect his notoriously corrupt, ethnically-based regime.

There are no guarantees of such forgiveness from future genera-tions, who might feel that their life chances had been adversely affected by the legacy of colonialism, and who, unlike Kenyatta, might also feel they had no chance of getting any closer to the sources of wealth and power. Indeed, the 'ominous silence' that greeted Charles's clumsy remark might suggest that there were others, even at the time, who doubted whether such clemency would automatically be forthcoming.

Perhaps the Commonwealth might yet come to the rescue of Britain, which currently seems to find it so difficult to have a sensible debate about its Empire. In many ways, the Commonwealth is the ideal forum for a debate at the highest levels about the impacts and legacies of colonialism. All of its members have been profoundly shaped by that history—from the UK as colonial hegemon to the tiniest of colonial dependen-cies; from countries shaped by British imperialism over centuries to those where its direct impact lasted little more than a genera-tion. Given the trends outlined above, in the years to come these issues will likely gain yet further significance in the discourse of international relations. The Commonwealth has a rare 'competi-tive advantage' in its ability to air and possibly help to reconcile wildly conflicting points of view.

Yet, as the quotation that opens this chapter shows, this is an opportunity that the Commonwealth has so far shunned in its eagerness to present itself as a 'modern' and 'relevant' organiza-tion. Rather than taking responsibility for an international con-versation about these questions, it still seems thoroughly in denial, insisting that its geographical composition is mere acci-dent, and that what really binds the Commonwealth together is a set of 'shared values'. This is certainly an approach that has suited British governments, even though it has limited their own influence within the organization, for fear that they will be accused of neo-colonial interference. But there is a serious problem with this denial of the shared imperial past: attempts to portray the Commonwealth as being united instead by 'shared values' have seen the organization tying itself in knots.

6

VALUES

In March 2013, readers of *The Mail on Sunday* were greeted with an arresting headline: 'Queen Fights for Gay Rights'. Her Majesty had not been marching arm-in-arm with Peter Tatchell. Nor had she attempted a citizen's arrest on Robert Mugabe or Vladimir Putin. Instead, she had just signed the Commonwealth Charter, a newly minted and supposedly comprehensive statement of the 'shared values' that bind the organization together. Yet the Charter makes no reference to 'gay rights' in any shape or form. Confused? Maybe we should retrace our steps a little.

The notion that the Commonwealth is united by 'shared values' sits rather uneasily with the longer-term evolution of the organization. Unlike the French, the imperial British did not tend to believe that their political culture embodied a set of universal values and that mankind would therefore benefit from its global dissemination. Their system had evolved to suit a particular set of local circumstances, including the 'character' of the nation's inhabitants. Even then, Britain was a union of separate kingdoms, including Scotland with its own distinct Church and legal system, and, until 1921, Ireland with a Catholic-majority population. The

Irish and the Scots had made a disproportionate contribution to the expansion of British imperial power, particularly in military terms but also—particularly in the case of the Scots—in the development of overseas trade and higher education.

It followed from this that the nation's culture and institutions were only really expected to take root in areas of significant British settlement. So instead of speaking of 'values', imperial enthusiasts tended to talk of the spread of the British 'character' or 'way of life'. The Tory politician L. S. Amery, one of the most influential advocates of Empire in the first half of the twentieth century, described it in 1935 as "the translation, into outward shape, under ever varying circumstances, of the British character, and of certain social and political principles, constituting a definite British culture or way of life, which, first evolved on British soil, have since been carried by our people across the seas."[1] The South African military and political leader Jan Smuts came slightly closer to a contemporary rhetoric of shared values. Writing at the end of First World War, he suggested that the newly emerging 'British Commonwealth of Nations' was based on notions of free-dom and cooperation "embedded in the British constitutional and Colonial system".[2] Smuts depicted it as a liberating and modern-izing force, juxtaposing it with Britain's wartime enemies, who represented the "last effort of old feudal Europe to block human progress". Yet accompanying such talk, whether by Smuts or some of the English policy-makers who helped to shape the notion of Commonwealth in the wake of the Second Boer War, was always a strong sense of racial solidarity between the sup-posed strongholds of 'Anglo-Saxon civilization'.

Certainly across most of their vast African and Asian territo-ries, the British were distinctly cautious about deploying the rhetoric of common culture and traditions. In India, for example, although they brutally repressed the rising of 1857, they tended not to buy into the missionary argument that the so-called

'Mutiny' had only happened because the subcontinent had not been thoroughly Christianized. British rule throughout much of India continued to be exercised via the Indian princes, whose susceptibilities would be offended and influence probably reduced by any attempt to spread the Good Word. Missionaries were viewed with some suspicion elsewhere in the Empire. In northern Nigeria, for example, British control was firmly based on the collaboration of a series of Muslim emirates. Here, the spread of Christianity was likely to be equally corrosive. Indeed, the whole project of 'indirect rule'—exercising control via local intermediaries—implied some need to respect indigenous beliefs, and to incorporate customary laws into the broader colonial framework of government—so long as they were not "repugnant to natural justice, equity and good conscience".

Even within the 'Empire of settlement', the direction of movement was towards greater autonomy rather than unity. An increasingly important element in the idea of dominion status was that its holders and particularly Britain did not interfere in each other's internal affairs. Under the circumstances, the monarchy became particularly important in holding the whole thing together. But even that, as we have seen, was in an ever-more watered-down form: first through the grudging official acceptance of a 'divisible monarchy' (under which the British king was quite separately king of Canada, of Australia and so on), and then, from 1949, through Commonwealth members' recognition of the monarch's nebulous status as 'Head of the Commonwealth'. The idea of the Commonwealth as an international family became a convenient way of making sense of this strange and incongruous agglomeration of states. There might be certain family resemblances and affinities to oil the wheels of social interaction, but there were also family members you would ordinarily avoid like the plague, were they not connected to you by remote bonds of kinship. In time, this "great imperial family", to whose service the then Princess Elizabeth publicly dedicated her life on her twenty-first birthday in 1947, gradually morphed into the 'Commonwealth family'.

The Commonwealth undertook the slow and tentative process of defining a set of 'shared values, against the unacceptably appalling actions of some of its member states. This idea of certain 'red lines' was back to the indirect rule-era doctrine of 'repugnance'. By far the most repugnant member of the family in the early post-war era was the Union of South Africa, which since the National Party victory of 1948 had been deepening and widening its already extensive practices of racial discrimination and separation under the policy of 'apartheid'. As decolonization took hold in Africa, and as the UK sought to encourage its colonies there to join the Commonwealth on independence, South Africa's membership became an increasing embarrassment to the organization. In the end, South Africa effectively triggered its own departure in 1961 after its white population voted in 1960 to become a republic. At the time, Commonwealth states that relinquished the Crown had to re-apply for membership; when it became clear that any such application was unlikely to be viewed warmly, South Africa simply walked, not to return until after the establishment of black majority rule in 1994.

Even after 1961, South Africa remained the spectre at the feast. To the profound unease of British Prime Minister Edward Heath, the first CHOGM, held in Singapore in 1971, provided the setting for a sustained attack on the UK government over its decision to resume arms sales to apartheid South Africa. What emerged from this furious row was the Commonwealth's first real statement of principles, the Singapore Declaration. It was a ringing condemnation of racial discrimination aimed squarely at South Africa and Rhodesia. In keeping with the temperament of one of the document's principal authors, President Kenneth Kaunda of Zambia, its language was rather more forthright than that used in many subsequent Commonwealth communiques. Racial prejudice was described as a "dangerous sickness" and discrimination as "an unmitigated evil of society". Yet the Declaration also bore the hallmarks of a classic diplomatic fudge, affirming, "No country will afford to regimes which practice racial discrimination assistance which in its own judgment directly contributes to the pursuit or consolidation of this evil policy". The phrase "in its own judgment" was apparently inserted by Pierre Trudeau of Canada, as a compromise addressing the UK's determination not to have its hands tied over supply of weaponry to the South African regime.

The de facto expulsion of South Africa at least opened the possibility of a less *laissez-faire* approach to the internal affairs of member states. Yet members continued to demand that the organization should not interfere in this sphere. What led to a significant change was another example of the old doctrine of repugnance—the transgressions of Idi Amin's brutal regime in Uganda. Although African states had opposed any outright ban on Amin's presence at the 1977 CHOGM in London, it was made clear to him that his presence would not be welcome; despite threats to gate-crash the summit, he stayed away. Sonny Ramphal recalls that, as Commonwealth secretary-general, he decided it was time to make a stand. He told Commonwealth leaders at the Gleneagles retreat during the 1977 CHOGM:

> There is a line beyond which abuse of human rights and human dignity anywhere in the world becomes the world's business. I don't know how you draw the line, and it hasn't been drawn yet, but there are situations when you know that, wherever that line is, it has been crossed, and that's Uganda. However that line has been drawn, it's been crossed. When it's crossed, it's the right of everyone—especially members of the Commonwealth—to condemn.[3]

As a result, leaders took the unprecedented step of including in the CHOGM's final communique a ringing denunciation of a fellow member state. It condemned Uganda for its "disregard for the sanctity of human life" and its "massive violation of basic human rights". The excesses of the regime, it stated, were "so gross" as to evoke condemnation by heads of government in strong and unequivocal terms.[4] At the same time, in typically evasive Commonwealth fashion, Amin was not mentioned by name.

Those Commonwealth leaders who had come to power by means of the ballot box had a mutual interest in arresting the disturbing trend towards military coups in the decades after independence. As such, another Commonwealth principle that emerged in this period was that leaders who had achieved power by unconstitutional means should have no place in its councils. Hence, after declaring itself a republic in 1987 following the second military coup of that year, Fiji was denied re-admittance to the organization. However, it was not until the fall of Communism that the Commonwealth began to take a more unashamedly close interest in the broader conditions within member states.

In the contemporary rhetoric of the Commonwealth, which suggests that the organization is united by shared values and shared institutions, there is a significant element of what historians have labelled 'the invention of tradition'. As we have seen, in practice the British were generally reluctant to try to implant their values and institutions except in their colonies of settlement. Consequently, the UK's imperial record is regularly turned back on it when it seeks to criticize breaches of democratic values in Africa. In 2005, President Yoweri Museveni of Uganda complained that "for the 70 years that the British were in Uganda there was no democracy."[5] Such accusations have built on the heady 1960s' broader rejection of 'shared values' rhetoric—and its Anglo-centric implications. As the Commonwealth began its rapid geographical expansion, there was a new embrace of pluralism. Ghana's Kwame Nkrumah told his fellow Commonwealth premiers at their meeting in 1964 that theirs was "no longer an association of like-minded countries deriving their institutions from Britain: the main bond was respect for each other's independence, and if it was to have any future strength its members needed to accept new obligations."[6]

The Birth of the Commonwealth Charter

The process of reimagining the Commonwealth as something bound by an historic respect for democracy, human rights and the rule of law really only gathered momentum following the end of the Cold War. When Commonwealth leaders met in Harare in 1991, there was a pervasive sense that Western liberal values had been vindicated by history. The declaration that emerged from the Harare summit, which the British government of John Major played a major part in shaping, spoke of "Totalitarianism … giving way to democracy and justice in many parts of the world". Unlike the Singapore Declaration, it championed the broader cause of human rights. It also preached the value of liberal economics:"There is increasing recognition that commitment to market principles and openness to international trade and investment can promote economic progress and improve living standards." The notion of market-based reforms as some sort of magic panacea for the Commonwealth's ills looked rather less convincing in 2013 than it did in 1991, and the Commonwealth Charter is notably silent on "the central role of the market economy" emphasized at Harare.

The current effort to codify Commonwealth values began in 2009, when the CHOGM in Trinidad and Tobago commissioned an Eminent Persons Group (EPG) to produce a report on how the Commonwealth might be revitalized. The announcement of this initiative was not universally welcomed. The Royal Commonwealth Society's 2010 survey 'The Commonwealth Conversation' noted that it was met with a mixture of delight, scepticism and downright anger by Conversation participants. Delight because many were hopeful that such a group could make a real difference at the highest level; scepticism because many felt they would probably produce a weighty tome which would be welcomed by Commonwealth leaders and then never acted upon; and anger because many felt that the response of a modern association to calls for reform should not be to set up an Eminent Persons Group, something which is seen as a stuffy and old-fashioned way of working.[7]

One participant in the survey warned against the appointment of a group of "Elderly Commonwealth luvvies". How he or she reacted when the membership of the group was announced is not recorded. The EPG in its final form consisted of ten members, chaired by Tun Abdullah Ahmad Badawi, the prime minister of Malaysia from 2003–9. The other nine members were drawn from Ghana, Jamaica, Pakistan, Uganda, Australia, the UK, Guyana, Canada and Kiribati. The group met formally on four occasions in London and Kuala Lumpur, the last in March 2011. It appointed as its rapporteur the Guyanan-born Sir Ronald Sanders, an experienced diplomat who had twice served as the high commissioner for Antigua and Barbuda in London. Sanders was also Sonny Ramphal's son-in-law. As such, he was recognized by the other members of the Group as having the most detailed grasp of the lore and history of the Commonwealth.

The Group submitted its detailed report to the Secretariat well in advance of the 2011 CHOGM. It contained no fewer than 106 recommendations, ranging across a wide range of topics, including good governance, the rule of law, human rights, trade, development and—most importantly—the functioning of the Commonwealth as an organization. It also included many recommendations either of marginal significance or too opaque and vague to carry much resonance. For instance:

Heads of Government should welcome the creation of the Commonwealth Youth Orchestra and express the hope that this venture will become the first of many initiatives that celebrate the variety and excellence of art and culture in all their forms throughout the Commonwealth (R.47)

[...]

Commonwealth governments should create a 'Commonwealth' page on their official websites including a list and contact details for all Commonwealth accredited organizations, and membership of Commonwealth professional networks and civil society organizations should be promoted through relevant Ministries and national umbrella organizations (R.85)

[...]

National sports federations should also be requested to commit themselves to establishing and strengthening linkages between sport, development and peace (R.105)

This slightly scattergun approach perhaps points to a tactical error by the EPG, allowing those who opposed some of the more significant reforms later to claim that the majority of recommendations had nevertheless been endorsed. Yet the Group did prioritize its recommendations, identifying fourteen key proposals. The first two were the drafting of a Commonwealth Charter, and the appointment of a commissioner for democracy, the rule of law and human rights. The terms in which these recommendations were framed deserve some detailed attention. On the first, the Group said the following:

A 'Charter of the Commonwealth' should be established after the widest possible consultation in every Commonwealth country. Civil society organizations should be fully involved with national governments in the process of pan-Commonwealth consultation, including in the organization of the process and assessment of its results. A task force should be appointed to analyse the findings of the national consultations and to make recommendations, on that basis, to Heads of Government. If the findings favour a Charter, the task force should be authorized to draft the final text.[8]

The idea of a Commonwealth Charter had apparently been suggested by Badawi, the group's chair. Sir Ronald Sanders, the rapporteur, believes that the idea emerged from Badawi's time in government:

> He was prime minister of Malaysia when ASEAN [the Association of Southeast Asian Nations] adopted a charter, very much a Malaysian idea. And he saw the success of that charter in the ASEAN context and therefore felt it was something that the Commonwealth could also adopt. Now he wanted more than just a charter that had a declaration of various things. He wanted a kind of organizational charter, something that defined the role of the Secretariat, defined the role of the Secretary General—you know went into that kind of detail, which is what I think the ASEAN charter does.[9]

Sanders pointed out that, while ASEAN was a treaty organization with a legal personality—making a charter of this kind entirely appropriate—the Commonwealth is an informal, voluntary association. Yet there was clearly an argument for seeking to amalgamate and streamline the various statements of principles that had been made since the Singapore Declaration of 1971. By the time the EPG was set up in 2009, these included the Harare Commonwealth Declaration, the Langkawi Declaration on the Environment, the Millbrook Action Programme on enforcing Commonwealth values, the Aberdeen Principles on Local Democracy and Good Governance, the Latimer House Principles of 2003 on the three branches of government, and the Trinidad and Tobago Affirmation of Commonwealth Values and Principles. And if the draft of the Charter could be developed in dialogue with NGOs from across the Commonwealth, this would both help to raise popular interest in the organization and make it more difficult for member governments to veto any of its more challenging elements. Hence the EPG's insistence that the Charter should only be produced "after the widest possible consultation in every Commonwealth country."

Yet doubts remained within the EPG about whether such a document, even one that appeared to command broad popular consent, would add much value to the Commonwealth if additional means were not devised to ensure that it was enforced. As its Australian representative, the distinguished jurist Michael Kirby, noted,

> Just to have a document called a charter, would seem to have been worthless, or at least unnecessary, when you had already statements in a succession of the closing resolutions of the Commonwealth Heads of Government at CHOGM meetings. There had been many such statements: the Singapore Declaration and so on. The charter would only be turned into something of practical use if you had an office-holder whose responsibility it was to be specially protective of charter values, and stimulating the education and other steps that would be required to make sure that the charter became an actuality.[10]

As such, the EPG saw the proposed creation of the separate office of 'Commissioner for Democracy, the Rule of Law and Human Rights' as an essential and indivisible corollary of the drafting of a new charter. It recommended:

> A Commonwealth Commissioner for Democracy, the Rule of Law and Human Rights should be appointed to provide well researched and reliable information simultaneously to the Secretary-General and the Chairperson of the Commonwealth Ministerial Action Group (CMAG) on serious or persistent violations of democracy, the rule of law and human rights in member states, and to indicate approaches for remedial action.[11]

Explaining the group's rationale in retrospect, Kirby pointed to the value of the new role, drawing on his recent experience of the functioning of the United Nations and the important part played by the UN high commissioner for human rights:

> It is sometimes difficult for the Secretary-General of the United Nations to do some things. However, if you have a guardian watchdog

who's biting at your heels every now and again, and causing an issue to come onto the agenda, and stirring the debates, and speaking from a point of view of principle, rather than pure pragmatism, it is more likely that the institution will work. Indeed, it is respecting the fact that the political head is going sometimes to be in an awkward situation, when criticisms on human rights, rule of law, or electoral democracy bases, are raised. The ultimate job of the Secretary-General is to keep the Association together, and functioning. The job of the Commissioner is to stand up for principles. That is sometimes awkward and difficult for the SG to do, as indeed it is in the United Nations.[12]

It was clear, however, that many Commonwealth heads of government would not welcome the creation of this new watch-dog, which was as likely to be snapping at their own heels as at those of the secretary-general. Nor was this the only recom-mendation liable to meet with resistance. As we know, the 1999 CHOGM had established a new post to be held between CHOGMs, the chair-in-office. Although the functions of the chair-in-office were ill-defined, there had been a broad expecta-tion that they would take an active role in new Commonwealth initiatives and would help to represent the Commonwealth at gatherings of world leaders and to boost its profile. Yet well before the EPG report appeared there was a general recognition that the experiment had not been particularly successful. Unlike the Queen, chairs-in-office had sometimes displayed a rather half-hearted approach to their role, which had grown in neither scope nor stature. This was certainly the feeling of the EPG, which recommended that the post be abolished. Instead, "The pre-existing system should be re-instituted under which the Secretary-General is the Chief Executive Officer of the Commonwealth, unambiguously responsible for gauging con-sensus from Heads of Government, acting as the organization's public voice and interlocutor, and accountable to member gov-ernments (R79)."

While there was expected to be considerable support for this in many quarters, at least one head of government was likely to resist it tenaciously. As we shall see in Chapter 7, President Mahinda Rajapaksa of Sri Lanka was determined that the 2013 CHOGM would take place in Sri Lanka. In the wake of the Sri Lankan civil war, during which government forces had been accused of major human rights violations, he badly needed the prestige of the chair-in-office role. As chair-presumptive at the 2011 Perth CHOGM to which the EPG was due to report, he was in an excellent position to veto the proposal.

In the light of this, and aware of the criticisms of the 'elitist' nature of an EPG, its members were keen that the production of their report should be a transparent process, and that it should be published and widely discussed well before the heads met in late October. In this way, the EPG would be able to gauge public support for their proposals and hopefully ensure that their recommendations carried a sense of popular legitimacy. In that way, it would be more difficult for particular Heads to scotch them. As the British representative on the group, the former foreign secretary Sir Malcolm Rifkind, recalled,

> We took the view that because we knew all along there would be some resistance to some of our more sensitive recommendations, we would have a better prospect if we generated a debate in the Commonwealth why we were sitting, why we were deliberating. People should know the direction we were moving. So that hopefully we would get endorsement from various parts of the Commonwealth family and the heads of government would be faced not just with a recommendation, but with something that clearly had support behind it. So we established our website, we gave progress reports from the very beginning on the way our thinking was going.[13]

Having submitted their report well ahead of the October summit, the EPG members waited patiently for the Commonwealth Secretariat to publish it—and waited, and waited. The Secretariat proved in no hurry to do so, and eventually ruled that it could not be published until ministers had had the chance to consider it. Thus began a very public farce, which was to culminate at the CHOGM itself. The report's publication was the subject of eager expectation amongst the small circle of Commonwealth cognoscenti in London and further afield. Being a small circle, not only did news quickly leak of the Secretariat's reluctance to publish, but illicit electronic copies of the report were soon circulating freely in Commonwealth milieus. Indeed, by the time of the meeting in late October, the only people present who seemed not to have read it were a number of prominent Commonwealth foreign ministers, who claimed to be unable to work though the numerous recommendations in the allotted time. Speaking to a fringe event on the eve of the CHOGM, the former Australian prime minister Malcolm Fraser commented that, although he wasn't supposed to have seen the report, he had; this won appreciative laughter from the many members of the large audience who had also read it.

Yet sarcasm turned to anger when it became clear that heads of government were likely to reject the proposal for a human rights commissioner. Signs that this might be the likely outcome became apparent in Perth before the summit had even formally convened. I heard one delegate, with good links to a number of Commonwealth governments, seriously suggest that it was likely to fail because the term 'commissioner' had overtones of colonial administration—'the district commissioner'—that might offend some heads. It occurred to me that, had the post been that of 'Commissioner for VIP Commonwealth Travel', it would probably have offended far fewer post-colonial sensibilities. Aside from this, the underlying position was depressingly clear: the decision to embargo the report had both restricted the ability of human rights groups to lobby for the post, and had led to confusion about its precise nature, offering ammunition to those who

opposed it. Fingers pointed at Trinidad and Tobago's prime minister, the outgoing chair-in-office, who became increasingly
defensive about her role in the process.

The members of the EPG who gathered at Perth to hear their
report being debated were to suffer a further blow: the secretary-
general, Kamalesh Sharma's own attitude towards the creation of
a Commissioner. Throughout this process, members of the EPG
had little sense that Sharma was in serious disagreement with the
broad direction of their report or with the specific recommendation for a democracy and human rights commissioner. According
to Kirby, the Australian representative,

> we believed that we had the support of the Secretary-General on that
> matter, because never once during the deliberations did Secretary-
> General Sharma indicate his disagreement with it. ... The Secretary-
> General sat at the table, and was there present during all of the
> debates. He was not a stranger who was up there in his room, wait-
> ing humbly for our recommendations. He participated.[14]

But, as Kirby recalls, "what all of us regarded as a key proposal
was torpedoed at a critical moment during the Perth CHOGM,
when the Secretary-General said he didn't agree with it, and
didn't think it was necessary."[15] So it was that on the second
morning of the summit, sick of being fobbed off with excuses for
the non-publication of the report and with their key proposal
mortally wounded, the patience of the Eminent Persons finally
snapped. They staged a 'polite' revolt, publishing it without the
approval of the heads of government or the Secretariat. According
to Kirby, the British representative Malcolm Rifkind took the
lead in this rebellion: "I think the rest of us were a bit inclined
to go along with the rules. But he'd had enough. He took the
view that the report should be disclosed. So he disclosed his
copy. After that, of course, the wall of the dam broke. The
report became public."[16] Rifkind concurs: "I'm afraid I was prob-

ably the main person responsible, but it wasn't just me, we were just so pissed off, excuse my language, that we called a press conference while the heads of government were in retreat."[17] Announcing the decision to the press, Rifkind described it as "disgraceful" that the findings had not been published before.

But it was too late. By the time of the concluding press conference on Sunday 30 October, when Australian Prime Minister Julia Gillard made what she could of the announcement that many recommendations had been accepted in principle and that many more referred back for further discussion, no one was really listening any more. Even the Western Australia media— and, indeed, CHOGM delegates anxious to get home—only wanted to discuss one thing: the temporary shut-down of Qantas Airlines. What coverage there was tended to be dominated by ministers' refusal to agree to a commissioner for human rights. Some on the EPG suspected that the fact that Sharma was standing for re-election in Perth was one reason for his failure to take a more courageous stand on their report. But the affair also seemed symptomatic of a more profound failure of governance within the Commonwealth. Kirby recalls that he and his colleagues on the EPG approached their task with an already rather jaundiced view of the Secretariat:

> We were inclined to think that the Commonwealth Secretariat was an ultra-cautious group of officials who were obsequious, and inclined to non-transparency in a way that was more reflective of the techniques of administration that existed during the British Empire, and out of harmony with the techniques of administration which the more modern members of the Commonwealth had introduced in their own administration, often reluctantly, and often against the strongest possible opposition of the public service.[18]

The handling of the report, and the actions of Sharma himself, only exacerbated Kirby's doubts about the effectiveness of the Secretariat. As he later explained, it's a timid, frightened, cautious bureaucracy. There's nothing really to put a burr under the saddle to stimulate the whole system. That is why whatever caused the Secretary-General to either change his mind, or keep his mind secret until the last minute, so that it did maximum damage to withdraw support from it amongst the Heads of Government, whatever caused him to do that, it was antithetical to the best interests of the Commonwealth. It was damaging to the Commonwealth Secretariat ... What [the Secretary-General] did was to strike a body blow at the guts of the central idea of the reform which the EPG put forward. And he did it in a way that respectfully, I thought, was dishonourable. More importantly, it deprived the reforms suggested of real teeth. It left the Charter hanging on the line as something limp and rather worthless. It's just more words, and it's not really an effective institution.[19]

A Failed Text

So the genesis of the Commonwealth Charter was not an auspicious one. Although heads of government supported this key recommendation of the report at Perth, it was born, as Peter Cook might have put it, "an only twin", without the accompanying recommendation that might have helped give it some substance.

What's more, while the idea of the Charter itself was approved, there was no subsequent attempt to base it on a widespread process of consultation, as the EPG had insisted would be essential if it was genuinely to be a 'People's Charter'. It had appended as an annexe to the report a preliminary outline of what such a document might look like, drawing on the text of previous declarations. This was largely the work of Michael Kirby. But it stressed that this was merely a possible starting point, to be "used as a basis for the Commonwealth-wide consultations". Yet this ambitious programme of consultation failed to materialize. Instead, the text of the Charter was largely drafted within the Commonwealth Secretariat. It was then agreed with Commonwealth high commissioners in London and foreign ministers in New York, before finally being signed by the Queen as head of the Commonwealth in March 2013.

The final version of the Charter also drew heavily on earlier Commonwealth declarations, so much so that particular turns of phrase used on previous occasions were simply inserted into the 2013 text. The Singapore Declaration of 1971 affirmed, "We believe that international peace and order are essential to the security and prosperity of mankind; we therefore support the United Nations and seek to strengthen its influence for peace in the world, and its efforts to remove the causes of tension between nations." The relevant passage in the Commonwealth Charter proceeds along similar lines, expanded and updated for the times: "We firmly believe that international peace and security, sustainable economic growth and development and the rule of law are essential to the progress and prosperity of all."

It is probably fair to say that the Commonwealth Charter is not a great piece of political prose. Indeed, far too often it is opaque and evasive. The 800th anniversary of Magna Carta in 2015 spawned a wide variety of conferences and seminars. For the Commonwealth Parliamentary Association, it provided an opportunity to consider the global influence of England's 'Great Charter', and the current state of human rights in the Commonwealth in the wake of its own Charter's endorsement. Unfortunately, inviting such comparisons succeeded only in highlighting the fact that that the Commonwealth Charter is a very pale imitation of Magna Carta.

Of course, that document largely reflected the interests of thirteenth-century England's landed elite. Yet at least King John's barons framed their demands in terms that were admirably clear and specific. Translated from the original Latin, its clauses regularly begin with such trenchant phrases as "no free man shall be", "no widow shall be", or "no constable may". Only in a minority of cases does it articulate its demands in terms of what might be called broader matters of principle—ones that have echoed down the ages. Even then, their power over the popular imagination owes much to the fact that they are expressed in such clear and unambiguous terms:

> (39) No free man shall be seized or imprisoned, or stripped of his rights or possessions, or outlawed or exiled, or deprived of his standing in any way ... except by the lawful judgment of his equals or by the law of the land.

> (40) To no one will we sell, to no one deny or delay right or justice.

By contrast, the language of the Commonwealth Charter rarely descends from lofty platitudes to specific demands, rights or expectations. Its language is willfully ambiguous, slippery and jargon-ridden, designed to suggest a consensus and a community of interest where no such things exist.

This all becomes painfully obvious when one tries to translate the sweet, insubstantial 'Commonwealth-speak' of the Charter into the good, plain, honest 'baron-speak' of Magna Carta. Take, for example, perhaps the most egregious linguistic sleight-of-hand in the document: the clause relating to the issue of discrimination. As we began by noting, the *Mail on Sunday* celebrated the signing of the Charter with the striking headline 'Queen Fights for Gay Rights'. It reported that "Sources close to the Royal Household said she is aware of the implications of the charter's implicit support of gay rights and commitment to gender equality."[20] This was apparently also the impression the Commonwealth Secretariat wished to convey.

Yet the relevant clause of the Charter not only makes no mention of LGBT rights, but actually makes very little sense at all. It states, "We are implacably opposed to all forms of discrimination, whether rooted in gender, race, colour, creed, political belief or other grounds." The phrase '*any* other grounds' might reasonably have been thought to apply to the LGBT community. But what other grounds? If my tenancy agreement warned that I could be evicted for failing to pay the rent or on 'other grounds', I suspect I would seek to have those specified before signing anything. If this really is about LGBT rights, and all signatories understand and support this, then why not say so? Translated into the language of Magna Carta, the relevant clause might read: 'No Commonwealth citizen will be punished for engaging in consenting, adult sexual relations.'

The answer, of course, is this: given that the majority of Commonwealth states continue to criminalize homosexual acts and show little inclination to take a more liberal stance, they would almost certainly have felt unable to sign the Charter. But they could and did sign a text with a discrimination clause so poorly drafted that it leaves the nature of their commitment completely unclear. Could this be an indication of how seriously member states take the Commonwealth and its 'values'?

As one of the minority of Commonwealth governments that does not criminalize homosexual activity, the UK might well have felt comfortable with an explicit assertion of LGBT rights. It would almost certainly, however, have been far less relaxed had other passages in the Charter been translated into Baron-speak. Take for example, the Charter's statement that "We are committed to the Universal Declaration of Human Rights and other relevant human rights covenants and international instruments." This is all well and good, but our baronial translators would probably demand that we grapple with specifics. So, how about "No Commonwealth state will employ or facilitate torture"? Suddenly Whitehall no longer seems so securely placed on the moral high ground.

Similarly, the Charter declares, "We are committed to an effective multilateral system based on inclusiveness, equity, justice and international law as the best foundation for achieving consensus and progress on major global challenges including piracy and terrorism." Surely this implies that no Commonwealth state will engage in illegal warfare against another nation state? But, again, that might have caused a certain amount of embarrassment rather close to home. As far back as 1971, the then prime minister of Australia, John Gorton, regretted that the Singapore Declaration didn't contain the words "the Commonwealth condemns any armed attack made by any nation upon any other nation". This sentiment didn't make it into any subsequent declaration of Commonwealth values. If it had, maybe our own nation would have found itself arraigned before the Commonwealth Ministerial Action Group. One could carry on endlessly, but suffice to say that one has only to transform a couple of the Charter's tortuous sentences into something more intelligible and concrete before one has a document that would never have won the unanimous endorsement of Commonwealth states.

Another way in which Magna Carta differs from the Charter is that it reflected the demands and interests of a specific group of people—albeit largely those of a narrow and powerful elite. By contrast, it is far from clear to what or to whom the Charter is responding. The key factor shaping its construction seems to be the desire to avoid the sorts of North-South divisions that tend to emerge when issues like human rights and good governance are discussed within a Commonwealth context. Hence, statements about human rights, democracy, non-discrimination and religious toleration, traditionally the priorities of the more affluent Commonwealth nations, are carefully balanced with items like sustainable development and access to healthcare, education, food and shelter, which tend to be higher on the agenda of developing nations. But does this really result in anything other than a lengthy and impossibly broad wish-list? Such is the standard criticism of CHOGM communiques, which tend to grow in ambition and prolixity in direct proportion to the waning influence of the Commonwealth itself.

Perhaps the key difference between the two charters is that Magna Carta had a clearly defined enforcement mechanism: a council of twenty-five barons "to keep, and cause to be observed with all their might, the peace and liberties granted and confirmed to them by this charter", if necessary even to the point of seizing the King's lands and property. As we have seen, the EPG recommended its own mechanism for monitoring violations of the Charter and for proposing remedial action: a 'Commonwealth Commissioner for Democracy, the Rule of Law and Human Rights'. Yet this concept had been strangled at birth.

Of course, the baronial council met a similar fate. King John almost immediately repudiated Magna Carta. Although the charter itself was re-affirmed in revised form in subsequent reigns, in all subsequent reiterations it notably lacked the clause establishing the council. Perhaps, then, the overriding historical lesson of Magna Carta, and in its more modest way of the Commonwealth Charter, is that rulers don't like signing up to documents that constrain their freedom of action, particularly if backed with the threat of coercion if they fail to comply. Why, then, has the Great Charter of 1215 endured in the national psyche?

A Failed Idea

In so far as Magna Carta exerted an influence over subsequent centuries of government both in the UK and overseas, it was not because of an external enforcement mechanism attached to it, but because it became embedded in both practice and popular imagination, although only after some bitter and bloody tests of strength. Perhaps, if the Commonwealth Charter had been the genuine 'People's Charter' intended by its progenitors in the EPG, there might have been some chance of it achieving this broader political resonance. After all, the 1975 Helsinki Final Accords on international relations and human rights and liberties were signed in spectacularly bad faith by a number of European and North American regimes who had no intention of changing their ways. Yet they spawned popular movements like Charter 77 in Eastern Europe, which were determined to use these declarations as a means of holding their governments to account.

There have been few signs of such take-up in the case of the Commonwealth Charter, and it may well be that it is simply too bland and cautious a document to have much chance of capturing the popular imagination. Nor is there any evidence of the Commonwealth Secretariat or the Ministerial Action Group making strenuous efforts to pursue member states that violate the Charter. There are some signs that the UK government has recognized it as a useful instrument for its own diplomacy. In January 2015, for example, British High Commissioner Andrew Ayre got into trouble with the government of Guyana for suggesting that its decision to prorogue the country's parliament was in breach of the Commonwealth Charter.[21] Such unilateral moves, however, run the familiar risk of accusations that Britain wishes the use the Commonwealth as a neo-colonial vehicle for the promotion of its own values and interests.

It might well be asked whether the Commonwealth has painted itself into a corner by generating these growing lists of supposedly shared values that it has an obligation to enforce. Isn't there an argument, one might ask, for agreeing that the notion of shared values is something of a myth; that the Commonwealth—like many other international bodies—contains plenty of countries with questionable records on human rights, democracy and the rule of law, and that the role of the organization isn't to preach or police, but precisely to encourage a dialogue between nations with very different political values? There are some pretty unpleasant states out there, but on the whole we have to deal with them—particularly if they're geopolitically powerful and/or potentially valuable trading partners.

Yet the history of the post-war Commonwealth suggests that such an ethical free-for-all simply isn't sustainable. There have always been states—like apartheid South Africa or Amin's Uganda—whose human rights records were so beyond the pale that they forced Commonwealth members to consider the ethical basis of association with them. Furthermore, the notion of human rights is undoubtedly of particular importance to the many weak and fractured states that the dissolved British Empire left in its wake, particularly to their ethnic and religious minority populations, whose interests can be threatened by the democratic—or undemocratic—will of the majority. Moses Anafu served in the Secretariat when the Commonwealth was attempting to refocus itself around values such as human rights and democracy; he suggests that this was in many respects as welcome to developing countries as it was to the West. It offered a guarantee against forms of external engagement by more powerful states involving support for corrupt or repressive regimes, in the interest of financial or strategic gains. It also meant that membership of the Commonwealth could be represented as a 'kite-mark' of international respectability: a sign to foreign investors that the political infrastructure of a member state was essentially sound. Anafu explains:

> Why has the Commonwealth developed along these lines? My take on it is as follows. One, the Commonwealth must move with the times. Rule of law, you know; respect for human rights, democratic and credible elections. If the Commonwealth doesn't have these things, it would have no credibility in the various countries.... When Cameroon applied—and this is very important—we had a delegation from the region, what used to be French Equatorial Africa. That's Cameroon itself, Congo-Brazzaville, and the Central African Republic. They sent a team to us, and you know what they said? They were sent by the Bar Associations of their respective countries to come—in their own words—"to support and reinforce Cameroon's

application" ... [That was] the first time I've heard this for Commonwealth membership ... I asked them, "Why? Why is it important to you? Why is Commonwealth membership so important to all of you?" And you know what? They put it very colourfully. They said, "Moses, we know that the Commonwealth is serious about human rights. France doesn't give a damn about human rights." They said, "In our countries, any head who tramples on his people but is on good terms with France, protects French capital and invest-ments, is a good man. He stays there forever. That is why we want Cameroon to join the Commonwealth, because Cameroon joining the Commonwealth is a big plus for human rights in our region."[22]

Anafu's present-day counterparts in Marlborough House would no doubt argue that, however imperfect it may be as a text, the endorsement of the 2013 Commonwealth Charter is part of a slow but important process, working through consensus towards a broad acceptance of an important set of values. And if member states currently fall short of these ideals, what matters is that they are moving in the right direction.

But if the Commonwealth is to become a sort of global secular religion organized around the principles of democracy, good governance and human rights, then symbolism matters. It would be inconceivable, would it not, for such an organization to allow an international pariah to host its biennial heads of government meeting and in the process act as its chair-in-office? But that is precisely what happened in 2013, the very year the Charter was signed. With this development, the Commonwealth threw its final reserves of credibility to the four winds.

7

THE ROAD TO COLOMBO

The phrase 'slow-motion car crash' is probably overused. But no other term so precisely conveys the experience of observing the events that led to the 2013 CHOGM in Sri Lanka. They deserve to be described in some detail, partly to illustrate the dangers that can be posed by an international organization that allows itself to be 'captured' by a highly motivated member state, perhaps as a Machiavellian guide to how such a capture might be effected, and possibly as a moral fable about the difference between piety and virtue. In the process, they will hopefully explain how an organization desperate to present itself as a champion of good governance, the rule of law and human rights allowed itself to be used as a 'soft diplomacy' vehicle by a regime that apparently respected none of those things.

The nepotistic Romanian dictatorship of Nicolae Ceauşescu was famously described as 'Socialism in One Family'. From 2005 to 2015, under President Mahinda Rajapaksa, Sri Lanka had its own unsavoury version of 'Democracy in One Family'. Alongside Mahinda himself, his brothers Gotabhaya and Basil held the ministerial portfolios for defence and economic development respectively, while another brother, Chamal, was speaker of the Sri Lankan parliament. When Rajapaksa took office, a brutal civil war had been going on for over two decades. It arose from claims that successive post-independent governments had favoured the interests of the Sinhalese ethnic majority over the Tamil minority based largely in the north and east of the country. These claims had led in 1976 to the creation of the Liberation Tigers of Tamil Eelam (LTTE), a guerilla movement dedicated to the creation of a separate, independent Tamil state. Despite various efforts to calm the situation in the north, including an unsuccessful intervention by Indian peace-keeping forces under an agreement between Indian Prime Minister Rajiv Gandhi and the Sri Lankan government, violence had flared once again from 1990.

The LTTE must surely feature amongst the most vicious terrorist groups in the history of the twentieth century. Its tactics ranged from targeted assassination to indiscriminate mass murder, from ethnic cleansing to child abduction. And it was not merely Sri Lankans who suffered. The former Delhi residence of the Indian prime minister Indira Gandhi, where she was assassinated in 1984, contains among its various exhibits the gruesome relics of another family member whose life was cut short: the shredded, bloodied clothes of her son, Rajiv, who was killed in Southern India in 1991 by a suicide bomber believed to have links with the LTTE. Two years later, the Sri Lankan president, Ranasinghe Premadasa, was to suffer a similar fate. The second half of the 1990s saw a further intensification of the civil war. An uneasy peace followed a Norwegian-brokered ceasefire in 2002. As though this man-made disaster were not enough, nature also directed its forces against Sri Lanka with terrible flooding in 2003 and a huge tsunami the following year, which claimed over 30,000 lives.

There were numerous breaches of the 2002 ceasefire, mostly instigated by the LTTE. But Mahinda Rajapaksa's narrow victory in the presidential elections of November 2005 brought in a regime prepared to pursue a ruthless campaign to extirpate the organization. Towards the end of 2006, it launched an operation to re-establish full control of Sri Lanka's east. In January 2008, it formally abrogated the ceasefire agreement and launched a massive offensive in the north. Between then and May 2009, when the Tamil Tigers forces finally conceded defeat, there was huge loss of life as civilians found themselves trapped between the Sri Lankan army and the embattled rump of the LTTE, which had no compunction about using them as human shields. The government demarcated separate No Fire Zones (NFZs) for fleeing civilians, but ultimately these were respected by neither side. A Panel of Experts on Accountability in Sri Lanka, established by the UN secretary-general in June 2010, reported,

> From as early as 6 February 2009, the SLA [Sri Lanka Army] continuously shelled within the area that became the second NFZ, from all directions, including land, sea and air. It is estimated that there were between 300,000 and 330,000 civilians in that small area. The SLA assault employed aerial bombardment, long-range artillery, howitzers and MBRLs [unguided missile systems] as well as small mortars, RPGs [Rocket Propelled Grenades] and small arms fire.[1]

In May 2009, the government claimed victory. The LTTE leadership had been eradicated and its reign of terror ended. As Rajapaksa's defenders never lost an opportunity to assert, he had delivered the peace that had eluded his country for over twenty years. Yet for thousands of Tamils it was the peace of the grave. As a UN Internal Review Panel noted,

> The final phase of the decades-long Sri Lankan conflict was catastrophic. The Panel of Experts stated that "[a] number of credible sources have estimated that there could have been as many as 40,000 civilian deaths". Some Government sources state the number was well below 10,000. Other sources have referred to credible information indicating that over 70,000 people are unaccounted for.[2]

While the final stages of the civil war attracted considerable international media coverage, once it was over the subject might easily have dropped off the news agenda. Sri Lanka was hardly a major focus for the foreign policy of the West and few there had more than the most sketchy grasp of the conflict's complexities. Certainly in the UK, this all changed in June 2011, when Channel 4 screened Callum Macrae's powerful documentary film *Sri Lanka's Killing Fields*. Broadcast late after the watershed, it contained explicit and harrowing footage of what appeared to be war crimes, including summary executions, perpetrated by Sri Lankan government forces in the course of the campaign against the LTTE. This general picture was corroborated by interviews with external observers of the conflict, including UN and human rights agencies staff, and was lent further weight by the fact that the film had been commissioned by respected independent news company ITN Productions, and was presented by Jon Snow of Channel 4 News.

The documentary drew predictable accusations of distortion and bias from the Sri Lankan government, which, as we shall see, even went to the lengths of producing a booklet refuting the various charges made in the original film and its sequel, *Sri Lanka's Killing Fields: War Crimes Unpunished*, which was broadcast in March 2012. Yet the regime could do little to repair the damage done to its reputation. Macrae's work was screened across the world and nominated for major media awards. Wherever it appeared, it generated powerful reactions. Whatever its flaws, it threw a spotlight on a period the Sri Lankan government was desperate to consign to history, instead presenting it to viewers with a visceral immediacy.

That it took a foreign news company to bring these allegations to international attention should come as no surprise. Although they were showered with abuse by the Rajapaksa regime and its apologists, and Macrae in particular claimed to have received death threats, he and his colleagues were relatively secure compared with any Sri Lankan journalist who attempted to delve too deeply into the activities of their government or the Rajapaksa family—a fine distinction in some cases. It was not difficult to discover stories of the harassment or even murder of locally-based reporters.

One particularly vivid example was even caught on tape. It would be farcical had not the broader context been so dark and chilling. In July 2012, Frederica Jansz, editor-in-chief of the Sri Lankan *Sunday Leader*, quizzed the president's brother and defence minister Gotabaya about some relatively trivial examples of his abuse of office. There was one allegation of a flight-load of passengers being bumped off a Sri Lankan Airlines plane so that a puppy intended for Gotabaya's wife could be flown from Zurich, and another in which a plane had been downgraded, with further inconvenience to passengers, to allow his daughter's boyfriend to fly it. Rather than denying the claims, he became abusive and threatening. Jansz published a full transcript of this and a subsequent conversation, to international bemusement and consternation. Here is one excerpt:

> Rajapaksa: Yes, I threatened you. Your type of journalists are pigs who eat shit! Pigs who eat shit! Shit, shit, shit journalists! Ninety percent of the people in this country hate you! They hate you! You come for a function where I am and I will tell people this is the editor of the *Sunday Leader* and 90% there will show that they hate you. I will put you in jail! You shit journalist trying to split this country—trying to show otherwise from true Sinhala Buddhists! You are helped by the US ambassador, NGOs and Paikiasothy [Saravanamuttu, human rights activist]—they pay you!
>
> Jansz: I hope you can hear yourself, Mr Rajapaksa.
>
> Rajapaksa: People will kill you! People hate you! They will kill you!
>
> Jansz: On your directive?

Rajapaksa: What? No, not mine. But they will kill you—you dirty fucking shit journalist.[3]

Given that Jansz's predecessor at *The Sunday Leader*, Lasantha Wickramatunga, had been shot in the head by killers on motorcycles who were never apprehended, it would have been highly unwise to have regarded this as an empty threat. Though, happily, this was not to be Jansz's fate, she did not—needless to say—last long on the newspaper. Two months later, a 72 per cent stake in *The Sunday Leader* was bought by an ally of the president. Shortly afterwards, Jansz was sacked as editor.

Clearly aware that it was in danger of becoming an international pariah state, the Rajapaksa regime employed the services of the now notorious British-based public relations company Bell Pottinger. The firm is well known for taking on 'challenging' clients, having acted in the past for the repressive governments of Bahrain and Egypt and for the Pinochet Foundation. In 2017, it found itself in the spotlight over its work for a firm connected with the Gupta brothers, Indian businessmen whose close relationship with South African President Jacob Zuma has led to corruption allegations. The extent of Bell Pottinger's involvement in the Rajapaksa regime's 'reputation management' was exposed by *The Independent* in 2011.[4] The report described Bell Pottinger's efforts to place articles favourable to the regime in the British and American press:

> The firm sub-contracted its work in the United States to the firm Qorvis, which placed an article by President Rajapaksa in the *Philadelphia Inquirer* in December 2009 entitled 'How Sri Lanka Defeated Terrorism'. In the piece the President suggested Sri Lanka had provided a "workable model" for defeating terrorism, from which the international community could gain "valuable insight".

David Wilson, the firm's chairman, even suggested to the newspaper's undercover reporters that Rajapaksa had used a text prepared by Bell Pottinger when he had addressed the United

Nations towards the end of 2010, in preference to the draft written by his own foreign ministry. Although Bell Pottinger apparently ceased its work for the Sri Lankan government at around
that time, the regime continued to employ similar 'news management' tactics. Macrae and Channel 4 became particular targets
of Sri Lankan government-sponsored propaganda. November
2013 saw the appearance of a book entitled *Corrupted Journalism:
Channel 4 and Sri Lanka*. Its anonymous author claimed to provide a detailed refutation of the allegations made by Macrae and
other regime critics and witnesses, often smearing them as
LTTE sympathizers. The book's publisher was a mysterious out-
fit called Engage Sri Lanka, which claimed to be UK-based,
although it provided no postal address. Both it, and a related
body under the name of Sri Lanka Media Watch, have websites,
but neither site names any particular individuals associated with
their organizations. Engage Sri Lanka also had a Twitter account,
which appears to have been active between December 2011 and
November 2013. Thereafter, the trail goes cold. Yet if these
public-spirited individuals were not in receipt of Sri Lankan government sponsorship and assistance then I, as Dorothy Parker
might have put it, am Marie of Romania.

Rajapaksa's most prominent cheerleader in the UK Parliament
was the former Commons deputy speaker Michael Morris, who
had been elevated to the Lords in 1997 as Baron Naseby. He was
chairman of the All-Party British-Sri Lanka Parliamentary
Group and a frequent recipient of Sri Lankan government hos-
pitality. With his ruddy complexion and trademark bow tie,
Naseby was the very image of the bluff English peer of the
Realm. To complete his bulldog image, he had a nice line in
Second World War analogies. In October 2013, he regaled the
House of Lords with the following heart-warming tale:

> After 26 years of war that decimated the top half of Sri Lanka, it is
> as bad as Germany was in 1945. There are huge problems of infra-

structure that are now being addressed. I hope that everybody who goes there will look at the way in which it is being rebuilt. There are new homes, new schools, the reopened railway line, and so on. We can travel up and down Sri Lanka, as the cook of another friend of mine did all the way from Jaffna by bus, without being stopped once or needing papers.[5]

Understandably, among the pro-government sections of the Sri Lankan press Naseby became the go-to person for 'sensible' British views on the country. But his close relationship with the Rajapaksa regime did not escape the attention of journalists in the UK. In June 2014, Peter Oborne accused him in *The Daily Telegraph* of having misled the House of Lords in a question he had asked the previous year about one of Macrae's films.[6] Naseby had claimed that there was "conclusive evidence that that film from Channel 4 features two key independent witnesses, so alleged, who were in fact fully paid-up members of the Tamil Tigers". Oborne questioned the claim, pointing out that its source was the "propaganda book" *Corrupted Journalism.*

Sri Lanka also had more powerful friends within the Conservative Party and the British government. In March 2010, Dr Liam Fox, then an Opposition spokesman, was criticized for failing to declare within the required time limit a visit to Sri Lanka funded by the Rajapaksa government. He had also failed to mention this and other sponsored visits when asking parliamentary questions about development assistance to the country.[7] Fox's Sri Lankan connections also fuelled the allegations around his relationship with close friend and advisor Adam Werritty, which led to Fox's resignation as defence secretary in October 2011. Earlier that month, he had had to explain to Parliament his role in an entity called the Sri Lankan Development Trust, which he had helped to establish. This, apparently, had two separate funds: the Sri Lanka Infrastructure Development Fund and the Sri Lanka Charitable Fund. Fox denied in the Commons that either he or Werritty had received any share of the Trust's profits. Lord Bell—whose firm, Bell Pottinger, had recently ended its relationship with the Sri Lankan government—told *The Financial Times* that he was not aware the Trust was active or that anyone had invested money in it. Yet it had apparently paid for at least three visits to Sri Lanka by Fox in 2008–9, when he was still in Opposition.[8]

Aside from mobilizing individual sympathizers, Sri Lanka had a more ambitious diplomatic goal, which it pursued as early as the final stages of the civil war: to host a CHOGM. This would provide a perfect opportunity to demonstrate that the country was back on its feet. As important as the event itself was the fact that, as leader of the host country, Rajapaksa would become chair-in-office of the Commonwealth for a two-year period, and thereby the organization's chief political representative on the world stage. How could any doubts then remain about the probity of someone so closely associated with a respected international body devoted to upholding human rights, democracy and the rule of law?

We can trace Sri Lankan lobbying for this objective at least as far back as 2007. At the 2005 CHOGM in Malta, heads of government both confirmed their intention to meet next in Kampala and formally accepted the Trinidad and Tobago government's offer to host the 2009 summit. With the venue for 2009 already agreed, when heads met in Kampala in 2007, Rajapaksa pressed for Sri Lanka to host in 2011. Secretary-General Don McKinnon, however, intervened to prevent any formal endorsement of the Sri Lankan offer. He later claimed that he had simply told Rajapaksa, "You will not get it. Don't push for it." As McKinnon explained, rather than leaving the matter in the hands of Commonwealth leaders, he felt he had a personal duty as secretary-general to preserve the integrity of the organization: "He [Rajapaksa] should never have got it, and that's when the Secretary-General has to protect the members who don't want to see it happen but aren't prepared to say so publicly."[9] At the end of the summit, government heads reaffirmed their decision to meet in Trinidad and Tobago in 2009, but, unusually, merely took note of Sri Lanka's offer to host in 2011.

Having publicly staked this claim in Malta, Rajapaksa returned to the issue when heads met in Port of Spain in 2009. By this stage, however, McKinnon had left office and been replaced by the more pliable Sharma. Nevertheless, as the seasoned observer of CHOGMs Derek Ingram noted, there remained considerable unease among government heads about Rajapaksa's offer. In the wake of the bloody civil war, concerns centred not only on the security of the conference but on the legacy of the conflict itself. Ingram recalled that there was "some rough talking ('blood on the floor', some said)."[10] In particular, British Prime Minister Gordon Brown and his Australian counterpart Kevin Rudd fought hard to prevent Sri Lanka from being allowed to host the 2011 summit. On the eve of the Port of Spain CHOGM, Brown briefed journalists that he was determined to block the bid. A Downing Street source subsequently told *The Guardian*, "We simply cannot be in a position where Sri Lanka—whose actions earlier this year had a huge impact on civilians, leading to thousands of displaced people without proper humanitarian access—is seen to be rewarded for its actions."[11] Rudd stepped in with an offer to host in 2011, which heads gratefully accepted. Nevertheless, Rajapaksa won a victory of sorts, securing agreement to host the 2013 gathering. The final communique recorded:

> Heads of Government accepted the offer from the Prime Minister of Australia to host the 2011 CHOGM. They also accepted the offers of the President of Sri Lanka and the Prime Minister of Mauritius to host the 2013 and 2015 CHOGMs respectively.

For Sharma, this was the end of the matter: the heads of government had spoken. He told the Commonwealth Oral History Project:

> In Port of Spain the firm decision was taken that these three meetings will be held. There was no provision for revisiting the decision. The situation was no longer open for consideration in Perth: it was a fixed decision of the Heads. There was not the slightest suggestion from any delegation at [the 2011 Perth CHOGM] that this decision by the Heads should be re-opened.[12]

This was a rather odd way of looking at the discussions at the 2009 and 2011 CHOGMs. At Port of Spain in 2009, the main priority for two of the largest Commonwealth budget contributors, Britain and Australia, had been to stop Sri Lanka from hosting the event in two years' time. When heads met again in Perth in October 2011, it was in the wake of the international outrage provoked by the screening of Callum Macrae's *Sri Lanka's Killing Fields*. Indeed, a series of developments over the previous two years had cast further doubt over the wisdom of allowing Sri Lanka to host in 2013. These were eloquently set out by my colleague, the distinguished South Asia expert Professor James Manor, in a pamphlet distributed at the Perth CHOGM.[13] It noted criticisms from a series of respected quarters that the Sri Lankan government had failed adequately to investigate human rights abuses committed in the final stages of the war. In May 2010, the regime had established a Commission on Lessons Learnt and Reconciliation, but this had been attacked by Human Rights Watch and the US State Department for its inadequate remit and lack of impartiality. Indeed, the UN secretary-general had seen fit to initiate his own investigation.

Some inside David Cameron's coalition government (2010–15) were equally worried. In 2011, the parliamentary secretary to the leader of the House of Commons wrote that "the Government continue to have grave concerns about human rights in Sri

Lanka, including in respect of disappearances, extra-judicial killings, arbitrary arrests and restrictions of free expression."[14] Meanwhile, Rajapaksa seemed determined to entrench his and his family's position. In September 2010, he secured the passage of an eighteenth amendment to the Sri Lankan constitution, which greatly enhanced the powers of the president and removed the restriction that he or she could only serve for two terms in office. In the light of all this, and of other recent signs that the regime remained corrupt and repressive, Manor's pamphlet presciently warned that "If the Commonwealth proceeds with the CHOGM in Sri Lanka in 2013, it will be seen as an endorsement of that government. It will do immense damage to the well-founded reputation of the Commonwealth as a force for decency and human dignity."

Even to an informed observer like Manor, then, the dangers of not revisiting that decision were glaringly obvious. Secretary-General Sharma was far more than merely an informed observer. He was the designated custodian of the Commonwealth's reputation, better placed than anyone to appreciate the risks. Given the weight of the EPG report as an agenda item for the 2011 CHOGM in Perth, there was never going to be space for a lengthy and contentious debate about Sri Lanka. But, ahead of the summit, another major contributor to the Commonwealth's budget, this time Canada, had already signalled that it regarded the issue as deeply problematic. It escaped no one's attention that Canada contained a highly vocal Tamil diaspora population of around 300,000, and doubts were expressed about whether Ottawa's stance was based on entirely altruistic motives. The country's prime minister, Stephen Harper, had announced in September 2011 that he would tell his fellow heads at the forthcoming CHOGM that, unless progress was made on human rights and other problems, "I will not as Prime Minister be attending that Commonwealth summit (in Sri Lanka in 2013). And I hope that others will take a similar position."[15]

Under the circumstances, the only sensible course of action for Sharma would have been to guide heads discreetly away from the decision they had made two years previously. This is not, however, what he opted to do. A typically encyclopaedic final communique, brimming with good intentions on a huge range of issues, simply reaffirmed their earlier decision that Sri Lanka should act as host in 2013. The Perth CHOGM also renewed Sharma's period in office for another four years. Whether or not a sense of insecurity about his future had shaped his behaviour at the 2011 summit was a question that intrigued observers at the time. In any case, it was clearly not a moment to start making enemies. Harper's ultimatum had left open the possibility that the controversy might go away if engagement with the Rajapaksa regime could be shown to be producing results—perhaps, then, the Sri Lanka issue was a can that could be safely kicked down the road for some time to come.

The only problem was that the controversy did not go away, and as the date of the 2013 summit loomed ever nearer, the opportunity to change course without a major loss of face on all sides was fading from view. 2012–13 saw a saga that forced even Sharma to speak out, when President Rajapaksa ratified the Sri Lankan parliament's impeachment of the chief justice, Shirani Bandaranayake. In November 2012, 177 MPs from Rajapaksa's ruling party had presented a motion to the parliamentary speaker, his brother, demanding Bandaranayake's impeachment. She was an unlikely dissident, widely regarded in legal circles as something of a lightweight whose rise to high office had owed much to her close links with the Rajapaksas. The reason for her fall from favour appears to have been that the Supreme Court, over which she presided, had ruled as unconstitutional two pieces of legislation that seemed likely to give the central government powers previously exercised by the provincial administrations.

By January 2013, the affair had turned into a direct conflict between the judiciary and the legislature, with the Supreme

Court and Court of Appeal ruling in Bandaranayake's favour, but a parliamentary select committee—from which opposition MPs had withdrawn shortly before its final ruling—upholding three of the five charges against her. Bandaranayake was removed from office on 13 January, when Rajapaksa ratified parliament's motion of impeachment. Having issued earlier statements expressing concern over this process, Sharma now announced that "the dismissal of the Chief Justice will be widely seen, against the background of the divergence between the Judiciary and the Legislature, as running counter to the independence of the judiciary, which is a core Commonwealth value."[16]

Yet, despite international echoes of this condemnation, the Commonwealth Secretariat remained adamant that the CHOGM later that year would go ahead in Colombo as planned. On 26 March, the secretary-general's spokesman, Richard Uku, confirmed the decision. He also announced that Sri Lanka would not be on the agenda at the upcoming meeting of the Commonwealth Ministerial Action Group (CMAG), the body set up in 1995 specifically to consider violations of Commonwealth principles by member states. Following his boss's line of reasoning, Uku claimed, "It was the Commonwealth Heads of Government that made the decision to hold the 2013 meetings in Sri Lanka. Such decisions are made at the Commonwealth Heads of Government level and not by CMAG."[17]

Even critics of the plan for Colombo to host tended to accept this as an authoritative statement of how the Commonwealth functioned. But how authoritative was it? The protocols for the organization of CHOGMs have never been the subject of any formal agreement by heads of government. In the absence of clear guidance, the Commonwealth tends to work on the basis of precedent; there simply was no precedent for the decision to hold a CHOGM in a particular member state being overturned due to concerns about that country's behaviour. In that respect, Sharma was on fairly firm ground. Yet there were other episodes in the organization's history suggesting that the secretary-general had greater freedom of movement than Sharma apparently wished to allow himself.

Although a CHOGM had never been relocated as a mark of disapproval, this is precisely what happened in the case of the 1981 Commonwealth finance ministers' meeting. This was due to take place in New Zealand, but was moved as a reproach to the government of Robert Muldoon, which had failed to prevent the apartheid-era South African Springbok rugby team from touring the country, in defiance of the 1977 Gleneagles Agreement. The Commonwealth secretary-general of the day, Sonny Ramphal, was personally outspoken in his criticism of Muldoon's policy.[18] In moving the finance ministers' meeting, however, Ramphal acted in the name of the heads of government. His ability rapidly to construct a consensus around this issue was presumably aided by the fact that the Springbok controversy erupted at a time when many Commonwealth leaders were gathered in London for the wedding of Prince Charles.

Of even greater relevance was the example of the CHOGM originally scheduled to take place in Brisbane on 6–9 October 2001. On 28 September, with only days to go before the summit, Secretary-General Don McKinnon announced its postponement, citing security concerns following the terrorist attacks in the US on 11 September. There was no vote on this by member states. Instead, McKinnon appears to have taken soundings and learned that a number of heads of government, including the prime ministers of the UK, Canada and India, no longer planned to attend. On that basis, he advised Australian Prime Minister John Howard to postpone the summit. Howard's press statement, announcing that he had reluctantly agreed to accept this advice, strongly implied that there was no consensus on the matter among member states, and certainly no general agreement that the meeting should not take place as planned.[19] Despite this, the prime minister of the host country was prepared to accept the secretary-general's recommendation to postpone.

Of course, Rajapaksa would have been highly unlikely to have agreed to any such change—then, the Commonwealth would have entered uncharted territory. But the precedent of Brisbane suggests that, in that case, Sharma might have sought a more formal expression of views from heads of governments about whether they wished to revisit their decision to award the next CHOGM to Sri Lanka. That was not a course he was prepared to take.

Uku's statement in March was clearly intended to dampen any expectation that CMAG would seek to intervene in the controversy on the basis of Sri Lanka's violation of key Commonwealth principles. Yet further ammunition was handed to the country's critics in April when, just over a week before CMAG met, the Commonwealth Law Conference in Cape Town urged Sri Lanka's suspension from the councils of the Commonwealth, on the grounds of serious breaches of judicial independence and the rule of law. It also asserted that staging the CHOGM in Sri Lanka would "tarnish the reputation of the Commonwealth". A resolution to this effect was ratified by the Commonwealth Lawyers Association, the Commonwealth Legal Education Association and the Commonwealth Magistrates' and Judges' Association.

CMAG met in London on the morning of 26 April. Knowing that it would dodge the issue of Sri Lanka, the Commonwealth Secretariat seemed to hope that the event would attract as little publicity as possible, and did not make arrangements for it to be followed by a press conference. It was at this point that the Institute of Commonwealth Studies (ICwS) made a small but, as it turned out, significant contribution to the saga. In conjunction with the Commonwealth Journalists Association, we arranged for the chair of CMAG, Bangladeshi Foreign Minister Dr Dipu

Moni, to speak at the Institute and answer questions on the afternoon of the meeting. This seemed to spur the Secretariat into action. At the very last minute—little more than a day before the meeting was due to take place—it announced that it was organizing its own news conference that day at Marlborough House, at 1.00pm. Meanwhile, the Bangladesh High Commission let us know that Dr Moni would prefer not to answer questions about Sri Lanka when she addressed our gathering later in the afternoon. It claimed that CMAG proceedings were confidential—a less than convincing explanation of Moni's reticence, given that the Commonwealth Secretariat had put out a same-day press statement outlining the discussions of the last CMAG meeting in September 2012.

They need not have worried, however. By the time she reached the Institute in the afternoon, the storm had passed, depositing a large quantity of something far less sanitary than fresh, clean rainwater on the heads of senior Commonwealth officials.

The term 'car crash' gives rise to a number of useful analogies. We have already noted the term 'slow-motion car crash', which nicely sums up the whole story of the 2013 CHOGM. The term 'car crash interview' has become a popular way to describe the spectacle of a major public figure disintegrating under media questioning. If one could speak, by extension, of a 'car crash press conference', this would be a perfect characterization of what happened when the secretary-general, his press spokesman and members of CMAG met the press on 26 April.

They walked straight into a brutal, pitiless ambush redolent of the final reel of *Butch Cassidy and the Sundance Kid*. Unlike Robert Redford and Paul Newman, however, Sharma and Uku did not come out with all guns blazing. The smart thing would probably have been to bore the audience into submission with a long account of what had actually been on the CMAG agenda. That, at least, would have used up some of the time available to the press. Instead, after only the most perfunctory of opening statements, the floor was opened to questions. Channel 4's foreign affairs correspondent, Jonathan Miller, asked Sharma whether the Rajapaksa regime embodied the values of the Commonwealth Charter, which the Queen had signed in the same building only six weeks before. After that came what he described in his subsequent report as a "barrage of questions", almost all of them focusing on Sri Lanka and why it had not been under consideration by CMAG.[20] At one point, desperate to solicit other points for discussion, Uku reminded the audience that this was "not a press conference about Sri Lanka per se." This would not be the last time he had to make a similar plea to journalists.

Meanwhile, CMAG member and Canadian Foreign Minister John Baird was busily briefing the press outside the press conference about Ottawa's frustration at the Secretariat's failure to intervene over the CHOGM. He told Miller, "We're appalled at Sri Lanka hosting this summit." Miller's report noted the concerns, which had also been expressed by the legal community, and concluded that the Commonwealth looked "isolated" over its apparent support for Sri Lanka, and risked becoming "irrelevant". For an organization rarely in the spotlight, this seemed to be testing to breaking point the old maxim that all publicity is good publicity.

There was an intriguing postscript to this public relations disaster. A few months later, in September 2013, Sharma was forced to respond to allegations that he had deliberately withheld from CMAG important information on Sri Lanka. It was claimed that he had obtained two independent legal opinions about the removal of Chief Justice Bandaranayake, both of which had pronounced the process unconstitutional. *The Sunday Times* noted,

> Two reports were commissioned by the secretariat, from a former South African chief justice, Pius Langa, and Sir Jeffrey Jowell, a London QC. Langa's report, submitted in March, was found in his

belongings after his death in July. In it he accused the Sri Lankan government of precipitating a "constitutional crisis of vast proportions" by trampling over Supreme Court objections to the impeachment, and of breaching Commonwealth values and principles. Senator Hugh Segal, Canada's special envoy to the Commonwealth, described the decision not to inform member nations of the report's contents as "Kafkaesque", adding: "Canada is deeply troubled." He said: "When you have an opinion from a former chief justice that is so categoric and so devastating, the notion that the Commonwealth just looks the other way and pretends it never happened is deeply problematic."[21]

In response to the allegations, Sharma admitted that the two reports had been received and did not seek to deny that Langa's verdict had been damning, but he explained that "Commonwealth Heads of Government agreed as recently as 2011 that CMAG and the Secretary-General's good offices' work should be complementary but should proceed along distinct tracks." The reports had been "confidential" and commissioned not as evidence for CMAG but to facilitate Sharma's own "quiet behind-the-scenes-diplomacy". As such, although they had not been "in any way concealed", Sharma strongly implied that he had not been under any obligation to pass them on.[22]

Leaving morality aside, in a purely legalistic sense Sharma's defence had a certain amount of substance to it. At the 2011 CHOGM, ministers had endorsed the recommendations of a report, published by the Secretariat in January that year, on ways of enhancing CMAG's effectiveness. 2011's ill-fated EPG report wished CMAG to identify an objective set of criteria that would automatically lead to a country being placed on its agenda. By contrast, the recommendations approved by the CHOGM left the onus on the secretary-general to brief CMAG on violations of Commonwealth principles and to invite it to take action. Such an invitation to action would normally only happen after two months of attempts to engage with the country concerned through the Secretary-General's "good offices"—and that period could be extended if they thought it required more time.[23]

This arrangement made sense in allowing for a period of quiet persuasion before adopting a more punitive approach. But it left CMAG both blind and impotent in circumstances where a secretary-general wished to shield a member state from sanction. Blind because, as the January 2011 report noted, "Given the sensitive role it discharges, CMAG's actions need to be based on the most reliable and objective evidence about a country situation, including the state of democracy, rule of law and human rights." Yet as the Secretariat's website currently notes, "[CMAG's] meetings are convened by the Commonwealth Secretary-General with the Commonwealth Secretariat providing secretarial support." As such, CMAG is highly dependent on the Secretariat for its information. For the secretary-general to fail to pass CMAG important legal advice indicating a major violation of Commonwealth principles was certainly at odds with the spirit of the January 2011 report. This stressed the need for CMAG to be more proactive, arguing, "The link between the Good Offices of the Secretary-General and the work of CMAG could be strengthened so as to provide greater complementarity between these roles. In this context, the authority of CMAG ought to be reinforced and further recognised."[24]

In this light, one might well ask why there was not more of an outcry at Sharma's (in)action across the network of civil society organizations that supposedly existed to promote Commonwealth values. Certainly, as we have seen, prominent associations representing lawyers, judges and magistrates were prepared to speak out, and the Commonwealth Journalists Association played a very honourable role in providing a platform for Sri Lankan journalists and opposition politicians to express their concerns. But some other prominent parts of the Commonwealth family were strangely silent. Why was this?

Much of the credit—if that's the right word—should go to Sri Lanka's 2011–14 high commissioner to the UK, Dr Chris Nonis. In 2012, he was named 'Diplomat of the Year' for Asia at the London Diplomatic Awards. On purely technical grounds, this accolade was well deserved. Diplomats and politicians across the Commonwealth have searched in vain for the secret of turning the organization into an effective foreign policy instrument. Nonis focused his energies on a single objective: bringing the CHOGM to Sri Lanka—thus securing the title 'Commonwealth Chair-in-Office' for his boss—and he succeeded. He certainly had the advantage of a fair wind in the form of a timid, risk-averse secretary-general. But he also made the weather, actively courting key Commonwealth official bodies and civil society organizations. As we have seen, the latter are overwhelmingly small, underfunded operations that can ill afford to refuse the assistance of influential patrons.

I became aware of this charm offensive soon after becoming director of the ICwS in 2009. It was generally quite an effort to persuade high commissions to engage with our activities. The Sri Lankans, on the contrary, seemed to be positively courting *us*. They were friendliness and cooperation personified. Indeed, one year we received not one but two corporate Christmas cards from them. One does not have to look far beyond Nonis's own website to appreciate the success of this technique.[25] He chaired the Commonwealth Secretariat's Board of Governors. He became deputy chairman of the Royal Commonwealth Society, the organization's most prominent cheerleader in London, with branches across the Commonwealth. He also became a trustee of the Ramphal Institute, a Commonwealth think-tank based at King's College London, and served on the International Advisory Council at Asia House. In terms of things royal, he chaired the Advisory Council for Sri Lanka of the British Asian Trust, one of the Prince of Wales's charities, and served on the Advisory

Council of the Queen's Diamond Jubilee Trust, a major Commonwealth-based initiative launched in February 2012.

Nonis was a wealthy businessman in his own right through his family firm, the Mackwoods Group, which operated in a wide variety of sectors from healthcare to agribusiness. Unusually, according to *The Colombo Telegraph*, Nonis did not distance himself from his personal business interests when he became high commissioner in 2011, instead remaining chairman of Mackwoods and continuing to oversee all major operations.[26] As a prominent businessman, Nonis was involved in some of Sri Lanka's major economic and developmental organizations, including its Export Development Board and its National Enterprise Development Authority. In that capacity, he also lent his services to the Commonwealth Business Council, acting as a member of its Board under chairman Mohan Kaul. The ICwS successfully resisted being incorporated in Nonis's web, and continued to provide a platform for critics of the Sri Lankan regime. Very soon, the corporate Christmas cards dried up.

There is always a danger of exaggerating the power that comes of the sort of personal vectors of influence that Nonis established in the Commonwealth community. For example, in June 2012, the admirably independently-minded political scientist Peter Kellner, who was Royal Commonwealth Society chair to Nonis's co-chair, certainly had little compunction about criticizing the Commonwealth's failure to pressure Sri Lanka, prophesying that the CHOGM there would be a disaster if the country's human rights record did not improve.[27] Nevertheless, it is probably fair to suggest that Nonis's close association with so many Commonwealth-related organizations had a chilling effect on debate about the record of the Rajapaksa regime and possible action against it. There was a time when he seemed an almost ubiquitous figure at Commonwealth gatherings. If he was not personally in the room, one could be sure that his minions from the High Commission would be present, busily taking notes, whenever and wherever Sri Lanka was discussed. While it might be hyperbolic to talk of an 'institutional capture' of the Commonwealth by the Sri Lankan government, Nonis certainly provided what a 'DIY kit' for this might look like.

In May 2013, it was announced that the Queen would not be attending the Colombo summit, but would be sending Prince Charles in her place. A spokesperson for the Palace claimed that this had nothing to do with concerns over the mounting controversy around the gathering. Rather, the reason was that "we are reviewing the amount of long-haul travel that is taken by the Queen. As a result of that she won't be travelling to the Commonwealth Heads of Government Meeting (CHOGM) later this year."[28] On the face of it, this was perfectly plausible excuse—the Queen had, after all, recently turned eighty-seven, and her husband was approaching his ninety-second birthday. It was entirely reasonable that she would be reluctant to undertake such a long flight, and it was known that she was keen for Prince Charles to take a more prominent role at major Commonwealth events (see Chapter 4).

In reality, though, both the Queen and her consort were in remarkably good health. Just days before the announcement was made, Prince Philip had rather proved the point by hopping over to Toronto for a three-day visit to mark his role as colonel-in-chief of the Royal Canadian Regiment. Two years on, both he and the Queen would attend the 2015 CHOGM on the admittedly much-nearer island of Malta. Until Colombo in 2013, the last time the Queen had missed a CHOGM was in 1971, when Edward Heath had formally advised her to do so. She had clearly been indignant at the prime minister's strictures, insisting that it was "her duty" to attend meetings of Commonwealth heads.[29]

In light of the Queen's passionate, life-long commitment to the organization, it was difficult to banish the suspicion that political considerations had indeed played a part in her decision. Had she given any indication of this, she would have found herself drawn into the controversy, and it would have embarrassed Commonwealth prime ministers determined to attend. If, on the other hand, she had gone to Sri Lanka, controversy of a different sort would have attached itself to her, and it would certainly have seemed anomalous, in the light of Harper's boycott, that the 'Queen of Canada' was attending the summit. Under the circumstances, pleading infirmity was by far the most attractive, and possibly the only option. Whatever the case, unlike most other participants in this disreputable saga, it was clear that the Queen's consistently sound instincts in Commonwealth affairs had not deserted her.

Meanwhile, fresh embarrassments kept coming. Following a week-long fact-finding visit to Sri Lanka in August 2013, UN Human Rights Commissioner Navi Pillay was forthright in her criticism of the Rajapaksa regime. She described to journalists the intimidation of Sri Lankans who had tried to speak to her, adding, "This type of surveillance and harassment appears to be getting worse in Sri Lanka, which is a country where critical voices are quite often attacked or even permanently silenced." It was, she noted, "particularly extraordinary for such treatment to be meted out during a visit by a UN high commissioner for human rights."[30] In October, as had become pretty much inevitable, the Canadian prime minister announced that he would boycott the summit. Ottawa also threatened to reduce its financial contribution to the work of the Secretariat. Meanwhile, Indian Prime Minister Manmohan Singh, caught between domestic pressure to stay away and a clear desire not to damage relations with Sri Lanka, wavered before announcing just five days before the CHOGM that he would be sending his foreign minister in his place. Two days later, the prime minister of Mauritius, Navin Chandra Ramgoolam, followed Harper in declaring a boycott of the summit because of lack of progress on human rights in Sri Lanka.

Even before these absences had been confirmed, there were signs that the Rajapaksa regime was seriously worried about low turnout of Commonwealth heads. Indeed, it was prepared to resort to some desperate remedies. On 29 October, *The Deccan Herald* announced that Sri Lanka's Wildlife Resources Conservation Ministry was offering each leader who attended the CHOGM the chance to 'foster' an orphaned baby elephant. The cost would be Rs 100,000 a month, but Commonwealth leaders would be able to name their elephant.[31] It is not recorded how many of them took up this offer.

In the end, fewer than half of the then fifty-three member states were represented by their prime ministers or presidents, with many sending deputies or foreign ministers in their place. This was a record low in the recent history of Commonwealth summits, even though it has proved a struggle at the best of times to persuade busy leaders to attend the biennial Commonwealth jamboree. Just at the point when the organization desperately needed to reverse this trend, it instead gave premiers an excellent reason for them to discover a diary clash. The British prime minister, David Cameron, was urged by the Labour Opposition to boycott the proceedings. He also came under direct pressure from the House of Commons cross-party Foreign Affairs Committee, which was chaired by one of his own backbenchers. Among the conclusions of its report on 'The role and future of the Commonwealth' published in November 2012, the Committee stated categorically:

> We conclude that continuing evidence of serious human rights abuses in Sri Lanka shows that the Commonwealth's decision to hold the 2013 Commonwealth Heads of Government Meeting in Colombo was wrong. We are impressed by the clear and forthright stance

taken by the Canadian Prime Minister, who has said he would attend the Meeting only if human rights were improved. The UK Prime Minister should publicly state his unwillingness to attend the meeting unless he receives convincing and independently-verified evidence of substantial and sustainable improvements in human and political rights in Sri Lanka.[32]

Cameron refused to commit himself in this way or, ultimately, to boycott the summit. Instead, he carried out a delicate balancing act. As promised, he travelled to the Tamil north of Sri Lanka immediately after the CHOGM opening ceremony, the first foreign leader to have done so since the country's independence in 1948. Accompanied by a large press contingent, he visited the offices of a newspaper and spoke to journalists who blamed the deaths of six colleagues on government-backed paramilitaries. He also visited a printing press that had been destroyed in an arson attack. He told reporters, "The pictures of journalists, shot and killed, on the walls, and hearing stories of journalists who have disappeared long after the war has ended— that will stay with me."[33] At the CHOGM itself, Cameron made a point of raising his concerns with Rajapaksa. Having done his duty in that respect, he then left a day early. On his return to the UK, he was able to claim that his visit had helped to highlight concerns around human rights and had allowed him to engage in a positive sense with the Sri Lankan government.

There was a widespread sense that Cameron had handled the event fairly deftly; but, of course, not everyone was convinced. The government-supporting sections of the Sri Lankan press were predictably hostile. They also lapped up an attack on Cameron by the British journalist Rod Liddle, headlined 'That's the president of Sri Lanka, PM, not one of your fags'. Equally predictable was the eagerness of Lord Naseby to be of service to the Sri Lankan government. Speaking in the House of Lords on 18 November, Naseby asked,

Is my noble friend aware that the reaction from the nearly 500,000 Sri Lankans living in the UK, whether they be Sinhalese, Tamil or Muslim, has not been at all positive? My e-mail has virtually collapsed because people are deeply concerned at the way in which the Prime Minister raised, in their view, an unbalanced view of what progress had been made, particularly the manner in which it was delivered to the President of Sri Lanka. I have to say that I partially share that concern.[34]

It would hardly have been surprising had Cameron come away from this encounter with the Commonwealth feeling battered and concluding that, far from being an asset to the UK, the organization had clumsily conjured up a completely unnecessary and embarrassing crisis. Although he had dealt with it fairly skilfully, it was bound to generate criticism whichever way he played the issue. This episode also demonstrated the difficulty Britain in particular faces when trying to use the Commonwealth to address issues around democracy, human rights and the rule of law. It is far too easy for repressive regimes and their apologists to portray any such initiatives as arrogant expressions of an imperial superiority complex.

Other Commonwealth leaders were far more cautious about doing anything to offend the Rajapaksa regime. Australia's Liberal prime minister, Tony Abbott, took a very different approach from his Canadian counterpart. He not only attended the summit, but was fulsome in lauding his host: "With peace has come more freedom and more prosperity—we are here to praise as much as to judge."[35] Abbott had his own domestic reasons for avoiding putting any pressure on the Rajapaksa regime. The former Labor foreign minister of Australia, Gareth Evans, clearly no admirer of Abbott, summed up the situation in the following terms:

Sri Lanka was a pretty good test for [the Commonwealth] and it failed fairly comprehensively, didn't it? There was a lot of help from

Australia, I have to say, behaving abominably. We played nice to the Rajapaksas, who were among the most abominable bunch of thugs in the universe, ... because we, under this new government, had an agenda about asylum seekers and refugees. We had a lot of people coming by boats from Sri Lanka, and we were highly dependent—or were seen as highly dependent—on cooperation with the Sri Lankan government to try and stop that at the source.[36]

Even by the prolix standards of CHOGM final communiques, the one that emerged from the 2013 Sri Lankan summit was particularly comprehensive in its range of subjects on which heads expressed their good intentions. Its ninety-eight points covered issues from "Sustainable Land Management" and "Governance and Management of Oceans" to "Transparency of Money Transfers" and the "Commonwealth Plan for Broadband", as well as, of course, old favourites like human rights and freedom of expression. Commonwealth supporters always seem bewildered at how little attention the international press generally pays to these sorts of fine sentiments. But journalists are always on the lookout for the 'real' story, and in the case of the Colombo summit, there was no question about what this was. The team from Channel 4 had turned out in full force, including McCrae, Miller and Snow. In a UK context, Cameron's dramatic trip north provided the main news story at the start of the summit. Thereafter, scheduled meetings with the press disintegrated into larger-scale versions of the disastrous news conference that had followed the CMAG meeting in April. Once again, Sharma's spokesperson Richard Uku found himself in the eye of the storm. The editor of the Commonwealth's *Round Table Journal* recalled,

At times Uku could be seen struggling to contain the avalanche of human rights-related questions directed at the Sri Lankan president. "Does anyone have questions that's [sic] not on Sri Lanka or human rights?" he was reduced to asking at one point. At another he lamented, "I see that I'm being consistently ignored when I call for questions on CHOGM."[37]

In Sri Lanka, however, Uku now found himself under fire both from journalists keen to probe into human rights abuses, and pro-Rajapaksa sections of the local press fiercely defensive of the government. Again, it was an utterly thankless task, and at the very least, Uku deserves credit for having used his influence to persuade a reluctant Sri Lankan government to allow Jonathan Miller and the team from Channel 4 into the country.

In retrospect, it was difficult even for supporters of the Commonwealth to put a positive gloss on what had happened in Colombo. Concluding his own account of the summit, Stuart Mole, chair of *The Round Table*'s editorial board, concluded,

> It was not just the credibility of Commonwealth values that was on the line in Sri Lanka—it was also the Commonwealth's reputation as an innovator, ideas-generator, consensus-builder, connector and campaigner. Colombo is not the first of the Commonwealth's 'lost' summits, and it will not be the last. But it has made the immediate road ahead that much harder to travel.[38]

In January 2015, the Commonwealth enjoyed an unexpectedly early release from the ignominy of having Rajapaksa as its chair-in-office when, to widespread surprise, he was defeated in the country's presidential elections. It would be comforting to be able to suggest that in some sense the Commonwealth's 'positive engagement' with Sri Lanka had helped to usher in a new age of pluralism and democracy. But the defeat of Rajapaksa, challenged by his health minister Maithripala Sirisena, came about largely as a result of a split within his own government. Senior figures had finally had enough of the regime's nepotism, authoritarianism and corruption. In the wake of his defeat at the polls, there were even reports that Rajapaksa had allegedly considered defying the result by staging a coup. In the event, however, he went quietly, pursued by allegations that during his time in office he and some family members had corruptly spirited billions of dollars out of the country.

It may be a matter of personal taste, but I have always had doubts about the morality of organizations that concentrate on passing well-meaning but ultimately empty resolutions and holding endless rounds of conferences on equally well-intentioned subjects without much thought as to what, if anything, they will ultimately achieve. Such meetings might well salve the conscience of their members. But arguably they also offer an illusion that meaningful results can be achieved without the hard bargaining and painful concessions that are the staple of everyday practical politics. Too often in recent years, the Commonwealth has epitomized this phenomenon. And we know all too well the way in which genuinely malign individuals can 'hide in plain sight' by attaching themselves to such organizations, confident that the sound of pious incantations will drown out rumours of their own misdeeds. That is undoubtedly what the Commonwealth allowed to happen in the case of the Sri Lankan regime, and this stain on its reputation will be difficult to erase.

8

EMPIRE 2.0?

Brexit

In the British referendum held on 23 June 2016, around 52 per cent of those who participated voted for Britain to leave the EU, and about 48 per cent to remain. As I tried to come to terms with what seemed to me an unmitigated disaster, there were always sympathetic friends at hand to make matters worse. "You're at the centre of things now," they said. "You must be very busy. Apparently the Commonwealth is the way of the future." To which, I'm afraid, my response was: "If the Commonwealth is the future then we're in even more trouble than I thought."

The irony of this is that, in the years leading up to the referendum, there were signs that the British political establishment had finally lost patience with the Commonwealth. This was apparent as late as the British general election of May 2015. Gone were the ritual invocations in party manifestos of its great untapped potential. In place of Labour's 1997 vow to give renewed priority to this "unique network of contacts linked by history, language and legal systems", or even its warm tribute in 2010 to "the enduring role of the Commonwealth—a unique organisation for fostering understanding and trust, spanning a quarter of the world's population", the party barely name-checked the Commonwealth in its 2015 manifesto. The Conservatives were a little more forthcoming, although they largely cut and pasted the words from their 2010 manifesto. Back then, they had promised to "strengthen the Commonwealth as a focus for promoting democratic values and development"; now they pledged to "strengthen the Commonwealth's focus on promoting democratic values and development."

The UK Independence Party (UKIP) predictably scattered references to the Commonwealth far more liberally than any other party—often as a tool to refute the claim that Britain was too small to survive outside the EU. Yet even UKIP had watered down its earlier commitment to the Commonwealth in 2015, dropping a startlingly ambitious proposal from its 2010 manifesto. This had promised:

> UKIP will seek to establish a Commonwealth Free Trade Area (CFTA) with the 53 other Commonwealth countries. The Commonwealth Business Council estimates that a CFTA would account for more than 20% of all international trade and investment, facilitating annual trade exchanges worth more than $1.8 trillion and direct foreign investment worth about $100 billion. Yet the Commonwealth has been shamefully betrayed and neglected by previous governments.

This was not, of course, the only promise that UKIP subsequently jettisoned. In a radio interview in January 2014, the party's then leader, Nigel Farage, famously said of the 2010 manifesto, "I didn't read it. It was drivel. It was 486 pages of drivel".[1] Certainly, as far as the idea of a Commonwealth free trade area is concerned, one would not want to disagree with him. Leaving aside all other objections—including the fact that Commonwealth members' economic interests were too diverse for a single trading model to be mutually acceptable—there was the simple fact that two of those members, Cyprus and Malta, were also members of the EU. As such, they, like Britain, would have to leave the Union before being free to agree to any such deal with the Commonwealth—a highly unlikely scenario.

Alongside the general marginalization of the Commonwealth in the 2015 election manifestos, one could also detect a more subtle change in its presentation, particularly by the more right-wing parties. The Conservatives, for example, promised to "uphold our Special Relationship with the USA and further strengthen our ties with our close Commonwealth allies, Australia, Canada and New Zealand." This was more than a little reminiscent of rhetoric during the inter-war period, when the Commonwealth was synonymous with the 'White Dominions'—territories of European settlement that supposedly felt a particular affinity towards the 'Mother Country'. To some extent, there has always been an 'inner' and an 'outer' Commonwealth, something of a guilty secret (see Chapter 3). Indeed, we have seen examples of this even in recent years. In 2012, for example, plans were announced for the UK and Canada to share some diplomatic missions around the world.[2] The 2015 Tory manifesto's passage on the Commonwealth had echoes of a proposal raised in 2013 by the then Conservative mayor of London, Boris Johnson, for Britain to establish a "bilateral mobility zone" with Australia and New Zealand, to make it easier for their citizens to live and work in the UK.[3] This was endorsed the following year by a report from the right-of-centre think-tank Commonwealth Exchange, which suggested adding Canada to the group.

UKIP, meanwhile, invoked the presence of the Commonwealth more frequently than the Conservatives in 2015, and even complained about the "blatant discrimination against Commonwealth countries" when it came to immigration. It promised to establish a Migration Control Commission charged with devising a system of "reciprocal arrangements" for countries that already had close links to the UK, including Commonwealth members. This seemed to leave open the possibility of an arrangement along the lines Johnson had suggested, which would have focused on the "old Dominions". What the UKIP manifesto did not do was to engage in any meaningful way with the activities of the contemporary Commonwealth. Indeed, it seemed more comfortable talking about an "Anglosphere" stretching from India to New Zealand to the Caribbean.

This very much foreshadowed the rhetoric during the EU referendum campaign the following year. Although the Commonwealth featured as an element in the snake-oil sold to voters by the Leave campaign, it was by no means the most potent ingredient. Indeed, Brexiteers struggled with the whole concept of the Commonwealth. On the one hand, it fed into their arguments that Britain had the opportunity to engage more actively with growing economies outside the EU. But it sat uneasily within a campaign which, by the end, had focused sharply on the issue of immigration. A valuable survey of the referendum by Eva Namusoke notes that the Commonwealth featured in the campaign not just as an issue, but also as a potential constituency to be wooed by the rival camps.[4] As in British general elections, non-British EU citizens did not have a vote in the UK whereas Commonwealth citizens did. In addition to this, there was a significant proportion of the British electorate of non-British Commonwealth extraction.

A 2015 Leave campaign flyer announced, "Our Commonwealth links are bound to be weakened much further if we stay in the Common Market." *The Daily Telegraph* marked Commonwealth Day in March 2016 with an article headlined 'Brexit will allow Britain to embrace the Commonwealth'. The pro-Brexit narrative made much of the idea that Britain had turned its back on the Commonwealth in the 1970s. As Namusoke notes, "The 1975 referendum [on remaining within the Common Market] along with the 1973 membership of the EEC have been described by leading Leave campaigners, including Conservative Member of the European Parliament (MEP) Daniel Hannan, UKIP leader Nigel Farage and former Mayor of London Boris Johnson, as the moment the UK 'betrayed' the Commonwealth."[5] And of course, the Commonwealth was frequently presented as a vast untapped market with which Britain could once more do a large proportion of its business. On the eve of the referendum, *The Daily Express* published an article by Paul Nuttall, the then deputy leader of UKIP, entitled 'Forget Brussels—the UK should be doing business with the Commonwealth'. Nuttall argued:

> The Commonwealth today contains fifty-three countries—compared to the EU's twenty-eight. It covers a quarter of the globe's landmass and contains a quarter of the world's people. Whereas the EU's proportion of world trade is shrinking, the Commonwealth's is growing. In 2013 the Commonwealth economy overtook the Eurozone's and by 2019 it will have overtaken the EU's as a whole, contributing 17.7 per cent in terms of global trade compared to the EU's 15.3 per cent. This is because the Commonwealth contains not only some of the most stable economies in the world like Australia and Canada, but also some of the fastest growing, like India, which is projected to be the second largest economy on the planet by the middle of this century.[6]

I doubt whether even the Royal Commonwealth Society or the Commonwealth Business Council have ever suggested that the mere fact of having more member states makes the Commonwealth superior to the EU. But in other respects, Nuttall was drawing from arguments that had frequently been propounded by both organizations.

In attempting to garner the support of Commonwealth citizens or Commonwealth-origin British voters, supporters of Brexit made tantalizingly vague promises that imposing restrictions on EU migration might be balanced by easing those on people from the Commonwealth. In February 2016, a letter

signed by eighty "patriotic Britons of Commonwealth background" was published by the official Vote Leave campaign. Its
signatories complained that "our immigration policy forces us, in
effect, to turn away qualified workers from the Commonwealth
so as to free up unlimited space for migrants from the EU ... The
descendants of the men who volunteered to fight for Britain in
two world wars must stand aside in favour of people with no
connection to the United Kingdom". A similar argument was
made by the pro-Brexit minister of state for employment, Priti
Patel. But it was refuted by the minister of state at the FCO,
Hugo Swire, who warned, "Our membership of the EU does not
prevent Commonwealth citizens from coming to the United
Kingdom. Anyone suggesting that it would be different or easier
is just raising false hopes by suggesting we would water down
those criteria".[7]

In a sense, the Commonwealth provided reassuring mood
music for a Leave campaign keen to demonstrate that Britain
would not be isolated in the world. Yet the actual promises about
what could be delivered through the organization were never well
defined. There was much talk of 'our friends' in the Commonwealth, but when mention was made of specific 'friends', they
tended to be the old white dominions. Not content with the
contemporary myth of the Commonwealth, the Brexit campaign
was apparently seeking to revive an older mythology of white-
British racial solidarity dating from the early decades of the
twentieth century. And on the crucial issue of the Commonwealth as an alternative trading partner, beyond a few hand-me-
down figures about its supposed economic potential, there were
few clues about how or why the volume of trade with member
states would be increased.

Beyond the inherent difficulty of making such a case, there
were probably two main reasons for this. First, with the exception of Liam Fox—who had not exactly wrapped himself in glory

in his dealings with the Rajapaksa regime in Sri Lanka—none of the leading figures in the Brexit campaign had hitherto displayed much interest in the Commonwealth, and their knowledge of how it operated seemed rudimentary at best. Boris Johnson was still doing penance for a comment in *The Daily Telegraph* fourteen years earlier: "It is said that the Queen has come to love the Commonwealth, partly because it supplies her with regular cheering crowds of flag-waving piccaninnies".[8] I always thought that a suitable punishment for such crass and ignorant references to the organization would be to make Johnson attend an endless round of Commonwealth-related meetings. For that reason alone, his appointment as foreign secretary in 2016 gave me a faint twinge of satisfaction.

A more serious impediment to 'weaponizing' the Commonwealth in the referendum was the particular direction taken by the Leave campaign in its final two months. One can point, fairly precisely, to the moment that Brexiteers admitted they had lost the economic argument for leaving the EU, and adopted a new strategy—one that ultimately helped them to victory. On 25 April 2016, Justice Secretary Michael Gove, a prominent Conservative Leave campaigner, warned in *The Times* that the UK would be threatened with an influx of millions of foreign workers if five prospective members—Macedonia, Montenegro, Serbia, Albania and Turkey—joined the EU.[9] This was the prelude to a far more aggressive use of the immigration issue by the Leave campaign, culminating a week before the referendum in Nigel Farage's unveiling of a new poster. Its slogan, "Breaking Point: the EU is failing us all", was superimposed on an image of a long queue of ostensibly Asian or Middle Eastern refugees. This kind of imagery sat uneasily with the Commonwealth's long history of anti-racism and its celebration of ethnic diversity. It also undermined promises that Brexit would ease restrictions on migration from the Commonwealth.

One can certainly point to some evidence that, alongside its broader slogan of "Take Back Control", the focus on immigration played far better with voters than the prospect of increased trade with the Commonwealth. This was supported by a referendum-day poll of over 12,000 people, conducted by Tory donor and election analyst Lord Ashcroft. In terms of the reasons respondents cited for their vote,

> Nearly half (49%) of leave voters said the biggest single reason for wanting to leave the EU was "the principle that decisions about the UK should be taken in the UK". One third (33%) said the main reason was that leaving "offered the best chance for the UK to regain control over immigration and its own borders." ... Only just over one in twenty (6%) said their main reason was that "when it comes to trade and the economy, the UK would benefit more from being outside the EU than from being part of it."[10]

Furthermore, when respondents who reported voting Leave were asked to rate a series of issues as forces for good or ill, the three issues considered to be forces for ill by the largest percentage were "Multiculturalism" (81%), "Immigration" (80%) and "Social liberalism" (80%).

The remarkably high Leave vote in Hull (see Chapter 1) fits fairly neatly into broader trends that emerged from this poll's granular data. For example, analysts observed an extremely close correlation between the proportion of university graduates in an area and the strength of its Remain vote; Hull conforms closely to this general pattern.[11] According to the Annual Population Survey in 2012, the proportion of its inhabitants with a university degree or equivalent professional qualification was only 22.9%, against a national average of 34.4%. Conversely, 16.2% of people had no qualifications at all, against a national average of 9.7%.[12] Hull is also predominantly white-British in its ethnic composition. 89% of its inhabitants classified themselves as such in the 2011 census, well above the average of 83% for England

and Wales as a whole, but slightly below that of the whole North East (92%). Again, this matches a correlation in the Brexit data between more nationally and ethnically diverse localities and a higher Remain vote. The North East region as a whole saw some of the largest votes in favour of Brexit among largely working-class communities.

As a Brexit stronghold, Hull became a focus of somewhat patronizing media interest when, in 2017, it embarked on a year as the UK's designated 'City of Culture'. Journalists were keen to discover why the city had apparently turned its back on continental Europe, the source of so much of what the British regard as 'high' culture. Their probings unearthed few expressions of warmth towards the idea of the Commonwealth. If there was a sense of nostalgia, the 'high seas' that lingered in the collective memories of the city were the grounds of its old fishing industry, which went into terminal decline in the 1970s. If there was any yearning to turn back the clock, it was to a time when the trawlers still provided plentiful employment.

In another reflection of broader national trends, the key issue motivating Hull voters seemed to have been immigration, as the *Guardian* journalist David Conn discovered when he spoke to residents of the city's Orchard Park housing estate. This is where I went to school between the ages of nine and thirteen. Even with my very limited experience of the wider world, I realized at the time that the residents of Orchard Park hadn't exactly won first prize in the lottery of life, and in the forty years since I left the school, the area has undergone further decline. It is now one of the most deprived wards in the country, with 50.2% of all children under sixteen classified as living in poverty, compared with 31.7% across Hull and 20.1% nationally.

One middle-aged woman told Conn that her neighbours had been motivated by resentment towards Polish immigrants who had moved to the estate, and had voted for Brexit because they "thought it would get rid of the foreigners". A local Labour councillor complained of "a strange fear of foreigners" among residents.[13] This was despite the fact that, according to the Office of National Statistics, between mid-2015 and mid-2016 there was a 22 per cent increase in international emigration from Hull, more than counterbalancing the 6 per cent increase in the number of international migrants arriving in the city from other countries.[14]

The importance of the immigration debate in Hull also fits neatly with the findings of political scientists who have sought to explain the Brexit vote. British Social Attitudes commissioned a survey in the wake of the referendum that looked for correlations between individual voters' views on different issues and their propensity to vote Leave. It found, perhaps not surprisingly, that attitudes to immigration were a significant determinate. Those who were worried about the subject voted overwhelmingly in favour of leaving the EU (73 per cent), against only 36 per cent of those who did not identify it as a concern. The author of the report, Professor John Curtice, believed that these attitudes were at the heart of the Brexit vote:

> for the most part the outcome of the referendum reflected the concern of more 'authoritarian', socially conservative voters in Britain— that is, primarily older voters and those with few, if any, educational qualifications—about some of the social consequences of EU membership, most notably in respect of immigration. In a society in which relatively few have ever felt a strong sense of European identity, the debate about EU membership seems to have brought that concern to the fore such that in the event a narrow majority voted to leave.[15]

Concerns about immigration, then, yes. But 'imperial nostalgia'? I very much doubt it. Instead, one detects a deeply entrenched sense of insularity, which decades of rhetoric about being members of the Commonwealth 'family' have done little to displace. Unlike the EU, however, the Commonwealth has not been the subject of obsessive attacks by the British tabloid press since the 1980s. And it can no longer be represented as a threat to what many Brexit voters appear to hold dear. From the 1962 Commonwealth Immigrants Act to the 1981 British Nationality Act, a series of laws gradually denied Commonwealth citizens their right to enter and settle in the UK. This means that the Commonwealth is no longer associated in the popular imagination with mass migration.

The Economic Myth of the Commonwealth

Whether or not it played a significant part in swaying voters in the 2016 referendum, the notion of the Commonwealth as a potentially huge trading opportunity for the UK was certainly frequently invoked. Once the result was announced, purveyors of this particular Commonwealth myth were busy celebrating. Less than a week after the poll, *The Daily Telegraph* carried an article by Lord Howell, chairman of the Royal Commonwealth Society, entitled 'A bright future awaits Britain post-Brexit in the Commonwealth markets'. The piece rehearsed a series of arguments that had been regularly trotted out by Commonwealth enthusiasts for two decades, including the idea of a 'Commonwealth Advantage' in terms of the ease and cost of trade, and the notion that the world's future growth areas would be outside the EU: "it is to Asia, Africa and Latin America we need to look for the big prizes, and the Commonwealth network is the gateway to many of these fast-growing new economies".[16]

In the light of the Brexit vote, Britain is now forced to take that sort of analysis more seriously than it had to before 23 June 2016. It is therefore worth considering how and why this view of the Commonwealth managed to gain such traction. The answer lies in part in a brief and not very well-substantiated 1994 *Round Table* article by the Australian scholar Katherine West, entitled

'Britain, the Commonwealth and the Global Economy',[17] The piece began with the proposition that, far from being a 'passport to prosperity' for the UK, Europe had "become an economic black spot, with double-digit unemployment, and the lowest rates of growth in the developed world." It suggested that the British government's "Eurocentric political rhetoric" tended to disguise the importance to Britain of markets outside the EU. West then moved to note "the spectacular economic growth" of Asian markets, suggesting again that "myopic concentration" on Europe on the part of British policy-makers was an impediment to the exploitation of these markets.

West posited the existence of a "Commonwealth business culture", based on a shared language, and on shared legal and accountancy practices. She invoked Samuel Huntington's 'The Clash of Civilizations' (1993) in support of this argument that there was a strong link between economic and cultural ties. The article acknowledged that the legacy of colonialism was a complicating factor in all this:

> Inevitably, to varying degrees, negative feelings of resentment survive from what some people still perceive as the unjustified oppression or at least insensitivity of aspects of British colonial rule, and to the extent that such criticism is publicly expressed it continues to give rise to feelings of guilt, or at least embarrassment, among many decision makers in Britain today.

Yet this obstacle, West suggested, was counter-balanced by widespread respect for "aspects of Britain's cultural and institutional influence".

The article might well have remained in well-deserved obscurity. One of the central planks of its case would be badly dented by 1997's disastrous crash in the Asian markets. In the meantime, however, West had found an influential champion in the form of David Howell, chair of the House of Commons Foreign Affairs Committee. West's work was one of the few academic sources cited in the Committee's April 1996 report on the future of the Commonwealth. *The Round Table* heralded the report as "authoritative" and noted that it was essentially "a rather bullish, basically investment- and trade-weighted essay". Among its central themes was the range of economic opportunities for Britain in the then booming Asian and Pacific markets.[18] Tony Blair's New Labour government, which took office in May 1997, initially seemed keen to run with this particular baton. The UK was about to host a CHOGM for the first time in twenty years, and the idea of the Commonwealth as an instrument to promote British trade seemed a useful way of fitting this rather creaking institution into New Labour's modernizing agenda. According to Blair's communications director, Alastair Campbell, at a Cabinet meeting in October 1997 immediately ahead of the Edinburgh CHOGM, Foreign Secretary Robin Cook "did a number on CHOGM, emphasising how we are trying to give it a bigger business and economic pitch."[19] As part of this broader commitment, the summit witnessed the birth of the Commonwealth Business Council (CBC), which in its early years commanded the support of some leading business figures in the UK and other member states.

Yet this new commercially-minded love affair between the Blair government and the Commonwealth was fairly short-lived. In the short term, Blair himself seemed disillusioned from virtually his first sight of the Commonwealth in action, irritated by the drawn-out and inconclusive nature of the Edinburgh CHOGM. Campbell records that, during the summit, Blair's thoughts were dominated by the entirely separate problem of agreeing his government's line on the European Economic and Monetary Union; the prime minister "said he was really frustrated having to spend so much time on CHOGM stuff when he ought to be sorting this damned statement."[20] In the longer term, and particularly following 9/11, Blair's attentions focused on Anglo-American relations and the

Middle East. Not only was the Commonwealth sidelined, but its high ideals sometimes came into conflict with the exigencies of the 'War on Terror'. For example, aid flows from the UK to Pakistan, a key ally in this strategy, increased fivefold between 2001 and 2004, despite the fact that Pakistan remained suspended from the Commonwealth over General Musharraf's failure to return his country to civilian rule.

Nevertheless, it was clear that promoting the notion of the Commonwealth as an under-utilized business asset was a way of persuading the British government to take it seriously. Over the next two decades, the Royal Commonwealth Society, the Commonwealth Business Council and the Secretariat pushed the idea vigorously. In particular, they suggested that there was a 'Commonwealth Effect' that rendered intra-Commonwealth trade cheaper and easier, an idea we can trace back to West's 1994 article. In 2015, the Secretariat published the latest set of data purporting to demonstrate this in its trade review, 'The Commonwealth in the Unfolding Global Trade Landscape'. The research for this report was overseen by Deodat Maharaj, deputy secretary-general for economic and social development at the Secretariat. Its message was that intra-Commonwealth trade was growing rapidly in significance: "In 2013, intra-Commonwealth trade, including in goods as well as services, stood at $592 billion, achieved through an average annual growth of almost 10 per cent each year since 1995. It is projected to exceed $1 trillion by 2020."[21] The report also claimed that "when bilateral partners are both Commonwealth members, they trade on average 20 per cent more", and that, compared with other country pairs, "the bilateral trade costs for Commonwealth partners are, on average, 19 per cent lower".[22]

These figures are now regularly rehearsed at Commonwealth gatherings, but there has been little objective analysis of this report. We might well be cautious in reading too much into its headline figures. First, as the study notes, there are wide variations in the extent to which individual Commonwealth countries trade with others. For some, the proportion is relatively low. The UK is mentioned in this context alongside Canada as countries "which are positioned close to large non-Commonwealth markets." By contrast, there are other member states, like Singapore, Malaysia and Lesotho, which enjoy greater geographical proximity to major Commonwealth trading partners, and so conduct a much higher proportion of intra-Commonwealth trade. Given both this and the fact that there are huge variations in the levels of trade conducted by individual member states, it is difficult to see what we can actually learn from an average figure for 'Commonwealth advantage' between two notional Commonwealth states. As Sir Ronald Sanders, a veteran of Commonwealth and international trade negotiations, notes,

> Six Commonwealth countries dominate exports to other Commonwealth countries. They are: Singapore 26%, India 20.37%, Malaysia 26.14%, Australia 10.9%, Britain 9.5% and Canada 6.7%. The other 45 countries between them account for the remaining 16% and they include big countries like Nigeria, South Africa, and Kenya in Africa, and Pakistan, Bangladesh and Sri Lanka in Asia. The small countries of the Caribbean and the Pacific account for less than 5% of all Commonwealth exports.[23]

Second, the study's numbers are questionable. It acknowledges that "because there are no standard measures of trade costs between countries", it is extremely difficult to test the hypothesis that they are lower between Commonwealth states. Consequently, it merely draws an inference from actual trade flows, and the results should perhaps be treated as extremely provisional. But even if we take the report's findings at face value, their implications are fairly modest as a basis for proposing major realignments in a country's trading patterns. The basic claim is that, after controlling for the major factors that generally determine trade flows, like proximity—and the study admits that the average distance between Commonwealth markets is 9,500 kilometres—member states are still 20 per cent more likely to trade with each other. This 20 per cent 'bonus' is unlikely to be of much economic significance, given the limited size of most bilateral trade between two Commonwealth countries.

In 2015, 44 per cent of UK goods and services went to the EU. By contrast, the entire rest of the Commonwealth received only 9.5 per cent of UK exports. This is because intra-Commonwealth trade figures have been shaped more by a mixture of hard economic reality and historical accident than by any so-called 'Commonwealth Effect'. From the mid-1950s to around the late 1980s, there was a fairly steady reduction in the proportion of total British exports and imports flowing to and from the Commonwealth. This was very much due to the revival of the economies of Western Europe, which had been devastated by the Second World War on the one hand, and the 1948 General Agreement on Tariffs and Trade on the other. This agreement began to unwind the UK's preferential trading agreements with its remaining colonies and with the Commonwealth.

Britain's entry into the EEC in 1973 did not see any marked change in this pattern of decline, partly because Britain's first application to join the EEC in 1961 had already given the UK's major Commonwealth trading partners, such as Australia and New Zealand, ample warning of the need to diversify. What EEC membership did herald was a roughly decade-long period when the UK's trade-in-goods deficit with the Commonwealth became a surplus, as the decline in imports outstripped that of exports.[24] From a historic low in the late 1980s, there has subsequently been a slight revival in imports from the Commonwealth, while exports have flatlined since the end of the '90s at just under 10 per cent.

In terms of the overall share of British trade conducted with Commonwealth countries, perhaps the single biggest factor in shaping the current pattern came down to sheer chance. In 1948, during a visit to Canada, the taoiseach of the Irish Free State, John Costello, announced that his country was leaving the Commonwealth. The move was unexpected and remains something of a mystery to historians of Irish foreign policy. The subsequent Republic of Ireland Act came into force in April 1949. Had Costello not been moved to make his announcement when he did, he would have witnessed the transformation of the Commonwealth's nature by the decision to allow India to remain as a republic. In light of that development, had Southern Ireland not already left the Commonwealth, there is at least a good chance that it would never have done so. In 2015, around 5 per cent of British exports went to the Republic of Ireland— had it remained a member, this alone would have made contemporary British trade with the Commonwealth around 50 per cent higher. This would no doubt have been presented as further evidence of the 'Commonwealth Effect'.

In terms of individual Commonwealth states, even the export figures to some of the UK's traditional and prosperous trading partners are relatively low: 1.6 per cent in the case of Australia and only 0.2 per cent for New Zealand. In terms of British trade, geographical proximity is obviously a key determinate, and although many Commonwealth states have large and growing populations, they tend to be relatively distant. The markets of the so-called BRICS countries (Brazil, Russia, India, China and South Africa), with their vast combined populations, will clearly play an increasingly important role in global trade in the years to come. But their distance from the UK means that they currently receive only 8 per cent of total British exports. Sir Simon Fraser, who served as permanent under-secretary at the FCO from 2010 to 2015, reflected on this issue in his February 2017 Tacitus lecture:

> Switzerland has about one third of the population of Canada, but imports twice as much from the UK. It is our third largest trade partner outside the EU, after the US and China. Over 70% of UK

agricultural exports go to the EU, where it is easier and cheaper to get them fresh to market. By any calculation, the trade strategy for Global Britain has to start with Europe and America ... Australia and New Zealand are keen for trade deals. The problem is that between them they account for less than 2% of our exports. When Australia made an F[ree] T[rade] A[greement] with the US, their trade grew about 70% over a decade, but academics suggest much of this was diversion of trade from other Australian partners. For the UK, early FTAs with Australia and New Zealand are desirable in political terms, but secondary in economic terms. Should they be a priority for deploying limited trade negotiating resources?[25]

As Fraser notes, so great is the UK's current dependence on trade with the European Union that "[i]f we were to lose 5% of our trade with the EU, we would need a 25% increase in our trade with the BRICS, or with the Commonwealth, to recoup that loss before any new gains were made." Nothing in even the most bullish reports from the Secretariat or the Royal Commonwealth Society suggests that this is remotely likely. Indeed, the proportion of British trade conducted with the Commonwealth has remained fairly stable since around 2008, irrespective of the increase in monetary value of intra-Commonwealth trade as a whole. Given that growth rates across much of the developing world have been hit recently by falling commodity prices, there seems little immediate prospect of any change here.

As my colleague Sue Onslow has noted, one of the most striking features of the run-up to the July 2016 Brexit referendum was that Commonwealth member states were virtually as one in wishing Britain to remain part of the EU.[26] To understand this uncharacteristic outbreak of unanimity, one needs to understand how much has changed since the 1960s. British membership of the EEC in 1973 entailed the termination of its existing preferential trading arrangements with Commonwealth members. In their place, the UK helped to negotiate the Lomé agreements, initially between forty-six African, Caribbean and Pacific (APC) states and the then nine member states of the EEC. They began by ensuring privileged access to the European market for commodities such as sugar and bananas and for some manufactured goods, and also included agreements on aid. The Lomé agreements were superseded in 2000 by the Cotonou Agreement, this time between seventy-nine APC countries and fifteen EU member states. As these agreements developed, they expanded in scope to embrace a range of other issues including debt relief and structural adjustment, and enshrined a number of conditions for receiving aid, in areas such as human rights and democratization.

With the establishment of the World Trade Organization in 1995 came new rules requiring the gradual phasing out of existing preferential trading agreements with the EU. This necessitated a fresh set of deals compatible with WTO regulations. The new aim was to establish Economic Partnership Agreements (EPAs) with APC countries. These were in the nature of Free Trade Agreements in that they offered full access to the EU market; but they also allowed APC partners a transitional period to open their own markets, offering APC producers some protection against cheaper European imports. Those countries that failed to negotiate EPAs, either individually or as part of a regional group, had to fall back on the EU's Generalized System of Preferences, which offered access to the EU market at reduced or zero tariffs on less advantageous terms than an EPA's.

Although the signatories to the original Lomé agreements did not include 'older' Commonwealth members, in recent years the EU has sought to establish trade deals with these areas as well. As EU law expert Steve Peers pointed out in 2015, this means that any notion of the Brexit referendum as a choice between Europe and the Commonwealth was a false one. In June 2016, the EU already had in place or was negotiating trade agreements with 90 per cent of non-EU-member Commonwealth countries, including the handful that accounted for the vast majority of intra-Commonwealth trade. Specifically, agreements were already in place with eighteen, deals agreed with another fourteen were awaiting ratification, and negotiations were underway with a further thirteen.[27]

In February 2017, for example, the European Parliament endorsed the Comprehensive Economic and Trade Agreement (CETA) between the EU and Canada. The hope is that, by eliminating around 98 per cent of export tariffs, the deal will give a 20 per cent boost to a trading relationship already worth around €60 billion a year. At least until it leaves the Union, Britain, as Canada's principal EU trading partner, will benefit considerably from this boost. The deal itself took around seven years to negotiate, and that process only began after several years of preparing the ground for talks. It may be another number of years before, as is necessary, all EU member states formally ratify the deal, and there are questions about whether the UK will remain bound by elements of the original agreement if this process is completed before it leaves the EU in March 2019. In other words, though it seems likely that this template would speed up the conclusion of a bilateral UK-Canadian agreement, even then it would be time consuming and labour-intensive. Nor does the CETA precedent bode well for the prospects of post-Brexit Britain swiftly negotiating a similar deal with the EU itself. Meanwhile, Singapore, which was the UK's leading Commonwealth export destination in the first three months of 2016, is also finalizing a trade deal with the EU from which the UK would stand to benefit.

In short, as far as the UK's future trading relationships with Commonwealth members are concerned, Brexit throws everything into confusion. There have been some suggestions that, purely on legal technicalities, the UK could simply continue to operate under EU trade agreements with Commonwealth and other affected states. Be that as it may, the UK would certainly face immediate challenges from other states on the grounds that WTO rules forbid it from discriminating between trade partners. The working assumption, therefore, is that the current EU agreements, which allow developing Commonwealth countries access to the UK market under advantageous terms, would lapse in Britain from the moment that Brexit takes effect. It will only be after that point that the UK has the legal capacity to negotiate trade agreements independently of the EU.

This means that many less developed Commonwealth countries that currently conduct a significant proportion of their trade with the UK will be hit by an immediate tariff hike. Given the finite resources available to the British government for complex trade negotiations, and that attention is likely to be focused on the more lucrative markets of Europe, Asia and North America, APC Commonwealth countries quite reasonably fear that they will be a relatively low priority for Brexit Britain. From the UK's perspective, even if there is the capacity and the will to put in place close bilateral equivalents of the EU's EPAs or Generalized System of Preferences, it seems highly unlikely that these would actually serve to boost trade with APC Commonwealth members. Many member states have already resisted the terms of EU EPAs, on the grounds that these threatened to make their own producers and manufacturers gradually more vulnerable to competition in the domestic market from European imports. While the EU itself was sympathetic to their concerns, it was bound by WTO rules that prevented it from granting privileged access to its own markets without corresponding reductions of tariffs by its trading partners. It seems extremely unlikely that APC Commonwealth members will prove any more enthusiastic about opening up their markets when the time comes for future bilateral trade talks with the UK. In this light, Brexiteer rhetoric about Britain reorienting its exports away from 'stagnant' European markets towards some of the developing world's most vibrant markets seems highly optimistic.

As British prime minister (2010–16), David Cameron made a series of high-profile visits to India with the explicit aim of fostering closer business links. On his trip in February 2013, he brought with him the largest trade delegation ever taken by a UK premier to any country in the world. One of the striking features of Cameron's public statements on these visits was his downplaying of the Commonwealth. At a press meeting at Unilever headquarters in Mumbai, although he spoke of the "huge ties obviously of history, and language and culture and business", he did not refer to the Commonwealth by name either in his speech or in his subsequent answers to questions.[28] Both Cameron and his speechwriters most likely realized that the organization as an idea holds little currency among Indian political and business leaders. Alongside this particular dog that didn't bark, Cameron's visits were marked by regular complaints from the Indian side about their students' and business representatives' difficulty in obtaining UK visas. It seems highly likely that this issue will feature prominently in any post-Brexit trade negotiations between Britain and India. Given the significant role of immigration issues in the Brexit referendum, this is likely to prove a major sticking point in talks.

There are a number of broader concerns about the future of post-Brexit Britain's Commonwealth relations. The EU as a whole represents an important market for many developing Commonwealth states. If Brexit damages the prosperity of other EU members, this is likely to have a detrimental effect on international trade, at the expense of countries struggling to increase their export earnings. Perhaps more significantly, the Commonwealth relationship was valued by many of its members precisely because of the significant role Britain played in major organizations such as the EU. Commonwealth discussions became a means of seeking to persuade the UK to use its influence elsewhere in ways that would serve the interests of developing nations. African countries, for example, were critical of the subsidies to European farmers provided by the Common Agricultural Policy, which they quite reasonably saw as placing their own producers at a disadvantage. As a long-time critic of the Policy, the UK was a valuable champion in these nations' efforts to lobby Brussels on the issue.

There are other ways in which British influence within the EU will be missed. Through its Aid for Trade programme and other initiatives, the EU channels a considerable amount of financial assistance to its trading partners in the developing world. As a major contributor—currently providing around £1.4 billion into the EU foreign aid pot—Britain has significant influence over how these funds are disbursed. Not only will Britain cease to exercise that influence after it leaves the EU, but its departure will obviously also create a major gap in the organization's aid budget. This is a major concern not only for some of the Commonwealth's poorer countries but also to the fourteen Overseas Territories, which remain under British sovereignty and as such are associated with the EU. When in July 2017 the House of Lords European Union Committee took evidence from representatives of the Territories, a number of them expressed concerns about the withdrawal of EU aid via the European Development Fund. Victor Banks, chief minister of Anguilla, noted that support from the Fund was his country's only major source of development aid, accounting for 36 per cent of Anguilla's capital budget in 2016.[29] This is another unforeseen consequence of Brexit. And with so many other more pressing matters to negotiate, it is quite possible that the British government may not prioritize plugging these sorts of financial gaps.

Meanwhile, attempts to chart a new economic course for Britain's economic relations with the Commonwealth have not got off to a particularly auspicious start. When Commonwealth trade ministers met in London in March 2017, there was a concerted push by both the Secretariat and the May government to talk up the prospects for post-Brexit trade deals. This inspired familiar rhetoric about the supposed 'Commonwealth Effect', with Secretary-General Patricia Scotland claiming that "Because we share common law, common language, common institutions and common parliamentary structures, that has given us a de facto advantage". This was something "which we as a Commonwealth are absolutely determined to exploit and to grow, and at this meeting today we were able to have a comprehensive opportunity to consider how in practice we do that."[30] The chairman of the Commonwealth Enterprise and Investment Council, Jonathan Marland, suggested that in the lead-up to the London CHOGM in April 2018 it might be possible to "develop a standard of rules—which could be a Commonwealth accord—[identifying] common business practices within the Commonwealth countries [that] countries can subscribe to." Like Baroness Scotland, he presented the Commonwealth as an area with substantial post-Brexit trading opportunities: "What easier and better place to trade than with countries who have shared associations for many years, where you speak the same language, where you have the same basic rule of law? That's why we need to come up with an accord that underlines that."[31]

One year ahead of the CHOGM, *The Times* added a note of dissonance to the mood music by running a story with the incendiary headline 'Ministers aim to build "empire 2.0" with African Commonwealth'. This referred to plans supposedly being discussed in Whitehall to encourage the creation of an African free trade zone, with which Britain would work closely. According to the article, "The 'empire 2.0' description was coined by sceptical officials worried about the high priority given to trade deals with Commonwealth nations." One unnamed Whitehall source rather cheekily referred to the planned free trade area as "covering 26 countries from the Cape to Cairo".[32] This invocation of Cecil

Rhodes's famous imperial dream (see Chapter 5) may have been particularly pointed. It was reported in July 2017 that Liam Fox had selected "a lithograph of British imperialist Cecil Rhodes" as one of the artworks to decorate his Department for International Trade.[33] Fox certainly seemed sufficiently rattled by the *Times* report to disavow the label 'Empire 2.0', telling Sky News, "That's not a phrase I would ever allow them [civil servants] to use".

Mention of 'Empire 2.0' drew condemnations from predictable quarters. For the former Indian minister and Congress MP, Shashi Tharoor, they could not have come at a better time. He had just published *Inglorious Empire* (see Chapter 5), and the *Times* story seemed to provide definitive proof of the UK's lack of contrition over its imperial record. Claiming that there was no contemporary awareness of British colonial atrocities or of "the fact that Britain financed its Industrial Revolution and its prosperity from the depredations of empire",[34] he predicted that the idea of a Commonwealth Free Trade area would go down "like a lead balloon" in India.[35] Meanwhile, writing in *The Guardian*, Kehinde Andrews argued that the UK government had "deluded itself into thinking that Britain can just install an update for empire and return to former glories on the world stage. But outside the EU and devoid of colonies, Britain will find that any nostalgic visions of empire are a mirage, providing nothing to sustain it."[36]

A House Divided

Just as the British government finally seemed to be taking the Commonwealth seriously, the organization began to suffer from the sort of negative publicity it had hitherto managed to avoid. By the time of the 2015 CHOGM in Malta, there was a widespread desire to turn a new page in the history of the Commonwealth and leave behind the lackluster Sharma era (2008–16). As a prelude to this new dawn, the organization opened the process of selecting his successor to a degree of public scrutiny. Previously, the appointment of Commonwealth secretaries-general had borne a marked resemblance to the election of a new Pope by the College of Cardinals. Behind closed doors at their biennial CHOGM, Commonwealth leaders had proposed names, scrutinized and bargained, until a successful candidate finally 'emerged'. 2015 was very different. After much speculation and some testing of the waters by potential candidates, by the time the government heads convened in November, three hopefuls remained who had very publicly thrown their hats into the ring.

The three candidates left standing were Mmasekgoa Masire-Mwamba, the Botswanan nominee; Sir Ronald Sanders of Antigua and Barbuda; and Dominica's Baroness Patricia Scotland. Masire-Mwamba was the quintessential 'safe pair of hands'. She had served loyally under Sharma as deputy secretary-general and was widely respected. She was likely to command the support of the majority of the organization's African members. Some felt, however, that she was too closely associated with Sharma to give the Commonwealth the fresh start it needed. The remaining two candidates were both nominees of the Caribbean. This in itself was rather odd. There was a general understanding that the position of secretary-general would rotate across the regions of the Commonwealth. Previous holders of the post had come, respectively, from Canada, Guyana, Nigeria, New Zealand, and India. Given that Canada and New Zealand both fell into the category of the realm of 'middle-aged white male', and that the former had been a serious critic of the organization in recent years, it was unlikely that Canada would be accorded another spin of the wheel. It seemed, then, to be 'the turn' of either Africa or the Caribbean. But there was also an expectation that leaders from these regions would put their heads together and come up with a single candidate for each. Yet as the 2015 CHOGM approached, neither Sanders nor Scotland displayed any inclination to step aside, and the Caribbean divided behind their two camps.

Born in Guyana, Sanders was a businessman and diplomat who had twice served as Antigua and Barbuda's high commissioner to Britain, in 1982–7 and 1996–2004. He had been knighted in 2002, and, as we know, served on the Commonwealth Eminent Persons Group that reported in 2011 on reforming the organization. Sanders was also Sonny Ramphal's son-in-law. Although originally from Dominica, Patricia Scotland's family had moved to the UK when she was only two. One of twelve siblings, Scotland's rise was a remarkable one. In 1991, she became the first black woman in the UK to be appointed Queen's counsel. She received a life peerage in 1997, taking the Labour whip in the House of Lords. She served in a number of ministerial posts in the Blair governments before being made attorney general by Gordon Brown in 2007.

While there were signs in the press of negative briefing against both Scotland and Sanders, it was the latter who undoubtedly sustained the greater damage. Virtually on the eve of the vote, *The Daily Telegraph* published a hostile story, repeating allegations of corruption dating back to a 2009 investigation in Antigua.[37] The report acknowledged that Antigua's police commissioner had confirmed to Sanders in June 2015 that there were no current or pending investigations against him, but reproduced papers from both sides: a statement from the lawyers claiming that this "conclusively exonerate[d] our client and, as far as he is concerned, represents the end of the matter", as well as original documents purporting to substantiate the original allegations. Coming so close to the vote, the *Telegraph* piece left no time for the Sanders camp to issue a more detailed refutation. Whether it swung any votes may never be known. But when heads met to consider the selection of a new secretary-general, Sanders was the first of the three candidates to be knocked out. It apparently required three rounds of voting before Scotland finally won, beating Masire-Mwamba by the narrowest of margins: twenty-six votes to twenty-four.

Scotland barely had time to settle herself into her new role before she found herself on the sharp end of even more hostile press attention. Interestingly, these stories only began once the EU referendum was safely out of the way. This may have been coincidence, but the negative press mostly came from *The Mail on Sunday* and *The Daily Mail*, the latter having campaigned vigorously for a Leave vote. Could it have been that *The Daily Mail* didn't want to tarnish the image of the Commonwealth—that supposedly 'natural' alternative to the EU—before the result was safely in the bag? Scotland had certainly not endeared herself to those pro-Brexit campaigners who had advocated leaving the EU as somehow a precondition for closer links with the Commonwealth. Whereas Sharma would probably have attempted to keep out of the debate altogether, Scotland made her personal position very plain. On taking office in April 2016, two months before the referendum, she told Reuters, "I say the Commonwealth offers a huge amount, but the Commonwealth does not set itself up in competition with Europe—we are partners". She went on, "As far as I can see, partnership is a much better way forward than separation for any of us". With regard to the UK's current membership of the EU, she added, "I haven't heard any Commonwealth country say they have an appetite for change".[38]

The press campaign against Scotland began with a *Mail on Sunday* headline on 3 July 2016: '"Baroness Brazen" under fire for handing £90,000 to Labour crony's firm to review her staff's efficiency—and £325,000 more to carry out the changes.' There were follow-up stories later in the month by both *The Mail on Sunday* and *The Mail*, and another spate of attacks in October and November. Meanwhile, their various allegations were taken up in the UK by right-wing blog Guido Fawkes and satirical magazine *Private Eye*. Two of the most prominent allegations against the new secretary-general related to the business of the Secretariat itself. The first concerned the fact that Scotland had brought in a consultancy firm, KYA Global, to advise on reforms to the Secretariat. The firm's director, Lord Patel, was a fellow Labour peer. This provided Scotland's critics in the media with the basis for claims of 'cronyism'; that normal procurement procedures had not been followed in comissioning the work from KYA Global, and that its fee would be as high as £415,000. The second major allegation concerning the Commonwealth claimed that extravagant embellishments to the secretary-general's official residence in Mayfair, approved personally by Scotland, were likely to be almost double the original refurbishment costs to around £450,000.[39] There were also claims about her salary and benefits demands and the cost of two advisors; allegations about the role of controversial PR consultant Anthony Bailey in her bid to become secretary-general; and suggestions that, in her early career, she had given legal advice to repressive governments, such as those of Kazakhstan and the Maldives.[40]

Of course, no Commonwealth scandal would be complete without a royal dimension. This was duly supplied in a report by the BBC's diplomatic correspondent, James Landale, in January 2017. The Palace had confirmed that the Queen would not, despite firm tradition, attend the evening reception at Marlborough House on Commonwealth Day in March. Landale suggested that "such are the concerns about Lady Scotland that some senior diplomats have even interpreted the fact that the Queen will not attend a major Commonwealth function in March as a signal of royal displeasure, something that is strongly denied." An unnamed "senior source" noted,

> The Queen has only got to nip down the road from Buckingham Palace to Marlborough House in a Bentley. It's not that hard. And yet she has decided not to come. The Palace are thinking there is so

much more to be done with the Commonwealth and yet they are lumbered with such poor leadership. The Commonwealth is stuffed.[41]

This final sentence might not have had a particularly regal tone to it. But concerns within the Palace about the leadership of the Commonwealth are undoubtedly long-standing. A few years ago, during the Sharma era, one of my colleagues found herself sitting next to a senior Palace aide at a formal dinner. His verdict on the Secretariat was that it was "risk-averse and rudderless", an icily alliterative phrase that lodged itself firmly in my memory.

Scotland submitted complaints against the newspapers printing these various allegations to the Independent Press Standards Organisation, a recently established body responsible for self-regulation. In June 2017, it ruled that, although there had been various inaccuracies in the reports, the papers had not in the main violated the body's editorial code of standards. This was despite the fact that they had certainly contributed to a misleading impression of personal extravagance on Scotland's part. She was keen to point out, for example, that her predecessor had signed off £276,000 for the renovation work on the secretary-general's official residence, and that the final bill was only £338,000, far less than the £450,000 figure carried in some reports. Furthermore, KYA Global had ultimately been paid £180,000, not the £415,000 posited in some artcles. In an interview with *The Guardian*, clearly intended to counter recent adverse publicity, it was suggested that being a black woman from the centre-left of British politics might well have made Scotland an attractive target to *The Daily Mail*.[42]

For some informed observers of Commonwealth politics, there were also other explanations for Scotland being targeted in this way. The first was that we were witnessing what one might call a powerful 'aftershock' of the accusations traded during the secretary-general's election campaign. The second was that we were also seeing a fightback by officials within the Secretariat, who felt threatened by Scotland's reforming agenda. As she prepared to take over her new role, a powerful message had been impressed upon her that Marlborough House needed a thorough shake-up if it was to improve on its recent lamentable performance. Bringing in trusted consultants and personal aides from outside, rather than relying on the Secretariat's existing staff, signalled clearly that Scotland was ready to deliver radical change. Could this have been the reason that Marlborough House suddenly seemed to be leaking like a sieve?

In June 2016 Ram Venuprasad was suspended from his post as deputy head of office to the secretary-general for passing information to the press. In his resignation letter a few months later, he added further detail to the allegations against Scotland. For some of her supporters, the criticisms were simply cries of pain from an organization that was being subjected to a thorough and timely overhaul. The former international development secretary, Andrew Mitchell, suggested to *The Guardian* that Scotland's troubles arose because "there are so many entrenched vested interests. And they will be out to get anyone who is serious about reform."[43]

Secretary-General Scotland, then, may well have been more sinned against than sinning. But the personal stories about her provided the press with a peg on which to hang more serious criticisms of the Commonwealth. Had she not already been in the spotlight, there might have been considerably less media interest in Whitehall's poor opinion of the Secretariat when it came to aid provision. As it was, at the end of 2016 journalists picked up on grievances that had long been bubbling under the surface and gave them particular prominence.

In 2011, the Department for International Development (DFID)'s Multilateral Aid Review had put the Secretariat on formal warning that its funding was at risk if it did not improve. It was subsequently placed in a 'special measures' programme, under which its performance was to be regularly reviewed. An interim report commissioned by DFID noted in 2013 that, while the Australian government had also expressed dissatisfaction with the Secretariat, these warnings had "not resulted in a clear response from the organisation, which has historically been slow to change."[44] As such, it won't have surprised many that DFID's major review of 2016, published in December of that year, was scathing. It concluded that "[w]hile the Commonwealth Secretariat has worked to sharpen its strategic focus and reduce the number of projects it manages, its commitment to delivering better value for money has not been demonstrated".[45] It added that the Commonwealth's implementing body—the Secretariat—continued to underperform, as it had done since the 2011 Multilateral Aid Review. "Improvement is essential if DFID is to continue to fund the organisation's Commonwealth Fund for Technical Co-operation. The Secretariat requires urgent organisational reform, while the Co-operation Fund needs greater strategic focus. The Secretariat and the Fund are both unsustainably reliant on UK funds".[46]

In short, this new era for the Commonwealth under Secretary-General Scotland appears so far to face the same dilemmas as those that have gone before. Arguably, her plight is that of being caught between an organization highly resistant to change, and a British government determined that it should be reformed.

CONCLUSION

SHATTERING THE MYTH

In October 2010, the former Conservative shadow foreign secretary, Michael Ancram, published a pamphlet setting out a new agenda for British foreign policy. The document, entitled 'Farewell to Drift: A New Foreign Policy for a Network World', acknowledged the contribution of Lord Howell, then the recently-appointed minister of state at the FCO, who "shared many thoughts with me and whose own ideas have inspired much of what I have written." The analysis Ancram presented did indeed closely reflect Howell's world-view: the forces of globalization were steadily undermining the significance of old-fashioned power blocs like the EU. Conversely, the Commonwealth, with its lack of treaty or constitution and its emphasis on collaboration and mutual support, was "a readymade vehicle for positive action within the network world."

> For too long the Commonwealth has been under-funded and under-appreciated by many of its members, including the UK. For us it costs only 20p per person per year, while the EU costs £52 per person per year. It urgently needs, with British help, encouragement and involvement to become a bolder organization that recognizes its own strengths. It could have associate members as well as new members; indeed some of the giants of the world like Japan could become

interested especially if it is based in the emerging powerhouse of India. It is in our interest to encourage such countries to become involved in the Commonwealth in one way or another.[1]

During the 2016 referendum campaign, Ancram duly pinned his colours firmly to the Leave mast.[2]

Ancram's encomium nicely encapsulated many elements of the British myth of the Commonwealth. This includes the tension between wishing to use the organization more effectively, and disavowing any wish to lead it. Ancram was not the first Commonwealth enthusiast to recommend moving headquarters to India, the most populous member state—but, over seven years since the publication of this pamphlet, that prospect is no less remote. With so many members of India's policy-making elite seeing the Commonwealth as little more than a quaint relic of British imperialism, there is little chance of them offering it this sort of flag-of-convenience. There was also something familiar in Ancram's ambiguous contrast between the supposed 20p cost of the Commonwealth, against the EU's £52. Were we supposed to conclude that the Commonwealth is better value for money, or simply that it is under-resourced? Commonwealth enthusiasts generally want to have it both ways: the Commonwealth has supposedly vast potential—witness the idea of Japan joining as an associate member—that could be augmented further with a little additional funding, yet membership will always remain cheaper than the EU, and not only in terms of the UK's direct financial contribution. Somehow, this mythical Commonwealth of the future will cost less than the EU in the vast number of hours required to negotiate its treaties and other formal agreements; it will not require members to make significant concessions in return for some collective good; and it will have only the most rudimentary of mechanisms to enforce its will.

In this light, the Commonwealth is the international relations equivalent of a homeopathic remedy: a cadre of staff so small as to be almost invisible when dissolved across an organization of 2.4 billion, which nevertheless does or could achieve miraculous results. But the promise of the Commonwealth can be seen in another, arguably far more realistic way: it is based on the prospect offered by charlatans and quacks throughout the ages—that of something for nothing. In the decades since the Second World War, the process of devising and agreeing mechanisms for European cooperation has indeed been time-consuming and expensive. Yet it has resulted in a series of concrete achievements, above all the creation of the world's largest free-trading bloc. Decisions made at an EU level affect the texture of daily life in its member states in the way that the Commonwealth's empty pronouncements do not. As a result, any contemporary survey of international relations since 1945 is likely to devote considerable space to the EU and little or none to the Commonwealth. Frankly, the EU matters, in the way that the Commonwealth simply does not.

Perhaps there is nothing wrong with this, so long as all members recognize the limitations of such a profoundly informal and tenuous association, and act accordingly: keeping it 'serviced' as Douglas Hurd has suggested, in case it seems capable at some future point of performing a useful function. The problem, as we have seen in the case of Sri Lanka, is that a stagnant organization with a weak leadership and an equally weak sense of ownership among its members is vulnerable to 'capture' by anyone willing to devote the necessary time and energy. Some would argue that this is precisely what the UK itself should be seeking to do. Yet, as we have seen, Britain is locked into an apparently eternal dilemma: while it can seek to shape the organization's priorities behind the scenes, any attempt to seek to 'lead' it is likely to reawaken accusations of residual imperial hubris.

This has long been apparent to those within the British government who engage directly with the Commonwealth. It is far less obvious, however, to the vast majority of people in the UK, who know the organization largely through occasional high-profile events such as the Commonwealth Games, and through the annual family 'round-robin' delivered in the Queen's speech. It is at this level, and in this specifically British context, that the myth of the Commonwealth is arguably at its most dangerous. It encourages perceptions of the organization as some sort of genuine global network with the UK at its centre, the other members ready to fall into line whenever Britain finally decides that it is time to resume a guiding role.

It was this combination of a widespread unfamiliarity with how the modern Commonwealth actually functions, and a lingering sense that it is in some sense a special asset to the UK, that allowed some in the Leave camp to present it during the 2016 referendum campaign as a direct alternative to the EU. This was despite the fact that the vast majority of Commonwealth members, and indeed the secretary-general herself, emphasized that membership of both organizations was not only wholly compatible but also mutually beneficial. The referendum result of 23 June 2016 marked the point when the Commonwealth ceased to be simply a puzzle in Whitehall—an itch the civil service didn't quite know how or where to scratch—and became a contributory factor in, arguably, Britain's greatest foreign policy disaster since the end of the Second World War.

What, then, should be the basis of the UK's future relationship with the Commonwealth? It could be argued that the referendum result has already ordained that this relationship will be an 'ever closer' one. But I doubt that. For the reasons explored in Chapter 8, Brexit is unlikely to enhance British trade with Commonwealth countries. Indeed, in the short term it may actually reduce it, as the UK struggles to replicate deals already in place under its EU membership. There may be closer trading and diplomatic relations with Australia and New Zealand, which represent the 'acceptable face' of the Commonwealth to many Leave supporters. But when it comes to the genuinely vast potential of the Indian market, a UK government committed to reducing immigration in the wake of the referendum vote is unlikely to make great strides in that direction. India seems likely to want a relaxation of visa restrictions on its nationals in return for trade liberalization. Certainly, the issue of immigration overshadowed Theresa May's visit there in November 2016, leading to accusations that the UK wanted India's business, but not its people. And whatever the future holds, invoking the name of the Commonwealth is unlikely to oil the wheels of any UK-Indian trade deal.

In the shorter term, there certainly was a temporary increase in the level of official UK engagement with the Commonwealth, as London prepared to host the April 2018 CHOGM, the first held in the British capital in over forty years. Then, until 2020, the British prime minister will also serve as the organization's chair-in-office. In January 2017, the government agreed to set up a dedicated unit within the Cabinet Office to coordinate preparations for this and to support a special inter-ministerial group, co-chaired by the foreign and home secretaries, to oversee the process. At the time of writing, as the summit approaches, the size of this unit is expected to rise to eighty. Whitehall is also investing in initiatives around a series of themes intended to generate outcomes during the prime minister's period as chair-in-office. This is certainly a major investment in civil service time, at a point when official resources are already stretched by the challenges of negotiating Brexit. The danger is that, with the enthusiastic backing of the Palace, the UK Government might aim for a 'quick win' in terms of newspaper headlines, the obvious one being a deal to secure headship of the Commonwealth for Prince Charles on his mother's death.

Could the UK actually abandon the Commonwealth altogether? In terms of the mechanics of actually leaving the organization run by the Secretariat, the process could be relatively straightforward—certainly infinitely more so than leaving the EU. But, politically, it is difficult to see that happening, particularly so long as the British monarch is head of the organization. As long as the UK continues to be a monarchy, it is also likely to remain part of a 'Commonwealth' of different realms sharing a common sovereign. The most the British government can and probably should do is to re-state publicly their long-held position—shared by the Palace—that it has no interest in perpetuating the monarchical system abroad, and that it is up to the peoples of the Realms to determine their own constitutional futures. That, at least, might puncture the sort of humbug about 'colonial liberation' we have heard in recent years in relation to the Realms.

A final Commonwealth press cutting, and one to break the heart of anyone who remembers the organization in the 1960s and '70s, when it seemed capable of establishing itself as a genuinely progressive force in global politics. In February 2017, *The Daily Telegraph* ran a piece under the arresting headline 'Exclusive: United States could become an "associate member" of the Commonwealth'. Almost inevitably, the story itself proved a little more mundane. It claimed:

> The Royal Commonwealth Society is making plans to open a branch in the United States, with a view to one day bringing America into the fold as an "associate member". The project, which is said to be backed by the Queen, has come about in part as a result of Donald Trump's fondness for Britain and the Royal Family.[3]

This is the sort of opening paragraph one might expect to read in a feature on one of the Internet's many satirical websites. But any comedic value was undermined by a genuinely unsettling detail. According to the story, the idea of a US branch of the Society was raised in a letter to Trump by its director, Michael Lake. This was then "hand carried by Andrew Wigmore, a close aide to Nigel Farage, and then delivered by the former UKIP leader." Lake told *The Telegraph* that plans to launch a US branch had been expedited by "opportunity of a new president, and the slightly dangerous but great fun opportunity that the 'Bad Boys of Brexit' offered".

It is not clear how much influence these 'Bad Boys' were able to exert over Trump, or whether the president himself played any part in the process. But in September 2017 it was announced that the Society's first US branch was indeed opening, in Mississippi of all places, with Governor Phil Bryant serving as its chairman.[4] Bryant, a right-wing Republican supporter of Trump, had recently courted controversy by refusing to back legislation to remove the highly divisive Confederate battle saltire from the State of Mississippi's flag. Needless to say, *The Telegraph* seemed unconcerned by this, boasting instead that the initiative was a boost for UK–US trade.

The whole publicity stunt was so crass and ridiculous that it managed to demean an organization that had already seemed to have shed its final ounce of dignity. We saw in Chapter 2 that the Royal Commonwealth Society's 2015 merger with 'Commonwealth Exchange' has marked a clear shift to the Eurosceptic right. But it is still genuinely shocking to see the Society using Farage as its messenger-boy to a US president whose own personal and political values—in so far as it is possible to pin them down—are repugnant to much of the world's population. Many of those in the UK who were associated with the Commonwealth in the early years of the Secretariat clung to the hope that it would help to make Britain a less insular, more inclusive and more tolerant society. Now, in 2017, we have Commonwealth-related stories in which Trump, Bryant, Farage and the other 'Bad Boys of Brexit' are the principal actors. At the same time, Eurosceptics, currently in the ascendant, are implicitly rehabilitating the racialized, early-twentieth-century notion of the Commonwealth as a cosy and exclusive white Anglo-Saxon club.

In short, we have little to fear from the reality of the Commonwealth, either as an organization that may limp along for a few more years, or as a collection of Realms, which may actually survive a little longer. The main danger to the UK, as was amply demonstrated in the 2016 EU referendum, is the myth of the Commonwealth. It is increasingly being commandeered by a grim collection of charlatans, chancers and outright villains. Our old comfort blanket has become toxic. It's time to grow up and set it aside.

NOTES

NOTE ON ARCHIVAL ABBREVIATIONS

Unless otherwise stated, all archival references are to the UK's National Archives. The following abbreviations have been used:

CAB: Records of the Cabinet Office
DO: Records created or inherited by the Dominions Office
FCO: Foreign and Commonwealth Office
PREM: Prime Minister's Office

PREFACE

1. Timothy M. Shaw, *Commonwealth: Inter- and non-state contributions to global governance* (London, Routledge, 2008).

1. "WHAT DOES THE COMMONWEALTH MEAN TO YOU?"

1. Bill Schwarz, *The White Man's World, Memories of Empire vol. 1* (Oxford, OUP, 2013).

2. MEET THE FAMILY

1. Commonwealth Oral History Project (COHP), interview with David McDowell (Part 2), 2 July 2014, available at: http://sas-space.sas.ac.uk/6120/2/David_McDowell_Transcript_2.pdf [Accessed 16/9/2017], p. 20.
2. Mark Mazower, *Governing the World: The History of an Idea* (London, Penguin, 2013), pp. 128–36. See also Mark Mazower, *No Enchanted*

Place: The End of Empire and the Ideological Origins of the United Nations (Princeton, Princeton UP, 2009).

3. Jim Tomlinson, 'The Empire/Commonwealth in British Economic Thinking and Policy', in Andrew Thompson (ed.), *Britain's Experience of Empire in the Twentieth Century* (Oxford, OUP, 2012), p. 219.

4. Madhav Khosla (ed.), *Letters for a Nation from Jawaharal Nehru to his Chief Ministers 1947–1963* (New Delhi, Penguin India, 2014), pp. 263–4.

5. Ibid., pp. 292–3.

6. See David W. McIntyre, 'The admission of small states to the Commonwealth', *Journal of Imperial and Commonwealth History*, 24/2 (1996), pp. 244–77.

7. Brook to Macmillan, 7 Dec. 1959, PREM 11/2910.

8. Lorna Lloyd, 'Britain and the transformation from Empire to Commonwealth: the significance of the immediate post-war years', *The Round Table*, 343 (1997), pp. 333–60.

9. As defined by Britain's own Nationality Act of 1948.

10. Ronald Hyam and Wm. Roger Louis, *British Documents on the End of Volume: The Conservative Government and the End of Empire, 1957–1964* (London, TSO, 2000), Pt 2, pp. 670–1. This and other documents in this multi-volume series are available via the website British Documents on the End of Empire: https://bdeep.org/.

11. Trevor Reese, 'Keeping Calm about the Commonwealth', *International Affairs*, 41/3 (1965), pp. 451–62, at p. 455.

12. W. David McIntyre, 'Britain and the Creation of the Commonwealth Secretariat', *Journal of Imperial and Commonwealth History*, 28/1 (2000), pp. 135–58, at p. 142.

13. Philip Murphy, *Monarchy and the End of Empire: The House of Windsor, the British Government and the Postwar Commonwealth* (Oxford, OUP, 2013), p. 124.

14. Ibid., pp. 143–4.

15. Ibid., p. 147.

16. Ibid., pp. 147–8.

17. Ibid., p. 151.

18. COHP, interview with David McDowell (Part 1), 24 June 2014, available

at: http://sas-space.sas.ac.uk/6120/1/David_McDowell_Transcript_1. pdf [Accessed 16/9/2017], p. 18.

19. COHP, 'Notes from Tony Eggleton: June 2014', available at http://sas-space.sas.ac.uk/5622/1/Tony_Eggleton.pdf [Accessed 16/9/2017], p. 2.

20. COHP, interview with David McDowell (Part 1), p. 7.

21. Matthew Battey, *Placing knowledge in a decolonising world: the Commonwealth Fund for Technical Cooperation (CFTC) and the histories of expertise for development 1965–1980* (University of London, PhD thesis, 2016).

22. Shridath Ramphal, *Glimpses of a Global Life* (Hertford, Hansib Publications, 2014), p. 386.

23. COHP, interview with Lord Hurd, n.d., available at http://sas-space. sas.ac.uk/5078/2/Lord_Hurd_Transcript.pdf [Accessed 16/9/2017], p. 9.

24. *Hansard, HC* Deb., vol. 120 cc. 921–2 (22 October 1987). The Inkatha Freedom Party, which had its power base in KwaZulu-Natal, had been founded in 1975 by Mangosuthu Buthelezi. During the 1980s it became increasingly hostile to the ANC and enjoyed covert support from the South African government, including training for its militias from the South African Defence Force. Buthelezi enjoyed a welcome ear from Mrs Thatcher and her supporters, who promoted him as a 'reasonable' voice in black South African politics.

25. Simon Allison, 'Analysis: The Khampepe Report, a crushing blow to SA's diplomatic credibility', *The Daily Maverick*, 17 November 2014, https://www.dailymaverick.co.za/article/2014–11–17-analysis-the-khampepe-report-a-crushing-blow-to-sas-diplomatic-credibility/#. WawHkoWcHIU [Accessed 8/1/2018].

26. COHP, interview with John Howard, 31 March 2014, available at http://sas-space.sas.ac.uk/5694/1/John_Howard_Transcript.pdf [Accessed 8/1/2018], p. 5.

27. COHP, interview with Kamalesh Sharma (Part 1), 9 March 2016, available at https://sas-space.sas.ac.uk/6528/1/kamalesh_sharma_transcript1.pdf [Accessed 8/1/2018], pp. 3–4.

28. COHP, interview with Sir Don McKinnon (Part 1), 27 February 2013, available at http://sas-space.sas.ac.uk/6061/1/Don_Mckinnon_Transcript_1.pdf [Accessed 8/1/2018], p. 15.

29. 'Commonwealth Nomenclature': Memorandum by the Prime Minister, Cabinet Paper (48) 307, 30 Dec. 1948.

30. Alex May, *The Round Table, 1910–66*. (University of Oxford, DPhil. Thesis, 1995), p. 1.

31. University of London Academic Council report to Senate, June 1943. Correspondence held by the Institute of Commonwealth Studies.

32. Timothy M. Shaw, *Commonwealth: Inter and Non-State Contributions to Global Governance* (London, Routledge, 2007).

33. Joanna Bennett, Dhananjayan Sriskandarajah and Zoë Ware, 'An Uncommon Association—A Wealth of Potential: The Final Report of the Commonwealth Conversation', Royal Commonwealth Society, 2010, available at https://www.thercs.org/assets/Research-/Commonwealth-Conversation-Final-Report.pdf [Accessed 16/9/2017], p. 42.

34. Ibid., pp. 45–6.

35. Richard Bourne, 'The Commonwealth and Civil Society', in James Mayall (ed.), *The Contemporary Commonwealth: An Assessment 1965–2009* (London, Routledge, 2010), p. 126.

36. Bourne, pp. 125–6.

37. Bennett et al., p. 49.

3. "WHAT IS IT GOOD FOR?"

1. Commonwealth Oral History Project (COHP), interview with Sandra Pepera, 7 August 2014, available at: http://sas-space.sas.ac.uk/5817/1/Sandra_Pepera_Transcript.pdf [Accessed 16/9/2017], p. 27.

2. COHP, interview with Martin Aliker, 22 May 2013, available at: http://sas-space.sas.ac.uk/5880/1/Martin%20Aliker%20Transcript.pdf [Accessed 16/9/2017], p. 1.

3. COHP, interview with K. Shankar Bajpai, 13 June 2013, available at: http://sas-space.sas.ac.uk/5998/1/K%20Shankar%20Bajpai%20Transcript.pdf [Accessed 16/9/2017], p. 11.

4. COHP, interview with Joe Clark, 23 April 2013, available at: https://sas-space.sas.ac.uk/5846/1/Joe%20Clark%20Transcript.pdf [Accessed 16/9/2017], p. 5.

5. COHP, interview with Bob Hawke, 31 March 2014, available at: http://sas-space.sas.ac.uk/6099/1/Bob_Hawke_Transcript.pdf [Accessed 16/9/2017], p. 11.

6. COHP, interview with Rashleigh Jackson, 27 January 2015, available at: http://sas-space.sas.ac.uk/6122/1/Rashleigh_Jackson_Transcript.pdf [Accessed 16/9/2017], pp. 27–8.

7. COHP, interview with Muchkund Dubey, 4 July 2014, available at: https://sas-space.sas.ac.uk/6432/1/Ambassador%20Muchkund%20Dubey%20transcript.pdf [Accessed 16/9/2017], p. 1.

8. COHP, interview with John Howard, 31 March 2014, available at: http://sas-space.sas.ac.uk/5694/1/John_Howard_Transcript.pdf [Accessed 16/9/2017], p. 3.

9. Ibid., p. 4.

10. COHP, interview with Jim Bolger (Part 1), 4 April 2014, available at: https://sas-space.sas.ac.uk/6134/1/Jim_Bolger_Transcript.pdf [Accessed 16/9/2017], p. 2. Bolger's chronology is, of course, a little faulty here. The UK made its first attempt to join the EEC in 1961. His broader point, however, still carries weight.

11. COHP, interview with Aliker, p. 21.

12. COHP, interview with Kamal Hossain, 8 December 2014, available at: http://sas-space.sas.ac.uk/6109/1/Kamal_Hossain_Transcript.pdf [Accessed 16/9/2017], p. 13.

13. COHP, interview with Neville Linton, 16 July 2013, available at: http://sas-space.sas.ac.uk/5782/1/Neville_Linton_Transcript.pdf [Accessed 17/9/2017], p. 27.

14. COHP, interview with Pik Botha, 13 December 2012, available at http://sas-space.sas.ac.uk/5806/1/Pik_Botha_Transcript.pdf [Accessed 17/9/2017], p. 3.

15. COHP, interview with Edward Seaga, 20 January 2015, available at: http://sas-space.sas.ac.uk/6056/1/Edward_Seaga_Transcript.pdf [Accessed 17/9/2017], p. 2.

16. COHP, interview with Hawke, p. 2.

17. R. W. Johnson, *South Africa: The First Man, The Last Nation* (London, Phoenix, 2006), pp. 195–6.

18. Joanna Bennett, Dhananjayan Sriskandarajah and Zoë Ware, 'An Uncommon Association—A Wealth of Potential: The Final Report of the Commonwealth Conversation', Royal Commonwealth Society, 2010, available at https://www.thercs.org/assets/Research-/Commonwealth-Conversation-Final-Report.pdf [Accessed 16/9/2017], p. 44.

19. Commonwealth Secretariat, 'Report of the Commonwealth Expert Team: The Gambia Presidential Election, 24 November 2011', 29 November 2011, http://thecommonwealth.org/sites/default/files/news-items/documents/TheGambiaPresidentialElection2011Final.pdf [Accessed 26/7/2017], p. 31.

20. COHP, interview with Kamal Hossain, 8 December 2014, available at: http://sas-space.sas.ac.uk/6109/1/Kamal_Hossain_Transcript.pdf [Accessed 16/9/2017], p. 12.

21. COHP, interview with David McDowell (Part 1), 24 June 2014, available at: http://sas-space.sas.ac.uk/6120/1/David_McDowell_Transcript_1.pdf [Accessed 17/9/2017], pp. 7–8.

22. COHP, interview with Kaliopate Tavola, 10 April 2014, available at: http://sas-space.sas.ac.uk/5803/1/Kaliopate_Tavola_Transcript.pdf [Accessed 17/9/2017], p. 17.

23. COHP, interview with Aliker, p. 22.

24. COHP, interview with Douglas Hurd, n. d., available at: http://sas-space.sas.ac.uk/5078/2/Lord_Hurd_Transcript.pdf [Accessed 17/9/2017], p. 3.

25. COHP, interview with Aziz Pahad (Part 2), 5 August 2015, available at http://sas-space.sas.ac.uk/5702/5/Aziz_Pahad_Transcript%20II.pdf [Accessed 17/9/2017], p. 2.

26. COHP, interview with Pepera, p. 28.

27. COHP, interview with K. Shankar Bajpai, 13 June 2013, available at: http://sas-space.sas.ac.uk/5998/1/K%20Shankar%20Bajpai%20Transcript.pdf [Accessed 16/9/2017], p. 11.

28. COHP, interview with Hurd, p. 10.

4. LONG TO REIGN OVER US?

1. Patrick Robinson, 'The Monarchy, Republicanism and the Privy Council: The Enduring Cry for Freedom', *The Round Table*, 101/5 (Oct 2012), pp. 448–50.

2. BBC News, 'Jamaica to break links with Queen, says Prime Minister Simpson Miller', 6 January 2012, http://www.bbc.com/news/world-latin-america-16449969 [Accessed 17/9/2017].

3. *The Daily Telegraph*, 23 March 2015.

4. C. E. Diggines, 'Constitutional Change in Trinidad and Tobago and the New Republic', 10 June 1976, FCO 6/1431.

5. Quoted in Crowe to Stewart. 24 Feb 1970, DO 127/140.

6. Peter Boyce, *The Queen's Other Realms: The Crown and its legacy in Australia, Canada and New Zealand* (Sydney, The Federation Press, 2008), pp. 225–8.

7. David Estep, 'Losing Jewels from the Crown: Considering the future of the monarchy in Australia and Canada', *Temple International and Comparative Law Journal*, 217 (1993), p. 230.

8. Oxford Analytica Brief, 8 November 1999.

9. Boyce, p. 70.

10. Ibid., p. 216.

11. Minutes of Prime Ministers' Meeting, PMM (49) 4th meeting, 27 April 1949, CAB 133/89.

12. Adeane to Clutterbuck, 26 Sept 1959, DO 35/5134. This letter was not, in fact, posted, but was presented to Clutterbuck by Adeane in October following a discussion between them.

13. Heath anticipated a row over British arms sales to South Africa and was afraid the Queen would become embroiled in this.

14. Julia Gillard, speech delivered at the Great Hall, King's College London, 5 October 2016, available at: http://juliagillard.com.au/articles/julia-gillard-speaks-on-the-future-of-the-commonwealth-in-london/ [Accessed 25/6/2017].

15. *Hansard*, HC Deb., vol. 540, col. 5WS, Written Ministerial Statement (6 February 2012).

16. Philip Murphy, *Monarchy and the End of Empire: The House of Windsor, the British Government and the Postwar Commonwealth* (Oxford, OUP, 2013), pp. 133–4.

5. GUILT

1. The Times, '50 years later: Britain's Kenya cover up revealed', 5 April 2011, https://www.thetimes.co.uk/article/50-years-later-britains-kenya-cover-up-revealed-npqhbd0cvgb [Accessed 19/2/2018].

2. For further information see David M. Anderson, 'Mau Mau in the High Court and the "Lost" British Empire Archives: Colonial Conspiracy or

Bureaucratic Bungle?', *Journal of Imperial and Commonwealth History*, 39/5 (2011), pp. 699–716; Mandy Banton, 'Destroy? "Migrate"? Conceal? British Strategies for the Disposal of Sensitive Records of Colonial Administrations at Independence', *Journal of Imperial and Commonwealth History*, 40/2 (2012), pp. 321–35.

3. Caroline Elkins, *Britain's Gulag: The Brutal End of Empire in Kenya* (London, Jonathan Cape, 2005) pp. xiii–xiv.

4. Bruce Berman, 'Mau Mau and the Politics of Knowledge: The Struggle Continues', *Canadian Journal of African Studies*, 41/3 (2007), pp. 529–45.

5. Charles W. Mills, *The Racial Contract* (Ithaca, NY, Cornell UP, 1997), p. 3.

6. John Torpey, *Making Whole What Has Been Smashed: On Reparations Politics* (Cambridge, MA, Harvard UP, 2006), p. 24.

7. Ibid., p. 16.

8. David Rieff, *In Praise of Forgetting: Historical Memory and Its Ironies* (New Haven, CT, Yale UP, 2016), pp. 63–4.

9. Bruce Gilley, 'The case for colonialism', *Third World Quarterly* (2017), DOI: 10.1080/01436597.2017.1369037. For the reasons described below, this is no longer available on the journal's website, but it can be accessed via Gilley's personal site, at http://www.web.pdx.edu/~gilleyb/2_The%20case%20for%20colonialism_at2Oct2017.pdf [Accessed 27/12/2017].

10. See the article's withdrawal notice: http://www.tandfonline.com/doi/abs/10.1080/01436597.2017.1369037 [Accessed 28/12/2017].

11. McDonald Centre, 'The Ethics of Colonial History', 2 December 2017, http://www.mcdonaldcentre.org.uk/news/ethics-colonial-history [Accessed 16/1/2018]; McDonald Centre, 'Ethics and Empire', n.d., http://www.mcdonaldcentre.org.uk/ethics-and-empire [Accessed 27/12/2017]. The first reference the author has found to this project on social media is from 14 December 2017.

12. *Cherwell*, 20 December 2017.

13. David Iliff, 'Ethics and Empire: an open letter from Oxford scholars', *The Conversation*, 19 December 2017, https://theconversation.com/ethics-and-empire-an-open-letter-from-oxford-scholars-89333 [Accessed 28/12/2017].

14. Guy Adams, 'Revealed: How Oxford University is "home to loud mouthed, Tory-loathing, anti-Israel academics who believe only they should have freedom of expression"', *Mail Online*, 23 December 2017, http://www.dailymail.co.uk/news/article-5207687/Oxford-home-Tory-loathing-anti-Israel-academics.html [Accessed 28/12/2017].

15. The Prince of Wales, 'A speech by HRH The Prince of Wales at The Overseas Service Pensioners' Association Farewell Reception', 8 June 2017, https://www.princeofwales.gov.uk/media/speeches/speech-hrh-the-prince-of-wales-the-overseas-service-pensioners-association-farewell [Accessed 20/9/2017].

6. VALUES

1. L. S. Amery, *The Forward Way* (London, Geoffrey Bles, 1935), p. 169.

2. Mark Mazower, *Governing the World: The History of an Idea* (London, Penguin, 2013), p. 133.

3. Commonwealth Oral History Project (COHP), interview with Sir Shridath [Sonny] Ramphal (Part 1), 23 November 2013, available at: http://sas-space.sas.ac.uk/5900/1/Shridath%20Ramphal%20Transcript%201.pdf [Accessed 18/9/2017], p. 12.

4. *The New York Times*, 16 June 1977.

5. Andrew Mycock, 'British Citizenship and the Legacy of Empires', *Parliamentary Affairs*, 63/2 (2010), pp 339–55, at p. 348.

6. Stuart Mole, 'From Smith to Sharma: the role of the Commonwealth Secretary-General', in James Mayall (ed.), *The Contemporary Commonwealth: An Assessment 1965–2009* (London, Routledge, 2010), p. 45.

7. Joanna Bennett, Dhananjayan Sriskandarajah and Zoë Ware, 'An Uncommon Association—A Wealth of Potential: The Final Report of the Commonwealth Conversation', Royal Commonwealth Society, 2010, available at https://www.thercs.org/assets/Research-/Commonwealth-Conversation-Final-Report.pdf [Accessed 16/9/2017], p. 50.

8. Commonwealth Secretariat, 'A Commonwealth of the People: Time for Urgent Reform', Report of the Eminent Persons Group to Commonwealth Heads of Government, Perth, October 2011, pp. 19, 149, 165, 175.

9. COHP, interview with Sir Ronald Sanders (Part 1), 12 November 2012, available at http://sas-space.sas.ac.uk/4915/1/Ronald_Sanders_Transcript_1.pdf [Accessed 18/9/2017], p. 20.

10. COHP, interview with the Hon. Michael Kirby, 28 March 2014, available at: http://sas-space.sas.ac.uk/5703/1/Michael_Kirby_Transcript. pdf [Accessed 18/9/2017], p. 4.

11. Commonwealth Secretariat, 'A Commonwealth of the People', p. 19.

12. Ibid., p. 6.

13. COHP, interview with Sir Malcolm Rifkind (Part 2), 12 March 2013, available at http://sas-space.sas.ac.uk/5079/3/Sir_Malcolm_Rifkind_ Transcript_2.pdf [Accessed 18/9/2017], p. 8.

14. COHP, interview with Kirby, p. 5.

15. Ibid.

16. Ibid., p. 10.

17. COHP, interview with Rifkind (Part 2), p. 9.

18. COHP, interview with Kirby, p. 7.

19. Ibid., pp. 8–9.

20. Simon Walters, 'Queen fights for gay rights: Monarch makes historic pledge on discrimination and hints that if Kate DOES have a girl, that means equal rights to the throne too', *The Mail on Sunday*, 9 March 2013, http://www.dailymail.co.uk/news/article-2290824/Queen-fights-gay-rights-Monarch-makes-historic-pledge-discrimination-hints-Kate-DOES-girl-means-equal-rights-throne.html [Accessed 25/1/2018].

21. *The Guyana Times*, 16 January 2015.

22. COHP, interview with Dr Moses Anafu (Part 3), 19 November 2014, available at http://sas-space.sas.ac.uk/6115/33/Moses_Anafu_ Transcript_3.pdf [Accessed 20/9/2017], p. 25.

7. THE ROAD TO COLOMBO

1. United Nations, 'Report of the Secretary-General's Internal Review Panel on United Nations action in Sri Lanka', November 2012, http://www.un.org/News/dh/infocus/Sri_Lanka/The_Internal_Review_Panel_ report_on_Sri_Lanka.pdf [Accessed 21/9/17], p. 11.

2. Ibid.

3. Oren Gruenbaum, 'Commonwealth Roundup', *The Round Table*, 101/4 (2012), pp. 303–10.

4. Melanie Newman and Oliver Wright, 'We wrote Sri Lankan President's civil war speech, say lobbyists', *The Independent*, 6 December 2011,

http://www.independent.co.uk/news/world/asia/we-wrote-sri-lankan-presidents-civil-war-speech-say-lobbyists-6272765.html [Accessed 17/1/2018].

5. *Hansard*, HL Deb., vol. 748, col. 723 (17 October 2013).
6. *The Daily Telegraph*, 3 June 2014.
7. BBC News, 'MPs' foreign visit rules breached', 23 March 2010, http://news.bbc.co.uk/1/hi/uk_politics/8580183.stm [Accessed 17/1/2018].
8. *TheFinancialTimes*,12October2011,https://www.ft.com/content/3d876284-f4f0-11e09023-00144feab49a
9. Commonwealth Oral History Project (COHP), interview with Don McKinnon (Part 2), 8 April 2014, available at http://sas-space.sas.ac.uk/6061/2/Don_Mckinnon_Transcript_2.pdf [Accessed 22/9/17], p. 20.
10. Derek Ingram, 'CHOGM Diary', *The Round Table* 99/406 (2010), pp. 23–6.
11. Nicholas Watt, 'Commonwealth vetoes Sri Lanka bid to hold 2011 gathering', *The Guardian*, 29 November 2009, https://www.theguardian.com/world/2009/nov/29/commonwealth-vetoes-sri-lanka-bid [Accessed 2/8/17].
12. COHP, interview with Kamalesh Sharma (Part 1), 9 March 2016, available at: https://sas-space.sas.ac.uk/6528/1/kamalesh_sharma_transcript1.pdf [Accessed 22/9/2017], p. 17.
13. James Manor, 'To Sustain the Commonwealth Commitment to Human Dignity: Reconsider the Award of the 2013 CHOGM to Sri Lanka', Commonwealth Advisory Bureau, October 2011, http://sas-space.sas.ac.uk/4844/1/111014_Opinion.Oct11.Jim_ManorSriLankaCHOGM.pdf [Accessed 2/8/17].
14. Ibid., p. 3.
15. Ibid., p. 5.
16. Commonwealth Secretariat, 'Dismissal of the Chief Justice in Sri Lanka', press statement, 13 January 2013, http://thecommonwealth.org/media/press-release/dismissal-chief-justice-sri-lanka [Accessed 3/8/2017].
17. Philip Murphy, 'Sri Lanka CHOGM 2013: With Whom Does the Decision Lie?', Institute of Commonwealth Studies blog, 26 April

2013, https://commonwealth-opinion.blogs.sas.ac.uk/2013/sri-lanka-chogm-2013-with-whom-does-the-decision-lie/ [Accessed 17/1/2018].

18. Sir Shridath Ramphal, 'How Muldoon let the side down', *The Times*, 5 August 1981.

19. Australian High Commission, India, 'Brisbane CHOGM to be postponed until new year', press release, 28 September 2001, http://www.india.embassy.gov.au/ndli/PA_18_01.html [Accessed 17/1/2018].

20. Channel 4 News lovingly recorded the scene. See Channel 4 News, 'Sri Lanka hosting Commonwealth meeting: opposition growing', 27 April 2013, https://www.youtube.com/watch?v=PF4ZmfhCq0E [Accessed 17/1/2018].

21. Nicola Smith, 'Let off for Sri Lanka on axeing of judge', *The Sunday Times*, 15 September 2013, https://www.thetimes.co.uk/article/let-off-for-sri-lanka-on-axeing-of-judge-bs9k9gx99tq [Accessed 17/1/2018].

22. Commonwealth Secretariat, 'Independent legal opinions on the removal of the former Chief Justice of Sri Lanka', press statement, 13 September 2013, http://thecommonwealth.org/media/news/independent-legal-opinions-removal-former-chief-justice-sri-lanka [Accessed 17/1/2018].

23. Commonwealth Secretariat, 'Strengthening the Role of the Commonwealth Ministerial Action Group (CMAG): Report of CMAG as adopted by the Commonwealth Heads of Government Meeting, 2011', 2012, http://thecommonwealth.org/sites/default/files/news-items/documents/120131.pdf, pp. 7–9 [Accessed 5/8/2017].

24. Ibid., p. 6.

25. See http://www.drchrisnonis.com/Dr-Chris-Nonis-Profile.aspx [Accessed 22/9/2017].

26. *The Colombo Telegraph*, 'Presidential Advisor Chris Nonis Mum Over His Rupees One Billion Heist', 5 July 2016, https://www.colombotelegraph.com/index.php/presidential-advisor-chris-nonis-mum-over-his-rupees-one-billion-heist/ [Accessed 6/8/2017].

27. Sujeeva Nivunhella, 'Inviting Rajapaksa was a "mistake" says RCS chief', *The Island*, 9 June 2012, http://www.island.lk/index.php?page_cat=article-details&page=article-details&code_title=54039 [Accessed 17/1/2018].

28. Martha Linden and Tony Jones, 'Queen to miss Commonwealth summit in Sri Lanka due to long-haul travel review—and will send Prince Charles instead', *The Independent*, 7 May 2013, http://www.independent.co.uk/news/uk/politics/queen-to-miss-commonwealth-summit-in-sri-lanka-due-to-long-haul-travel-review-and-will-send-prince-8605684.html [Accessed 17/1/2018].

29. Philip Murphy, *Monarchy and the End of Empire: The House of Windsor, the British Government and the Postwar Commonwealth* (Oxford, OUP, 2013), p. 130.

30. BBC News, 'UN's Navi Pillay attacks Sri Lanka human rights record', 31 August 2013, http://www.bbc.co.uk/news/world-asia-23899082 [Accessed 30/6/2017].

31. *The Deccan Herald*, 'Lanka to name stray baby elephants after Commonwealth leaders', 29 October 2013, http://www.deccanherald.com/content/366025/lanka-name-stray-baby-elephants.html [Accessed 17/1/2018].

32. House of Commons Foreign Affairs Committee, 'The Role and Future of the Commonwealth', Fourth Report of Session 2012–13', 15 November 2012, https://publications.parliament.uk/pa/cm201213/cmselect/cmfaff/114/114.pdf [Accessed 17/1/2018], p. 5.

33. Rowena Mason, 'Tamils hail David Cameron as "god" but Sri Lankan president is not a believer', *The Guardian*, 15 November 2013, https://www.theguardian.com/world/2013/nov/15/david-cameron-visits-tamils-sri-lanka [Accessed 17/1/2018].

34. *Hansard*, HL Deb., vol. 749, cols 772–3 (18 November 2013).

35. *The Sydney Morning Herald*, 16 November 2013.

36. COHP, interview with the Hon. Gareth Evans, 27 March 2014, available at http://sas-space.sas.ac.uk/6063/1/Gareth_Evans_Transcript.pdf [Accessed 22/9/2017], p. 16.

37. Venkat Iyer, 'CHOGM Diary', *The Round Table*, 103/1 (2014), pp. 13–16.

38. Stuart Mole, 'Colombo Notebook', *The Round Table*, 103/1 (2014), pp. 17–22.

8. EMPIRE 2.0?

1. BBC News, 'Nigel Farage: 2010 UKIP manifesto was "drivel"', 24 January 2014, http://www.bbc.co.uk/news/uk-politics-25879302 [Accessed 19/1/2018].

2. BBC News, 'Britain and Canada to have joint diplomatic missions overseas', 26 September 2012, http://www.bbc.co.uk/news/uk-politics-19697052 [Accessed 19/1/2018].

3. Peter Dominiczak, 'Britain must look "beyond" the EU and focus on links with the Commonwealth', *The Daily Telegraph*, 25 August 2013, http://www.telegraph.co.uk/news/politics/10265602/Britain-must-look-beyond-the-EU-and-focus-on-links-with-the-Commonwealth.html [Accessed 19/1/2018].

4. Eva Namusoke, 'A Divided Family: Race, the Commonwealth and Brexit', *The Round Table*, 105/5 (2016), pp. 463–76.

5. Ibid., p. 464.

6. Paul Nuttall, 'Forget Brussels—the UK should be doing business with the Commonwealth, says PAUL NUTTALL', *The Daily Express*, 22 June 2016, https://www.express.co.uk/comment/expresscomment/682269/Brussels-UK-business-Commonwealth-PAUL-NUTTALL-Ukip-trade [Accessed 19/1/2018].

7. Namusoke, pp. 466–8.

8. Boris Johnson, 'If Blair's so good at running the Congo, let him stay there', *The Daily Telegraph*, 10 January 2002, http://www.telegraph.co.uk/comment/personal-view/3571742/If-Blairs-so-good-at-running-the-Congo-let-him-stay-there.html [Accessed 19/1/2018].

9. BBC News, 'EU migration: UK to face "free-for-all", Michael Gove warns', 25 April 2016, http://www.bbc.co.uk/news/uk-politics-eu-referendum-36126993 [Accessed 19/1/2018].

10. Lord Ashcroft, 'How the United Kingdom voted on Thursday … and why', Lord Ashcroft Polls, 24 June 2016, http://lordashcroftpolls.com/2016/06/how-the-united-kingdom-voted-and-why/ [Accessed 19/1/2018].

11. Martin Rosenbaum, 'Local voting figures shed new light on EU referendum', BBC News, 6 February 2017, http://www.bbc.co.uk/news/uk-politics-38762034 [Accessed 30/6/2017].

12. Hull City Council, 'Hull at a Glance—2014. Economic Update Report', n.d., http://www.hullcc.gov.uk/pls/portal/docs/PAGE/HULL_ MEANS_BUSINESS/HMB_BUSINESS/HULLATAGLANCE%20 2014.PDF [Accessed 30/7/2017].

13. David Conn, 'Hull after Brexit—will the City of Culture regret voting out?', *The Guardian*, 3 April 2017, https://www.theguardian.com/ politics/2017/apr/02/hull-after-brexit-will-the-city-of-culture-regret-voting-out [Accessed 30/7/2017].

14. ITV News, 'Hull's population at highest level since 1997', 20 July 2017, http://www.itv.com/news/calendar/2017–07–20/hulls-population-at-highest-level-since-1997/ [Accessed 30/7/2017].

15. NatCen Social Research, 'The vote to leave the EU: Litmus test or lightening rod?', n.d., *British Social Attitudes* 34, http://www.bsa.natcen.ac.uk/media/39149/bsa34_brexit_final.pdf [Accessed 30/7/2017], p. 20.

16. Lord Howell, 'A bright future awaits Britain post-Brexit in the Commonwealth markets', *The Daily Telegraph*, 29 June 2016, http:// www.telegraph.co.uk/news/2016/07/29/a-bright-future-awaits-britain-post-brexit-in-the-commonwealth-m/ [Accessed 19/1/2018].

17. Katharine West, 'Britain, the Commonwealth and the Global Economy', *The Round Table*, 83/332 (1994), pp. 407–17.

18. *The Round Table*, 85/339 (1996), pp. 259–63.

19. Alastair Campbell, *The Alastair Campbell Diaries, Volume II, 1997–1999* (London, Hutchinson, 2011), p. 187.

20. Ibid., p. 191.

21. Commonwealth Secretariat, 'The Commonwealth in the Unfolding Global Trade Landscape: Prospects, Priorities Perspectives', Commonwealth Trade Review 2015, http://thecommonwealth.org/sites/default/ files/inline/Commonwealth%20Trade%20Review%202015-Full%20 Report.pdf [Accessed 19/1/2018], p. xx.

22. Ibid., p. xxi.

23. Sir Ronald Sanders, 'Commonwealth Free Trade: A British straw man?', Sir Ronald Sanders blog, 17 March 2017, http://www.sirronaldsanders. com/viewarticle.aspx?ID=593 [Accessed 19/1/2018].

24. House of Commons Library, 'UK-Commonwealth trade statistics', 6 December 2012.

25. Sir Simon Fraser, 'The World is Our Oyster? Britain's Future Trade Relationships', The Tacitus Lecture 2017, 23 February 2017, http://worldtraders.dev.amediatek.com/wp-content/uploads/2017/04/Tactitus2017.pdf [Accessed 11/7/2017].

26. Sue Onslow, 'What Brexit means for the Commonwealth', Institute of Commonwealth Studies blog, 7 July 2016, https://commonwealth-opinion.blogs.sas.ac.uk/2016/what-brexit-means-for-the-common-wealth/ [Accessed 19/1/2018].

27. Steve Peers, 'The EU or the Commonwealth: a dilemma for the UK—or a false choice?', EU Law Analysis, 29 November 2015, http://eula-wanalysis.blogspot.co.uk/2015/11/the-eu-or-commonwealth-dilemma-for-uk.html [Accessed 19/1/2018].

28. David Cameron, 'David Cameron's speech at Unilever offices in Mumbai', 18 February 2013, https://www.gov.uk/government/speeches/david-camerons-speech-at-unilever-offices-in-mumbai [Accessed 19/1/2018].

29. Lord Jay of Ewelme to Rt Hon David Davis MP, House of Lords European Union Committee letter, 13 September 2017, http://www.parliament.uk/documents/lords-committees/eu-select/Correspon-dence-2017–19/11–09–17-Overseas-Territories-letter-to-David-Davis-MP.pdf [Accessed 19/1/2018].

30. Dan Roberts, 'Drive to replace UK-EU trade links with closer ties to Commonwealth', The Guardian, 10 March 2017, https://www.the-guardian.com/global-development/2017/mar/10/drive-to-replace-eu-trade-links-with-closer-ties-to-commonwealth-economies [Accessed 19/1/2018].

31. Dan Roberts, 'Drive to replace UK-EU trade links with closer ties to Commonwealth', The Guardian, 10 March 2017, https://www.the-guardian.com/global-development/2017/mar/10/drive-to-replace-eu-trade-links-with-closer-ties-to-commonwealth-economies [Accessed 19/2/2018].

32. Sam Coates, 'Ministers aim to build "empire 2.0" with African Commonwealth', The Times, 6 March 2017, https://www.thetimes.co.uk/article/ministers-aim-to-build-empire-2–0-with-african-com-monwealth-after-brexit-v9bs6f6z9 [Accessed 19/1/2018].

33. Ben Quinn, '"Three Brexiteers" chase buccaneering spirit of empire in choice of art', *The Observer*, 2 July 2017, https://www.theguardian.com/politics/2017/jul/01/three-brexiteers-chase-buccaneering-spirit-of-empire [Accessed 19/1/2018].

34. Jon Snow, 'MP Shashi Tharoor on the consequences of Britain's imperial past', Channel 4 News, 2 March 2017, https://www.channel4.com/news/mp-shashi-tharoor-on-the-consequences-of-britains-imperial-past [Accessed 19/2/2018].

35. Iain Dale, 'Former Indian Minister: "Empire 2.0 Will Go Down Like A Lead Balloon In India"', LBC, 6 March 2017, http://www.lbc.co.uk/radio/presenters/iain-dale/empire-20-will-go-down-like-a-lead-balloon-india/ [Accessed 19/2/2018].

36. Both cited in Sanders.

37. David Blair, 'Exclusive: leading candidate to be Commonwealth secretary general alleged to have received $1.4m in fraud against Antiguan government', *The Daily Telegraph*, 25 November 2015, http://www.telegraph.co.uk/news/worldnews/centralamericaandthecaribbean/antiguaandbarbuda/12017407/Exclusive-leading-candidate-to-be-Commonwealth-secretary-general-alleged-to-have-received-1.4m-in-fraud-against-Antiguan-government.html [Accessed 19/1/2018].

38. William James, 'New Commonwealth chief says "don't put us against EU" in Brexit debate', Reuters, 4 April 2016, http://uk.reuters.com/article/uk-britain-eu-commonwealth/new-commonwealth-chief-says-dont-pit-us-against-eu-in-brexit-debate-idUKKCN0X11FR [Accessed 19/1/2018].

39. A useful summary of these two main allegations against Scotland in the press, and of her responses to them, can be found in two separate Independent Press Standards Organization (IPSO) rulings. IPSO found the Mail on Sunday to be in breach of standards over its reporting of the KYA Global matter, but found no breach by the *Mail Online* over the reporting of the official residence refurbishments. See IPSO, '13840-16 Baroness Scotland v The Mail on Sunday', 8 June 2017, https://www.ipso.co.uk/rulings-and-resolution-statements/ruling/?id=13840-16 [Accessed 20/2/2018]; and IPSO, '13841-16 Baroness Scotland v Mail Online', 8 June 2017, https://www.ipso.

co.uk/rulings-and-resolution-statements/ruling/?id=13841-16 [Accessed 20/2/2018].

40. Laura Hughes, 'Baroness Scotland hits back at accusations she oversaw extravagant refurbishment of official residence', The Telegraph, 4 November 2016, http://www.telegraph.co.uk/news/2016/11/04/baroness-scotland-hits-back-at-accusations-she-oversaw-extravaga/ [Accessed 19/2/2018]; Vanessa Allen, 'Labour peer turns down a job with £160,000 salary, Mayfair mansion and chauffeur-driven car ... because men before her were paid even MORE', The Daily Mail, 7 October 2016, http://www.dailymail.co.uk/news/article-3827801/Baroness-Scotland-rejected-160k-pay-men-got-more.html [Accessed 19/2/2018]; Ian Gallagher and Ned Donovan, 'Pressure mounts on Baroness Brazen as her PR advisor is stripped of a second knighthood over "irregularities"', The Mail on Sunday, 30 July 2017, http://www.dailymail.co.uk/news/article-4743222/Baroness-Brazen-s-PR-advisor-stripped-knighthood.html [Accessed 19/2/2018]; Guy Adams, 'Baroness Hypocrite: How the Blairite law chief with an illegal immigrant cleaner has cosy links to two vile despots that raise grave questions about her suitability to be new boss of the Commonwealth', The Daily Mail, 16 April 2016, http://www.dailymail.co.uk/news/article-3542759/Baroness-Hypocrite-Blairite-law-chief-illegal-immigrant-cleaner-cosy-links-two-vile-despots-raise-grave-questions-suitability-new-boss-Commonwealth.html [Accessed 19/2/2018].

41. BBC News, 'Concerns raised over Commonwealth leadership', 26 January 2017, http://www.bbc.co.uk/news/uk-38760133 [Accessed 20/2/2018]

42. Anushka Asthana, '"It's unfair to call me Baroness Brazen"—inside Lady Scotland's refurbished home', The Guardian, 7 August 2017, https://www.theguardian.com/politics/2017/aug/07/unfair-lady-scotland-inside-refurbished-home-commonwealth [Accessed 19/1/2018].

43. Ibid.

44. Coffey International Development, 'UN and Commonwealth Reform Study, Main Report (Final Draft)', February 2013, https://assets.publishing.service.gov.uk/media/57a08a0740f0b649740003aa/61063-IDEVREAN12017GB_MainReport_Final_11Feb2013.pdf [Accessed 19/1/2018], p. 21.

45. Department for International Development, 'Raising the standard: the Multilateral Development Review 2016', December 2016, https://www.gov.uk/government/uploads/system/uploads/attachment_data/file/573884/Multilateral-Development-Review-Dec2016.pdf [Accessed 23/7/17], p. 18.

46. Ibid., p. 36.

CONCLUSION: SHATTERING THE MYTH

1. Rt Hon Michael Ancram QC, 'Farewell to Drift: A New Foreign Policy for a Network World', Global Strategy Forum, October 2010, http://www.globalstrategyforum.org/wp-content/uploads/Farewell-to-Drift-.pdf [Accessed 19/1/2018], p. 27.

2. Michael Ancram, 'After 40 years of being lied to, it's time to leave the EU', *The Daily Telegraph*, 26 April 2016, http://www.telegraph.co.uk/news/2016/04/25/after-40-years-of-being-lied-to-its-time-to-leave-the-eu/ [Accessed 23/9/2017].

3. Ruth Sherlock, 'Exclusive: United States could become an "associate member" of the Commonwealth', *The Daily Telegraph*, 23 February 2017, http://www.telegraph.co.uk/news/2017/02/23/donald-trumps-love-royal-family-may-see-united-states-join-commonwealth/ [Accessed 30/9/2017].

4. Ben Riley-Smith and Chrostopher Hope, 'Boost for UK-US trade links as Royal Commonwealth Society opens Mississippi office', *The Daily Telegraph*, 16 September 2017, http://www.telegraph.co.uk/news/2017/09/16/boost-uk-us-trade-links-royal-commonwealth-society-opens-mississippi/ [Accessed 30/9/2017].

INDEX

INDEX

INDEX

Baird, John, 180
Bajpai, K. Shankar, 57, 79
Baker, Herbert, 9, 117, 119, 133
Baker, Steve, 50
Balfour, Arthur, 22, 86
Bandaranaike, Sirima Ratwatte
    Dias 'Sirimavo', 90
Bandaranaike, Shirani, 175–6,
    180–81
Bandaranaike, Solomon West
    Ridgeway Dias, 90
Bangladesh, 65, 73, 75–6, 178–9,
    207
Banks, Victor, 215
Barbados, 59, 89, 115
Barber, Anthony, 70
Barrow, Adama, 75
Barrow, Errol, 59
Battey, Matthew, xiii
Beatles, The, 11
Beaverbrook, Lord, see Aitken,
    William Maxwell
Beckles, Hilary, 115
Belgium, 17
Bell Pottinger, 168, 171
Bell, Timothy, Baron Bell, 171
Bengal Famine (1943), 107
Berlin Wall, 121
Beyond the Fringe, 49
Bible, x–xi
Biggar, Nigel, 124–6
bilateralism, 62–3, 206–8
Blair, Anthony 'Tony', 14, 64,
    114, 205–6, 219
Bodleian Library, Oxford, 7

Boer War, Second (1899–1902),
    22, 44, 67, 117, 138
Bolger, James 'Jim', 63
Botha, Pieter Willem, 70, 72
Botha, Roelof Frederik 'Pik', 70
Botswana, 70, 76–7, 218
Bourne, Richard, xiii, 49
Bowie, David, 12
Boyce, Peter, 93, 95
Brandt, Willy, 33
Brazil, 209
Brewer, Karen, 47
Brexit, x, 17, 61, 81, 106, 122,
    132, 193–217, 225–32
BRICS (Brazil, Russia, India,
    China and South Africa), 209,
    210
Brisbane, Queensland, 177–8
Britain's Gulag (Elkins), 112, 113
British Asian Trust, 183
British Broadcasting Corporation
    (BBC), 11, 12, 89, 221
'British Commonwealth', 43
British Empire, 2–11, 13, 21,
    43–4, 55–6, 103, 105–35
    architecture, 9, 13, 117, 119,
        133
    and Christianity, 124, 139
    Colonial Office, 85, 123
    Colonial Service, 130–34
    Colonial Society, 43
    decolonization, 6, 7, 10, 23–8,
        55, 68, 84, 88, 91, 105–35
    divide-and-rule, 129
    Dominions, 22, 30, 43, 61, 62,
        86–7, 139, 195, 196, 198

INDEX

INDEX

INDEX

INDEX

INDEX

INDEX

INDEX

INDEX

INDEX

INDEX

INDEX

INDEX

INDEX

INDEX

INDEX

INDEX

INDEX

INDEX

INDEX

United Nations, 34, 78
  Centre on Transnational
    Corporations, 71
  Development Programme
    (UNDP), 32
  High Commissioner for
    Human Rights, 147–8
  Rajapaksa's address (2010),
    168–9
  Sri Lanka, 165, 168–9, 173, 186
  Trusteeship territories, 85
  Universal Declaration of
    Human Rights (1948), 156
United States, 16
  banking, 71, 72
  Central Intelligence Agency
    (CIA), 14–15
  Cold War, 65
  Commonwealth associate
    membership, 230–31
  identity politics, 107, 116
  Imperial Cricket Conference
    membership, 45
  and monarchy, 95
  and Organization of American
    States, 72
  Revolutionary War (1775–
    1783), 21
  Second World War (1939–45),
    45
  September 11 attacks (2001),
    177, 205
  slavery, 107, 114, 116
  and Sri Lanka, 173
  United Kingdom, relationship
    with, 195, 205–6, 230–31

Vietnam War (1955–75), 131
War on Terror, 206
Universal Declaration of Human
  Rights (1948), 156
Universities Bureau of the British
  Empire, 44
University College London, 115
University of Cape Town, 117
University of London
  Congress of the Universities of
    the Empire (1912), 44
  Institute of Commonwealth
    Studies (ICwS), x, xi, xii,
    1–2, 8, 10, 45, 51, 88, 178–
    9, 183, 184
University of Reading, 2
Ussher, James, x–xi

Vancouver, British Columbia,
  34–5, 71–2
Venuprasad, Ram, 223
Viceroy's Palace, Delhi, 9
Victoria, Queen of the United
  Kingdom, 84–5
Victoria, Australia, 94
Victorian era (1837–1901), 5
Vietnam War (1955–75), 131

Wales, 84
War on Terror, 206
Weisweiller-Wu, Lara, xiv
Werritty, Adam 170–71
West Indies Federation (1958–62),
  91
West, Katherine, 203–5, 206

INDEX